ON SPORTS

OTHER BOOKS BY FREDERICK C. KLEIN

The Education of a Horse Player (with Sam Lewin)
News and the Market (with John Prestbo)
Lem Banker's Book of Sports Betting (with Lem Banker)
Bulls, Bears and Other Sports (editor)

ON SPORTS

Essays and musings by
Wall Street Journal columnist
Frederick C. Klein

Bonus Books, Chicago

91   90   89   88   87   5   4   3   2   1

Library of Congress Catalog Card Number: 87-70663

International Standard Book Number: 0-933893-34-5

Text illustrations: Joel Davies

Bonus Books, Inc.
160 East Illinois Street
Chicago, Illinois 60611

Printed in the United States of America

To Paul, Mike, Jessie, Marc and Andy

Contents

Foreword

It was the morning after I had read the galley proofs for *On Sports,* a collection of Fred Klein's columns. I was home, entertaining Mr. Marv Rotblatt, my insurance man who in years gone by had been a major league pitcher with the Chicago White Sox. More accurately, Mr. Rotblatt was entertaining me. He is a man of rare good cheer and with a seemingly endless fund of stories.

Suddenly, it occurred to me that this same Mr. Rotblatt had been the subject of one of Fred Klein's pieces. "Look at this," I told him. "You're in this book."

Mr. Rotblatt was surprised and pleased, of course, with the discovery he soon would be bound in hard cover. He took the proofs and began reading aloud. It should have taken about two minutes. "Playing Rotblatt" runs 800 to 1,000 words. It took much longer. After every few paragraphs, Mr. Rotblatt stopped and burst into laughter. And at each pause, he said, "Hey, this guy is funny."

Fred Klein is funny. No question about that. He also has an excellent eye and ear and, better yet, can spot a good anecdote at 1,000 yards. This is among the several qualities that set him apart. He neither hurries his readers, nor himself. His is a leisurely stroll through the sports scene.

In "Playing Rotblatt," for example, he neither tells us that Mr. Rotblatt had an outstanding changeup curve nor does he bury us under a stack of statistics. Instead he explains how the students at Carleton College, who had adopted Mr. Rotblatt and named a baseball league for him, awaited his visit to their campus with concern:

> They shouldn't have worried; Mr. Rotblatt had been to college and was hip. He appeared on campus wearing (among other garments) sun glasses and a loud sports shirt, carrying his White Sox traveling bag and puffing a big cigar. At a softball game staged in his honor, he pitched, he hit homeruns batting right and lefthanded, and entertained between innings with a juggling routine he'd learned while barnstorming with the old House of David team.
>
> He drank beer and leered at the girls, and at a banquet that night he wowed 'em with an hour of baseball stories and off-color jokes. After all, you don't make a living selling insurance without a gift of gab.

Mr. Klein also has a gift which is readily apparent: the desire— more than a desire, it's a necessity—to go beyond the final score and exhume the body. I have read thousands of baseball stories, for example, but other than a single line in the record book—most triples, one season, 36, John Wilson—had never read or seen a complete sentence on Mr. Wilson, or, for that matter, on triples. Mr. Klein introduces us, not only to Mr. Wilson but with an explanation of why the so-called three-bagger has become an "endangered species."

In speaking of his column, Mr. Klein says he "nibbles at the edges." I like that. Sports in general has had a tremendous growth in the last quarter of a century. The boom is reflected in the daily newspaper sports sections. Considerably more newsprint, two and three times as much as 30 years ago, is devoted to sports. To fill this space, specialists now abound, authorities on baseball, football, basketball, etc., who seldom stray from the area of their expertise.

But, often it's the generalists such as Mr. Klein who offer the most interesting view. The reporter anchored to a specific beat has advantages—among them a greater depth of knowledge about the team and sport he is covering. But Fred Klein will beat them every time. Not only does he have a natural curiosity, which is essential, but he arrives at the ballpark without baggage. He is not burdened with what happened yesterday, or last week, or the final score of the game he has come to see.

He attends a spring training baseball game between the

Montreal Expos and the Los Angeles Dodgers in Vero Beach, Florida. While the other reporters are watching from the press box, busy taking notes and keeping score, Mr. Klein is sunning himself in a box seat behind the plate:

> I sit with Ed Vargo, a National League umpire for 24 years and now an umpire-supervisor. "Who's the best ump in the game?" I ask. "Nobody," he says with a straight face. "They're all very good."

In this one terse paragraph, we are offered the equivalent of a full-length essay on the code of major league umpires. Obviously, some umpires are better than others. Some are better when they work the plate calling balls-and-strikes; others have better judgment on the bases. But for public consumption all are equal. Or as Mr. Vargo explained, "They're all very good."

I will remember Mr. Vargo's comment considerably longer than the score of the game.

Mr. Klein is not an "insider." He travels the world but never attaches himself to a ball-club. That's for the "beat" writers whose assignment is to report how and why the winning touchdown was scored, or whether Reggie Jackson swung at a curve or a 97-mile-an-hour fastball. Instead as Mr. Klein says, he "stands back a step and attempts to capture the flavor of the event."

During the fifth game of the 1985 World Series, Avron Fogelman, then the rookie co-owner of the triumphant Kansas City Royals, caught a foul ball. After the game, does Mr. Klein join the stampeding herd and rush to the clubhouse to interview the winning pitcher? Of course not. The reaction and quotes from winning pitchers are predictable. But the odds of catching a foul were 2,650-to-1. He relays this information to Mr. Fogelman and tells him, "If that could happen anything could."

Mr. Fogelman agrees: "My opinion exactly! I've been going to games for 35 years and I never came close to getting a foul ball before. I knew it had to mean something good."

The Chicago Bears destroyed the Boston Patriots 46-10 in the 1986 Super Bowl game. Always the observer, Mr. Klein provides the most telling testimony on the proportions of the rout:

> At the end of the third quarter, with the Bears ahead 44-3, vendors already were in the stands selling pennants that proclaimed the team to be champions of the National Football League.

Lou Carnesecca, basketball coach at St. John's University, insisted his wardrobe, or more specifically, a brown, red and blue crew-neck sweater was among the reasons for his team's success. To prevent the winter chill from worsening a persistent cold, Carnesecca began wearing the sweater at mid-season. The sweater not only snuffed the sniffles but, according to Carnesecca, was responsible for a remarkable 13-game winning streak.

Mr. Klein reports the results of the investigation:

> "What happens to the sweater between games?"
>
> "I never touch it," Carnesecca explained. "Two big guys—they go about 6-foot-4 or 6-foot-5—take it from me right after the game and put it in a plastic bag. I don't get it back until the next game."
>
> "Do they keep it in a bank vault?"
>
> "Are you kidding? You know what happens in banks these days."

As a lifelong sportswriter, I know what happens on the nation's sports pages. The scores are provided along with the usual wooden quotes from the participants. Fridays, I look for *The Wall Street Journal*. Not for the stock and bond prices but for Mr. Klein and the "flavor of the event."

Jerome Holtzman

Preface

E
•

very newspaper writer yearns to see his stories published in book form for the simple reason that you can't wrap garbage in a book. An anthology, moreover, is evidence that some sort of after-life might be possible. If a newspaper column from 1977 can make it back, surely there is hope for us.

It is testimony to the attraction of sports in the United States that this collection of my *Wall Street Journal* stories ("The Least-Worst of Klein" was one suggested title) focuses solely on that subject. I joined the *Journal* in 1963, and for 20 years was a "real" newspaper reporter, writing on subjects as various as business (of course), labor, politics, education, science and religion. I covered the steel workers and mine workers unions from Pittsburgh, profiled the likes of writer William F. Buckley and fashion-designer Bill Blass from New York, and, from Chicago, added a few chisel strokes to the crumpling of the Richard J. Daley Democratic political machine.

It was all interesting enough, and I guess my bosses liked it because they kept paying me. No bindery, however, saw fit to respond. The strongest reaction any of my stories engendered concerned a 1972 piece on how scholars at the University of Chicago were laboring to compile a definitive dictionary of the Assyrian language. I noted that not only hadn't Assyrian been written or spoken in some 2,000 years, but that the ancient Middle Eastern tribe itself had long since disbanded. In fact, it turned out that Chicago was home to a small but feisty band of people who call themselves Assyrians, and who let me and the *Journal* know of their existence in no uncertain terms. I even was denounced by name in an editorial in their community newspaper. If it weren't for the honor, I'd just as soon have read the funnies.

I have been a sports fan since I was able to dial a radio, and my introduction to journalism came as sports editor of my high school newspaper. I also wrote sports in college and on the small-town papers in Illinois and Michigan that were nice enough to employ me in my student and early post-graduate days. In my mid-20s, I resolved to put away childish things and set my career, as it were, on a different, more serious path. Fortunately, I wised up before it was too late.

My first sports piece for the Journal was a 1966 page one profile of Arnold Palmer, the golfer, who was just then emerging as the first jock-tycoon of the modern sports-business-entertainment world of Sportsbiz. The *Journal* hadn't had too many sports pieces before that, and the response was favorable. Occasional sports stories followed, by me and other reporters, the early ones justified by a business twist, the later ones, increasingly, standing on their own merits. By 1970, enough sports-related pieces had appeared in the paper to prompt Dow Jones Books, owned by the same company that owns the *Journal*, to publish a book of them. Another such book followed four years later.

On a couple of occasions, the *Journal* had looked into the possibility of doing something regular about sports. In Ira Berkow's excellent biography of the great Red Smith (*Red*, Times Books, 1986) it is recounted that in 1967, after his *New York Herald Tribune* flagship folded, Red's son Terence contacted the *Journal* about hiring Red as a daily sports columnist, but that Vermont Royster, then the editor of the editorial page, regretfully declined the proposal on grounds of space. In 1975, at the request of managing editor Fred Taylor, I did a brief study of the feasibility of the paper putting out a daily or weekly sports page. It was quickly obvious that the *Journal's* early-evening deadlines and lack of weekend editions ruled out daily coverage. A weekly page also was nixed, apparently because it was thought that not much in the way of meaningful news on so vast a subject could be produced once a week.

Nonetheless, I was convinced that sports of some sort deserved an airing in a newspaper whose readership was about 85 percent male, and I proposed to the editorial page features editor that I do a weekly column that would regard the subject with "a more distant eye" than that employed by sports columnists on other dailies. I must confess I wasn't sure what that meant when I first said it, and I'm still not, although I have heard my approach called "soft-core sports." The first editor I approached replied in the negative, but sometime later his successor, Tom Bray, found my letter lying around and okayed a once-a-month effort. The name "On Sports," not catchy but to-the-point, was agreed upon.

The deal was that I would write the column in addition to my regular reportorial duties, and not spend any of the paper's money doing it. That wasn't exactly what I had in mind, but I said okay anyway. "On Sports" was launched on Jan. 7, 1977, with a piece on football gambling. I sabotaged the once-a-month rule early on, but the no-travel one stood, so most of the early columns were essays.

"On Sports" went on the road, and became a full-time job for me, in September of 1983, when the *Journal* began its daily "Leisure & Arts" page. My column was a charter member, along with movie reviews by Julie Salamon and coverage of the finer arts by Manuela Hoelterhoff. It's high-toned company for a sports column, but what the heck. My regular day is Friday, and I usually also do a Monday, Tuesday or Wednesday piece about an event the weekend before.

Sharp-eyed readers will notice a stylistic change in the column that coincided with its moving to "Leisure & Arts" from the main editorial page: the dropping of the "Mr." before the names of athletes and coaches. To be sure, it might seem awkward to write that Mr. Payton scored a touchdown, or that Mr. Perry made a tackle. Still, in denying jocks the dignity of the honorific, the *Journal* placed them in a category otherwise occupied only by convicted felons. On second thought, maybe it's deserved.

Now, *The Wall Street Journal* is a considerable publication, and its daily paid circulation of close to two million is the largest in the United States. But I quickly learned that in the world of sports it carried about as much weight as *Women's Wear Daily*. My first request for credentials to cover a major event, the 1983 baseball World Series, didn't elicit so much as a reply from the teams involved, and it took an 11th-hour call to the office of Commissioner Bowie Kuhn, about whom I'd done an earlier page-one story for the paper, to get me in. Similarly, the first time I sought a press pass to cover a National Football League game, the home team's publicity director told me to come ahead, but left nothing for me at the pass gate on game day. "I thought it was a joke," he said of my request when I called him from a pay phone in front of the stadium.

Covering any new beat is like doing research among gorillas in the jungle—once they get used to seeing you around they'll toss you a banana—and before long I had gained access to the press boxes. Many athletes, however, still are amused that I wish to speak with them. "What does *The Wall Street Journal* wanna talk to me for? I don't own no stocks. Haw, Haw, Haw!" they guffaw. I usually laugh, too, but only because they're too big to hit.

In fact, "On Sports" is only occasionally about the business side of the games people play, or other extraneous issues. I don't know if sports are a microcosm of life, or vice versa. I do know that they are a form of human endeavor like any other, that just about everyone can play or watch them, and that a reporter who observes them carefully can learn, and describe, a lot about how humans compete. Sports aren't so serious that you can't joke about them, and when the game is done you know who has won or lost, which is more than you can say about many things.

You can't cover a subject as varied as sports in a couple of thousand-word pieces a week, so "On Sports" mostly nibbles at its edges, looking for small pictures that might illuminate the big ones. I write as an outsider rather than an insider, a fan rather than an expert. Everyone who blunders into my column amid the art, movie, dance, and book reviews, might not understand the jargon of the sports pages, so I try to keep it to a minimum. Similarly, I always try to mention, prominently, what sport I'm writing about; you'd be surprised how many sports stories omit that piece of information. I toss in technical explanations whenever I feel they won't lard-up a narrative, and I'll occasionally address a piece specifically to the non-fan (see "Sports Talk with a Non-Fan," p. 243). About the nicest compliments I get are from people who tell me they read my stuff even though they don't follow sports.

Except for six or seven years with the *Journal* in the benighted eastern outposts of Pittsburgh and New York, I'm a lifelong Chicagoan, and the bittersweet histories of that city's teams permeate my outlook, for better or worse. Probably worse.

I have other prejudices that find their way into my columns. In the pages to follow you will find more stories about professional sports than the college variety. That is because I think one has to hold his nose before covering the college games, and I find myself less and less willing to do so. Big-time sports colleges recruit athletes with the promise of a "free" education, and then cheat them by keeping them so tied up with conditioning, practices, travel and games that the kids don't have time to pursue one. In rereading my columns on the subject, only some of which are reprinted here, I find I have become repetitive on this point, but that doesn't bother me because I don't think it can be made too often.

You will find no stories about hockey and only one about automobile racing ("Long Day at the Indy 500," p. 237) in this book. That is because I don't care for either sport. Professional hockey used to be a good game, but the number of teams has far outstripped the ability of its sparsely populated home country of Canada to stock them, and on-the-ice brawling seems to have grown from an occasional irritant to the game's *reason d'etre*. At least boxers keep their gloves on when they fight. As for auto racing, the less said the better. The American Medical Association should look into it.

I admit to some ambivalence about international sports extravaganzas such as the Olympics or Ted Turner's 1986 Goodwill Games in Moscow. I don't buy the argument that athletic competition leads to friendship between nations or peoples. To the contrary, every international event I've attended has been marred by biased decisions and wholesale manipulations of the rules by officials, and recent Olympics have been noteworthy mainly as stages for political boycotts. On the other hand, I've also seen some nice things, like the Russians who leaned out of the stands at Druzhba Arena in Moscow to touch the massive shoulders of American heavyweight wrestler Bruce Baumgartner after he'd won the gold medal at the Goodwill Games, or the American and Romanian woman (or, more accurately, girl) gymnasts huddled giggling together before the individual-event finals in the 1984 Olympics at Los Angeles. Maybe the good overbalances the more-numerous bad.

It's tough to prove it by reading the typical, big-city sports section, but American men and women of average ability participate in sports in large numbers. I am one of them, and I am not loath to share my experiences with my newspaper's readers ("True-Life Adventures"). Not incidentally, when a story is in the offing, the

Journal picks up the bill for my expenses, which has expanded my horizons in that department.

Mostly, I regard sports as fun, and try to reflect that feeling in my columns. The best thing about being in what some in the profession call the "toy department" is that, as long as you get the score right, you can fool around a little. I don't know anyone who writes for a living who can honestly claim that he enjoys it (Red Smith used to say that writing was "the price I pay for the wonderful job I have"), but when the subject is sports, you can come close.

———————

I'd like to thank my editors at *The Wall Street Journal* over the life of "On Sports": Tom Bray, for buying my act; Dan Henninger, for laughing at my jokes; and Ray Sokolov, for keeping me on a long leash. Thanks also to the following, in no particular order: the late Robert Sink, the late Bert Bertine, Harv Wittenberg, Bill Mullendore, Dick Emmons, Seymour Shlaes, Jon Laing, Lee Berton, Felix Kessler, Russ Boner, Jerome Holtzman, Fred Seidner, Ira Silverman, Lem Banker, Jimmy Snyder, Bill Young, Seymour Siwoff, John McWethy, Sam Lewin, Bill Blundell, John Lawrence, Nat Sobel, Aaron Cohodes, Ellen Slezak, and, of course, my wife, Susie.

HARDBALL

Part 1

Wilbur Wood and His Knuckler

e who are middle-aged, of average height and overweight, however slightly, have few people in big-time sports with whom we can identify. Basketball is out entirely. So is football, now that George Blanda and Sonny Jurgensen have retired. The news that the four male singles semi-finalists in the recent Wimbledon tennis tournament averaged 21.2 years of age was disquieting in the extreme to those of us who like to think that the experience and guile that come with age count for something in sports' upper regions.

Thus, it was with a good deal of pleasure that we greeted the return to regular duty last month of one of the handful of athletes who seems even remotely like ourselves: pitcher Wilbur Wood of the Chicago White Sox. He had been out of action since May of 1976, when a line drive hit by Ron LeFlore of the Detroit Tigers broke his kneecap (ouch!).

Mr. Wood is 35 years old, baldish, round of build and placid of nature. Roger Angell, who writes about baseball for The New Yorker magazine, once described his appearance on the mound as that of "an accountant or pastry cook on a holiday." My own view is that he looks more like the clerk in the hardware store who knows all about tools.

Whatever, our affection for Mr. Wood is made complete by the fact that the sole effective weapon in his pitching arsenal is the knuckleball, that soft, curious pitch that looks so easy to throw but is so hard to hit. Which of us has not experimented with this piece of baseball exotica while playing catch with our kids? Which of us has not thought that given enough practice, we, too, could baffle the mighty of the major leagues with Mr. Wood's apparent effortlessness?

Any discussion of the knuckleball must begin by stating that the pitch is misnamed. The ball isn't gripped with the knuckles at all; rather, the pitcher digs the nails of his first two fingers into the ball just behind the seams and pushes it forward with very little wrist action. The ball has no spin of its own, relying on the air currents around home plate to give it its deceptive motion. It can flutter, dip, break left or right, or go straight, in which case it usually winds up being hit into the bleachers. No one, least of all the pitcher, can predict what any particular knuckleball will do.

The second thing that must be said is that the knuckleball really is fairly easy to throw. Just about every player in the majors fools around with it. Baseball people say that Mickey Mantle, the former New York Yankee slugger, had an especially good one.

What is difficult about the pitch is controlling it—getting it over the plate with regularity. This is as much an intellectual achievement as an act of physical dexterity, something that is rare in sports.

Pat Jordan, a one-time minor-league pitcher turned author, explained it well in his autobiography, *A False Spring*. He wrote: "A [knuckleball] pitcher has no control over the peregrinations of the ball. To be successful, he must first recognize this fact and then decide that his destiny still lies only with the pitch and that he will throw it constantly no matter what."

Professional athletes like to take the bull by its horns, as it were, so it should come as no surprise that the adoption of the knuckleball as a bread-and-butter pitch is almost always an act of desperation. That's the way it was with all four of the present big league practitioners of the art: Mr. Wood, Phil Niekro of the Atlanta Braves, Charlie Hough of the Los Angeles Dodgers and Bruce Dal Canton of the White Sox.

Mr. Wood was signed out of high school in 1960 by the Boston Red Sox as a conventional fastball-curveball pitcher, but after spending parts of five seasons in the majors with only one win to show for his efforts it became clear to him that he had better try something else. When he was purchased by the White Sox in 1967 he turned to the knuckler, which he had thrown off-and-on since his school days.

It was, he relates, "a make-or-break thing for me. If the knuckler didn't work, it was back to my father-in-law's plumbing and heating business" in his hometown of Lexington, Mass.

The knuckler worked. He stuck with the White Sox as a relief pitcher, and in 1968 he won 13 games in that capacity and was named American League "Fireman of the Year." He became a starter in 1971 and won 20 or more games for four straight seasons. His career victory total of 150 at mid-season ranked him behind only Emil "Dutch" Leonard (191) and Atlanta's Mr. Niekro (170) among all the knuckleballers who have ever pitched. Given a long-enough career (easy-throwing knuckleball pitchers can continue in the majors until well into their 40s; Hoyt Wilhelm lasted until he was 49) he could surpass them, too.

Mr. Wood throws the knuckler upwards of 80% of the time, mixing in an occasional fastball for variety. A calm, patient man who must think awhile before declaring whether he'd rather be pitching or pursuing his hobby of fishing, he has accomplished his surrender to his pitch with grace.

"I can't control what the ball will do, so I don't worry about it," he says. "When I'm on the mound I concentrate on aiming for the center of the plate waist high and releasing the ball the same way every time. It doesn't matter who's at bat or what the score is. I've never been hit hard when the pitch was going right."

And when things don't go right, well, that's the way it is in knuckleball business. After a losing performance, Mr. Wood usually tells reporters that *he* was doing what he always does. It was just that the ball didn't cooperate.

• *July 22, 1977*

Ain't Nothing
Like a Triple

S
•

o you think you know baseball, huh? Then tell me this, without peeking at the next paragraph: Who holds the major-league record for most triples in a single season?

The answer is John Owen Wilson, who socked 36 three-baggers for the Pittsburgh Pirates in 1912.

Mr. Wilson's feat is one of the most remarkable in the long history of the game; no other player has ever hit more than 26 triples in a season. Yet it remains unknown to all except the most industrious Figure Filberts.

Even today, when nostalgia is the rage, no one much cares about Mr. Wilson's achievement, or about Mr. Wilson himself. His file in baseball's Hall of Fame at Cooperstown, N.Y., consists of a few statistics and an ancient newspaper clipping, source and date unknown. The only lengthy article about him on hand at The Sporting News, baseball's long-time bible, was published in October 1962 to commemorate the 50th anniversary of his record.

What is known about Mr. Wilson is this: He was born in Texas in 1883 and died there in 1954. He played in the big leagues from 1908 through 1916, first with the Pirates and then with the St. Louis Cardinals. He was tall, and swift afoot, but had a reputation for being erratic at the plate; his single-season batting averages ranged from .227 to .300 and his lifetime mark was .269.

Before coming up to the big leagues, Mr. Wilson

performed for a time for a team of deaf and mute players, although he was neither deaf nor mute. His nickname was "Chief," but the Hall of Fame lists his ancestry as "English-Irish" and makes no reference to his having Indian blood. His nature was decidedly reticent.

The point of all this isn't to revive the memory of Mr. Wilson, although that isn't a bad idea. It is to revive the memory of the triple, which is far and away baseball's most exciting play but which has become a rare, if not endangered, species in what was once called the national pastime.

How rare is the triple? Well, in 1921, a record 694 such blows were struck in the American League, whose eight teams played a total of 616 games. That's an average of 1.12 triples a game.

Last year, 14 American League clubs, playing 1,134 games, hit 644 triples, or .57 a game, the most for any league since the majors expanded beyond 16 teams in 1961. Less than one triple every two games has been the norm over the last 30 years or so, and the last individual to hit as many as 20 in a season was Willie Mays, who did it in 1957.

What is responsible for this sorry state of affairs? All of the things that make present-day baseball what it is, or isn't. For this we have no less an authority than Lew Fonseca, who led the American League in batting in 1929 with a mark of .369, and has spent some 60 of his 79 years in the game in one capacity or another.

"First off, you've got the ballparks," says Mr. Fonseca, a gruff-voiced man who for the past eight years has been a batting instructor for the Chicago Cubs. "Today they're mostly symmetrical, but back then a lot of them were odd-shaped, with deep center fields. A good hit could roll a long way.

"Then you've got the way the outfielders play. These days, the style is for them to play deep, very deep. In the old days, outfielders like Tris Speaker prided themselves on how shallow they could play. They caught a lot of short shots that are singles today, but if one got by it was an easy double or triple.

"Mostly, though, you've got to remember that the triple is a line-drive hit, and to hit liners consistently you've got to make good contact with the ball. When I played, most players used 35- or 36-ounce bats with thick handles. You could get good wood on the ball even if you didn't hit it perfect. Now, almost everybody uses a lighter, whippier bat with a skinny handle and a fat end, and swings for the fences. It's not right for most players, but they do it anyway and they're not about to change. Why should they? Homers are what they're paid for."

To get the best idea what we fans have lost from such trends, we must turn to the arts, specifically to Philip Roth's 1973 book, *The Great American Novel*. The critics didn't care much for it, but I liked it fine. It had baseball, humor and sex. In other words, it had everything.

My favorite part was when Luke "The Loner" Gofannon, one of the book's superstar heroes (greater than The Babe!), had just completed a particularly strenuous bout of lovemaking with Angela Whitling Trust, the ageless beauty whose husband owned the Tri-City Tycoons, the best team in all of baseball.

To her feverish questionings, The Loner admitted that he loved her more than stolen base, a shoestring catch, a fastball letter-high and a little tight, and even a home run. ("Smack a home run and that's it, it's all over," he explained.)

But when she asked him if he loved her more than a triple, he replied, "I can't tell a lie, Angela. There just ain't nothing like it."

● *July 21, 1978*

Playing Rotblatt

T
he periodic readership surveys this newspaper commissions show that quite a few of you out there have been to college. Thus, it is safe to assume that you have had at least a brush with the blend of the cynical and grotesque that's known as "college humor," and can appreciate what is to follow.

There is, in Northfield, Minn., an institution called Carleton College. It's a small college, and yet there are those who love it. Some of my best friends are Carleton grads. They tell me it's an excellent school, one of those "Harvard of the Midwest" sort of places, whatever that means.

Back in 1964, some of the boys at Carleton, finding themselves in need of exercise, formed an intramural slow-pitch softball league. Considering it infra dig to announce to their fellows that they intended merely to play softball, they determined to fashion their own version of the game. They also thought it would be cute to name it after a former major leaguer so obscure that his identity would test trivia buffs.

The rule changes they adopted were these: Walks weren't permitted, a batter could hit an unlimited number of foul balls, and while only 10 men at a time could play the field, everyone on a team's roster who showed up had to be given a regular turn at bat. The player they chose to name the game for was Marvin J. Rotblatt, whom one of the league's founders remembered from a boyhood baseball-card collection.

Mr. Rotblatt was superbly qualified for the honor, the lads agreed. He was short (5-foot-7), stocky, lefthanded and had a funny name, and his record as a big-league pitcher was a truly forgettable four wins and three losses scattered over parts of three seasons with the Chicago White Sox of the late 1940s and early '50s.

So the game of Rotblatt was launched, and for two years the Carletonians played happily at it. The only fly in the ointment was that Mr. Rotblatt was so obscure (and so perfect for the purpose) that some at the college thought he'd been invented. When an officer of the league discovered in 1966 that the ex-pitcher was alive, well and selling insurance in Chicago, the city of his birth, he invited him to come to Carleton to dispel the notion he was a legend. Mr. Rotblatt accepted.

According to a Carleton historian of the period, Mr. Rotblatt's visit was awaited with some trepidation. I suspect that was because some of the youths weren't sure he would appreciate their brand of fun.

They shouldn't have worried; Mr. Rotblatt had been to college and was hip. He appeared on campus wearing (among other garments) sun glasses and a loud sport shirt, carrying his White Sox traveling bag and puffing a big cigar. At a softball game staged in his honor, he pitched, hit homeruns batting right and lefthanded, and entertained between innings with a juggling routine he'd learned while barnstorming with the old House of David team.

He drank beer and leered at the girls, and at a banquet that night he wowed 'em with an hour of baseball stories and off-color jokes. After all, you don't make a living selling insurance without a gift of gab.

His appearance was acclaimed as an unblemished triumph. "We all had tears in our eyes as he left," the Carleton historian wrote.

Since then, Mr. Rotblatt has been adopted by Carleton, and vice versa. He appears every several years at Rotblatt banquets in Northfield and at Carleton alumni affairs around Chicago.

One such luncheon was held the other day. Mr. Rotblatt was there, mainly to give the benediction of his presence. The guest of honor was Ballard Smith, a Carleton alum, class of '66, and former Rotblatter who had accomplished something Marvin never did:

making it big in the bigs. Last year, Mr. Smith was named president of the San Diego Padres of the National League.

Mr. Smith, a pleasant young man, gave a brief speech, the rough title of which was "from Rotblatt to the majors." He told of his joy in playing Rotblatt at Carleton, of his law school days and of his struggles as a young lawyer and district attorney in Meadville, Pa., a small town near Pittsburgh. The story of his ascendancy to the Padres' presidency was wholly in the spirit of Rotblatt. "I married the boss's daughter," he said, the boss being Ray Kroc, the hamburger baron and owner of the team.

Mr. Rotblatt beamed, proud that one of his boys had made good. Not one to let an opportunity pass, he later collared Mr. Smith and was last heard describing to him the wonders of a group insurance plan he'd worked up.

● *June 3, 1980*

Winning
the 'Oriole Way'

T he 1983 World Series was preceded by a spate of articles on the physics of baseball that concluded that it was well-nigh impossible to hit a well-thrown pitch.

After intensive study, scientists concluded that not only can baseballs really be made to curve, but that they also can be persuaded to dip, flip and flutter in various marvelous ways. The surface of the bat—round—is the wrong shape for solid contact with the elusive spheroid, and it rotates away from the ball at impact, which ain't good either.

Furthermore, a researcher at Carnegie-Mellon University found that it is "physiologically impossible" for a batter to keep his eye on a pitch until it strikes his bat the way coaches have been preaching for years. The best a hitter can do is follow the ball until it's five feet or so from the plate and then take an educated guess where it'll wind up.

Looked at that way, what the Baltimore Orioles' pitchers did to the Philadelphia Phillies' hitters in the just-finished Fall Classic could be regarded as a tribute to the literacy of the latter: They didn't know how hard their job was until they read about it. It's more probable, though, that the O's simply have one of the best staffs of hurlers ever assembled, and that they picked the best possible time to prove it.

The Orioles' achievement in holding the National

League champs to nine runs in their five-game World Series triumph was remarkable enough, but it becomes downright incredible when added to their handling of the power-hitting Chicago White Sox in the four-game American League pennant play-off. In those nine games the Baltimore pitchers did this:

—Held the Phils to a team batting average of .195—54 points under their regular-season mark—and the White Sox to .211—51 points under theirs.

—Permitted a total of 12 runs, only 10 of which were earned.

—Threw three shutouts and allowed only a single, unearned run in another contest.

—Held their opponents scoreless in 69 of 82 innings, and allowed more than one run in only one inning.

The pitchers who accomplished these feats were starters Scott McGregor, Mike Boddicker, Mike Flanagan and Storm Davis, and relievers Sammy Stewart, Tippy Martinez and Jim Palmer. None except Martinez has thrown even one pitch for another major-league team. The rest were either signed originally by the Orioles or acquired in trades from other teams' minor-league clubs and then trained to hurl the Oriole way. When people talk about the "Orioles' system" (and you've probably had it up to here about that by now), what they really mean is the care and feeding of pitchers.

"We have different standards in evaluating pitching talent than most teams," said Ray Miller before the series' opener in Baltimore last week. He's a longtime minor-league bullpen rat who has been the O's pitching coach for six years and spent four more campaigns teaching in the team's farm chain.

"Other teams look for power pitchers—kids with great arms. We'll take one of 'em if we can get him, but there aren't that many around. Mostly, we go for kids with good mechanics, by which I mean sound throwing motions. Given a choice between a kid who can throw 90 miles per hour with bad mechanics, and a sound kid who can throw 85, we'll take the sound kid.

"Then we give them our three rules of pitching: work fast, throw strikes and change speeds. Working fast keeps the defense on its toes. Throwing strikes saves the arm and puts the pressure on the batter. Changing speeds is what pitching's all about.

"Notice there's nothing in there about throwing hard or striking people out. We don't care much about strikeouts, and we don't want our guys throwing hard. If a hard-thrower gets in trouble, what can he do, throw harder? We want our guys to save their hard stuff for situations when they really need it."

Between chews from an enormous wad of tobacco, Miller laughed at the "junk ball" label that has been stuck on the Orioles' staff. "We've got guys who can throw fast, like Stewart and Davis, and we throw about 60% fastballs, just like the other teams. The difference is that we get the other 40% over the plate. When your off-speed stuff is working, it makes an 85-mph fast-ball look like 105. And all that talk about 'junk' gives us an extra edge."

I thought that game two of the series best exemplified what Miller was talking about. The O's pitcher was Mike Boddicker, a 26-year-old rookie. Going for the Phils was Charles Hudson, 24, and also in his first year.

Boddicker stands 5 feet 11 inches tall, weighs 172 and looks a bit frail for a major-league hurler. He'd put in five full seasons in the O's minor-league chain, and was called up after opening day only because of injuries to Palmer and Flanagan. He throws mostly curves and change-ups. Hudson is a strapping 6 feet 3 inches tall and throws a heckuva fastball. He had spent just two years in the minors before making the jump to the Bigs.

Hudson zipped the O's for four innings, but in the fifth they timed his hummer for four straight hits and three runs. That was the ballgame (the final score was 4-1), because the Phils never figured out Boddicker. He walked none and gave up just three hits, only one of which was solidly struck. The Phils' only run was unearned. It was the best-pitched game of the Series, for my money.

There were, of course, other factors in the Baltimore triumph. If team happiness contributes to success (and I'm not at all sure it does), the Orioles had a big edge. Phils' veterans Pete Rose, Gary Matthews and Garry Maddox spent the Series grumbling about the platooning tactics of their manager, Paul Owens, while the O's tolerated the same treatment from their skipper, Joe Altobelli, with apparent equanimity. "Accepting being platooned is a sign of maturity," the O's John Lowenstein told one post-game press conference with only a hint of a smile.

More to the point, the Phils used ace pitcher Steve Carlton in the final game of the play-offs against Los Angeles and thus could get him to the mound just once against the O's. Having Carlton ready for game two after the Phils' opening-game win might have changed things.

But probably not, because the Orioles' pitchers just outnumbered their foes. Young Boddicker put it well after his win. In answer to a reporter's question, he said he felt no particular team pressure to win because if he didn't, someone else would. "The reason it took me six years to make this club," he said, "is because there were so many good pitchers ahead of me."

● *Oct. 18, 1983*

Year of the Cubs (?)

CHICAGO

"I don't care who wins as long as it's the Cubs"
—Bert Wilson, Chicago Cubs' broadcaster, 1940's.

T his has been a memorable season for the Chicago Cubs, and people who know that I'm a lifelong Cubs fan have asked me numerous times during its course when I was going to write about the team. Invariably, my answer was, "Later."

I didn't put them off from lack of interest, but from fear. I believed that as soon as I began to take the Cubs seriously as pennant contenders, even in my mind, they would revert to historic form and collapse. I didn't want to take even part of the blame for that.

I suspect that, for all their apparent current optimism, most Cubs fans felt much the same way. Thirty-nine years in the baseball wilderness had inoculated us against hope. George Will celebrated the Cubs in an August column in Newsweek magazine in which he quoted Saul Bellow, Nelson Algren, Joseph Epstein and John Wesley, but never once did he say flat out that he thought the Cubs were gonna win. Even as our heroes' magic number approached zero, we fans remain wary.

My own conversion to overt confidence came only last Friday afternoon in a chilly, overcast Wrigley Field. The Cubs, 7½ games in front with 16 left, led the second-place Mets 3-0 and had loaded the bases with two outs in the sixth inning. The batter was Jody Davis, our tall, popular, country-boy catcher.

The 36,000 in attendance grasped the possibilities

of the situation, and began chanting "Jo-dee, Jo-dee" as Davis strode to face Brent Gaff, the Mets' pitcher. Gaff threw and—pow!—Jody walloped the first pitch into the center-field stands, putting the game and, probably, the race out of the Mets' reach.

Cubs' manager Jim Frey has been opining right along that God is too busy to pay attention to the Cubs (there's a presidential election campaign on, you know), but I'll bet even he glanced upward after that one.

The Cubs have owed their long history of ineptitude mainly to the ownership of Philip K. Wrigley, their president from 1932 until his death in 1977. Arthur Daley once wrote in the New York Times that Mr. Wrigley was "the noblest creature ever to enter the game." He was sportsmanlike, gracious and modest—everything a baseball executive shouldn't be.

The positive side of the Wrigley regime was its devotion to Wrigley Field, the nicest ballpark in the world. The negative side was its cavalier attitude toward winning. The Cubs were among the last major league teams to develop a farm system. They traded good players who were personally troublesome and kept fan-favorites long after their usefulness had ended.

Hypnotized by the cozy dimensions of Wrigley Field, Cub management always stocked up on power hitters while neglecting speed. The Cub heroes of the postwar years—Hank Sauer, Ernie Banks, Billy Williams, Ron Santo and Dave Kingman—were sluggers all. The last Cub to lead the National League in stolen bases was Stan Hack, in 1939, with 17. When they chanced upon a swifty, the Cubs would speedily trade him. Remember the Brock-for-Broglio deal?

In the 38 seasons since their last pennant in 1945, the Cubs set a record for consecutive second-division finishes with 20 (1947-66) and played .500 ball or better just 10 times. They did, however, have one good year: 1969. With Banks, Williams and Santo hitting, and Ferguson Jenkins and Ken Holtzman pitching, they sprinted to an 8½-game mid-August lead in the NL East.

But those Cubs were unused to success, and behaved inappropriately. Santo took to clicking his heels on the field after victories, and pitcher Dick Selma led cheers from his bullpen seat. Agents seeking endorsements besieged the clubhouse. I'm afraid we fans made things worse with our overenthusiasm. It all proved exhausting, and the Mets swooped past the Cubs in September to win by eight.

The Cubs turnaround dates from October 1981, when Tribune Co., a locally based newspaper and television empire, bought the team and brought in Dallas ("I Have No Patience") Green from the Philadelphia Phillies to run it.

Green is only occasionally sportsmanlike and gracious, and never modest. He stomped into Chicago and declared the team's 105-year history null and void, proclaiming a "new tradition." He hired pugnacious Lee Elia as his field manager.

The pair wasn't an immediate hit. The Cubs finished fifth in 1982 and 1983, and Elia distinguished himself mainly by a postgame tirade in which he blasted the long-suffering Chicago fans as "nickel-and-dime people" and "country suckers." (The tape of his full, unexpurgated outburst is baseball's biggest underground best seller.) He was canned last August.

The calm Frey now reigns in the dugout (his motto is, "You don't celebrate until it's New Year's"), but winning hasn't mellowed Green. Just the other day, a fan called a radio show on which Green was appearing. The man blessed Green for the job he'd done, but asked about rumors that the Cubs wanted to trade a starting outfielder for a left-handed pitcher.

"What rumors? I never started any! It's people like you that get those stupid things started!" Green exploded. The fan meekly apologized and hung up.

Green turned the Cubs around with a series of trades that almost completely changed their roster. The only holdovers to figure prominently in the pennant push are catcher Davis, first baseman Leon Durham and relief pitcher Lee Smith.

Green can't get his fill of Phillies. He acquired second baseman Ryne Sandberg, shortstop Larry Bowa, pitcher Dick Ruthven and outfielders Bob Dernier, Gary Matthews and Keith Moreland from his former employer. Dernier and Sandberg give the team the kind of speed and sharp defense the old Cubs never had.

Veteran third baseman Ron Cey came from the Dodgers, and pitchers Steve Trout, Dennis Eckersley and Scott Sanderson came from the White Sox, Boston and Montreal, respectively. Green's masterstroke was obtaining pitcher Rick Sutcliffe from Cleveland last June 14. Sutcliffe has won 15 games and lost one since joining the club. His presence alone should give the Cubs an edge in any post-season action.

Still, true Cub fans can always find something to worry about, and this season is no exception. We fear that, like the White Sox last year, a divisional championship may be the limit of the Cubs' potential. We recall that Detroit, the team we're likely to meet if we do get to the World Series, was the villain of the 1945 go-around. We're still steamed about Bowie Kuhn's ruling that deprived us of the four-games-to-three home-field edge in any Series as punishment for the sin of refusing to play night games at Wrigley Field.

But, what the heck, those are trifles. The time is now, and now is the time.

"It might . . . it could be . . . IT IS!"
> —*Harry Caray, present Cubs' broadcaster.*

I hope.

● *Sept. 21, 1984*

Note: The Cubs never made it to the World Series, losing to the San Diego Padres in the National League playoffs.

Tigers Take It

DETROIT

I
•

f there were a baseball statistical category called Season-Winning Hit, its 1984 leader would be Howard Johnson of the Detroit Tigers, with one.

On April 3, in the Tigers' opening-day game at Minneapolis, Johnson doubled home Chet Lemon in the third inning to put his team in front, 1-0. The Tigers beat the Twins in that one and didn't spend as much as a day behind another team the rest of the way en route to the world championship they clinched here Sunday night.

As it turned out, Johnson's days of championship-season glory would be few. The 23-year-old third baseman performed well enough through June, but then a slight shoulder injury and outside breaking pitches proved his undoing. He saw little action thereafter, and appeared in the Series only as a pinch hitter in game five.

Nonetheless, the memory of that April moment warmed his post-Series celebration. "I hit a high fastball off Al Williams," he recalled. "The ball hit the top of the right-field fence about six feet fair. This is a nice time to think about it, you know."

Thus began one of the rarest of feats in the game with the longest of seasons—a wire-to-wire triumph. No team had accomplished it since the 1927 New York Yankees of Ruth, Gehrig and Lazzeri, and only five did it before that. The Tigers won 104 times during the regular season, blitzed the Kansas City Royals in three straight in the American League play-offs, and exorcised the San Diego Padres four games to one in the World Series.

It would be nice to report that the '84 Tigers belong in the company of baseball's great teams, but that would be stretching things. Statistically, they weren't outstanding. Only one everyday player hit better than .300 during the regular season (Alan Trammell at .314) and no pitcher was a 20-game winner. And the Padres managed to outhit them, .265 to .253, in the series.

According to Dick Tracewski, this Tiger squad might not have beaten the 1968 one that claimed this city's last baseball crown. "Denny McLain won 31 games for that team, and Willie Horton hit 36 homers. No one on this bunch did that," noted Tracewski, who played shortstop for the 1968 team and is a coach with this one.

Faced with such discrepancies, baseball men tend to fall back on obscurities like team "chemistry" and "character," and those terms were bandied about plenty here. As usual, they weren't satisfying. Everyone, after all, has chemistry (we're 90-some-percent water) and even losers can possess character by ordinary definitions.

Rather obviously, the Tigers started with a generous quantity of garden-variety talent. Shortstop Trammell, second baseman Lou Whitaker, catcher Lance Parrish, outfielders Lemon and Kirk Gibson and pitchers Jack Morris and Willie Hernandez might not be shoo-ins for Cooperstown, but they'll do for now. The Wyatt Earp-mustached Morris stood out in the Series with his two complete-game victories. Even though Trammell was splendid, I thought that Morris, not he, deserved the Series Most Valuable Player award.

Less obviously, the Tigers possessed the sort of bottom-of-the-lineup productivity that brings victory in these days when no team has a monopoly on Big T talent. "We're a lot like the Baltimore team that won last year," opined Tracewski before the Series started. "They had their stars, sure, but it was the play of the platoon guys like John Lowenstein, Jimmy Dwyer and Gary Roenicke that put them over. For us, it was Larry Herndon, Milt Wilcox, Ruppert Jones and Marty Castillo. Let's face it. Their play varies from year to year. This year they came through, and so did we."

Indeed, if this World Series is remembered for anything, it will be for the play of its average-guy participants. Herndon, a right-handed-hitting platooned outfielder, won game one for his team with a two-run homer. Knock-around Kurt Bevacqua (seven teams in a 13-season Major League career) got San Diego even in game two with a three-run shot. In game three, journeyman veteran Wilcox was the winning pitcher, and Castillo got the game-winning hit, also a home run.

Trammell's two home runs scored one for the stars in game four, and muscleman Gibson's two huge blasts provided most of the fifth-game fireworks. But it was Rusy Kuntz, a reserve outfielder, who got the game-winning RBI in the finale with a short fly to right field that scored Gibson from third in the fifth inning.

The 1984 Series also proved again that just because a contest is important doesn't mean that it will be well played. The baseball was seldom beautiful and mostly wasn't even plain. In the third game, won by the Tigers, 5-2, Padres' pitchers tied a World Series record by walking 11, and the two teams left a total of 24 runners on base to set a mark. They don't keep records for pitchers' tosses to first base to hold runners and the number of 3-2 counts on hitters, but if they did two more marks might have been set in that one.

There were no late rallies and precious few late runs. In each game, the team that led after five innings won. After game four, with his team ahead three games to one, Tiger manager Sparky Anderson lamented that the nation had yet to see the "real" Tigers in the Fall Classic. His team's robust performance in its 8-4 win Sunday remedied that, somewhat.

The Series' central mystery, as impenetrable as the floor plan of the Renaissance Center here, was why the Padres' starting pitching was unspeakable and their relievers all but unhittable. San Diego starters were battered for 17 runs (16 earned) in 10⅓ innings. None lasted more than five innings, and two failed to complete a single frame. Yet once Padres manager Dick Williams went to his bullpen, Andy Hawkins, Dave Dravecky, Greg Harris and Craig Lefferts, whose previous accomplishments had been modest, stopped the Detroit merry-go-round cold.

The sole exception was in the seventh inning of game five, when Williams yanked Leffers for his relief ace, Goose Gossage. Detroit led 4-3 at the time. Parrish smacked the mighty Goose's second pitch for a left-field home run, and the next inning Gibson mashed a three-run job to right. But that's the kind of Series it was.

● Oct. 16, 1984

Squeezing the
Grapefruit League

ALONG I-95, SOUTH FLORIDA

Writing about baseball spring training on the East Coast of Florida isn't all suntan and soda pop. There's also I-95.

On the plus side, this link in our great interstate highway system is free (i.e. no tolls) and runs past all the training camps. The minus is that it usually takes a while to get there on it.

The engineers who laid out I-95 set the tone for the roadway by mixing left-lane turnoffs with conventional right-laners around Miami in a way that necessitates some truly breathtaking lane changes. State highway officials chipped in by positioning traffic signals just before on-ramps and just beyond off-ramps so that it's tough to get on the thing, and tough to get off.

The folks who use the road (mostly out-of-staters, Floridians claim, but I doubt it) do their part by striving continually to create the perfect gapers' block. They'll brake to ogle a dented beer can.

But at the ballpark such irritation always fades quickly in the warmth of the day and the good feeling that suffuses the activity. Fans, relieved of the obligations of partisanship by the fact that the games don't count in the standings, feel free to cheer good plays by both teams. Players, temporarily liberated from the relentless travel that takes the joy out of big-time sports, can be, well, playful. Even team owners exhibit occasional good humor. Here is some juice from a recent tour of the Grapefruit League, eastern branch.

Monday, March 4—The Montreal Expos, training at West Palm Beach, have a wondrous machine that launches towering pop flies for their catchers to pursue, that being a difficult task for fungo batsmen. One catcher in the line of 10 or so executes a somersault before making his play. His mates decide it looks like fun, and they do somersaults, too, in turn.

Wednesday, March 6—The Baltimore Orioles play an intrasquad game in their park in inner-city Miami before a crowd of about 50 people, who are let in free. Eddie Murray, their high-priced slugger, comes to bat in inning one against pitcher Mike Boddicker and points at the center field wall, like Babe Ruth did. Boddicker does what Charley Root should have done to Ruth. He walks him.

After the game, manager Joe Altobelli makes his players run the bases hard a half-dozen times to work up a sweat. The Orioles have eight bona fide major league outfielders in camp, two more than they probably can keep. It's no wonder that Gary Roenicke, scrapping to hold his spot in the O's pasture, leads the chase.

Sunday, March 10—The Texas Rangers visit the Expos at West Palm. They lead 8-1 early, but are engulfed in a 10-run Expo eighth. Behind me in the stands, two players' wives exchange notes on the trials of bringing children to spring training.

"Having an infant with you in a motel room is no fun," says one. ". . . (her husband) says he's going to have to move out to get some sleep."

"Our 10-year-old's school back home won't excuse kids for any sort of trip," says the other. "We had to have the team doctor write a note that he's sick this week."

Tuesday, March 12—The New York Yankees play the Rangers in the latter's tiny home field at Pompano Beach. George Steinbrenner, the Yanks' owner, sits three rows behind the home-plate screen and draws most of the fans' attention.

When a Yankee makes a miscue in the field or on the bases—and several do—people in the crowd yell "Trade him, George." Mickey Rivers, formerly a Yank and now a Ranger, pinch hits and singles sharply. "Nice deal, George! Thanks a lot!" a Ranger fan bellows.

Steinbrenner sits with some cronies, chatting and ignoring the barbs. After the final out of a Ranger victory that puts his team's spring mark at 0-5, he arises, turns to the multitude, and shrugs. Someone asks him if he plans to stay in the area for the rematch between the two teams the next day at the Yanks' base at nearby Fort Lauderdale. "I'll stay as long as the Pepto-Bismol holds out," Steinbrenner answers.

Wednesday, March 13—The Expos play the Los Angeles Dodgers at the large Dodgertown complex in Vero Beach. It's the nicest of the spring-training facilities here, featuring a golf course, swimming pool, tennis courts and motel-like housing in addition to the usual ball fields.

Streets are named for such Dodger heroes as Walter Alston, Jackie Robinson and Sandy Koufax. The Dodgers, unique in baseball for their money-making skills, turn a buck here, too, by running a conference center on the grounds when it's not being used for baseball.

On a side diamond before the major-league contest, some Dodgers' minor leaguers play a team from South Korea that's visiting Florida. The Dodgers try to be good hosts, but they can't help giggling at the repeated guttural barks of the Korean catcher as his pitcher struggles through a six-hit, four-run inning. I ask a Korean-looking spectator what the catcher is saying. "He's telling the pitcher to improve his performance," is the smiling reply.

The Dodgers' big leaguers enter their stadium for their game after a full house of fans has assembled. Manager Tom Lasorda comes last. As he strolls in alone from right field, a recording of "Hail to the Chief" is played on the park's p.a. system. Lasorda regally doffs his cap to waves of applause. Apparently, it's a ritual here.

I sit with Ed Vargo, a National League umpire for 24 years and now an umpire-supervisor. Who's the best ump in the game? I ask. "Nobody," he says with a straight face. "They're all very good."

Friday, March 15—The Braves play the Dodgers at West Palm. It's a 3-2 yawner win for the Dodgers, highlighted only by the valiant efforts of Pedro Guerrero, their muscular third baseman, to defend himself from ground balls.

The star of the day is Dan Deshaies, a young minor-league umpire up for a look behind home plate. When he calls a strike, he takes a crossover step to his right, pumps his right arm and vigorously, and emits a roaring "EEERAAAW!" The crowd loves it, and soon is calling "EEERAAAWS" with him. The recollection is enough to make almost bearable the two-hour ride on I-95 back to my Fort Lauderdale hotel, 50 miles away.

• Mar. 22, 1985

Missouri Loves Company

TORONTO

I. n a year in which Villanova, Michael Spinks and Ivan Lendl have triumphed, it is fitting that the Kansas City Royals and the St. Louis Cardinals will contest the baseball World Series beginning tomorrow night.

The Royals and Cards entered their respective league championship playoffs favored to spend late October in seasonal retirement. The Cards reinforced their underdog status by dropping their first two playoff games to the Los Angeles Dodgers, and the Royals did them one better by falling behind the Toronto Blue Jays three games to one.

Turns out they were just setting up their foes for the kill. In a memorable baseball doubleheader Wednesday separated by some 2,000 miles, the Cards broke the one-time Bums' hearts, 7-5 in the L.A. sunshine and the Royals bummed out an entire nation by ousting the Jays in the seventh game of their set here at night.

I must admit that I was sorry to see the Jays go. Their presence would have finally put the "world" into the World Series, and given us two national anthems for the price of one. Also, with the Jays in it, naming this Series would have been fun. A set between the Blue Jays and the Cards, for example, could have been labeled "One for the Birds," or, maybe better, the "Beer Barons' Polka," the Cards being the property of the Anheuser-Busch folks and the Jays that of Labatt.

On the other hand, "Missouri Loves Company" ain't a bad tag for the games we're gonna get. (OK, no more puns.)

I fear, though, that however clever we sportswriters are in naming this Series, the weatherman might upstage us. Baseball's powers-that-be have decreed the first all-night-game World Series. In addition, the week late start of the regular season and the expansion of the league-championship playoffs to seven games from five will make this the latest-starting post-season baseball test since the 1981 players' strike brought two rounds of league playoffs and an Oct. 20 opening date between the Dodgers and New York Yankees.

The '81 arrangement was temporary; the present one is permanent. It has been dictated by television ratings and ad dollars, the main motors of modern sportsbiz. ABC-TV, which will air the proceedings, explains that putting the Series on at night will mean about a half-dozen more ratings points, or almost five million more viewing households, than the traditional weekend day games. That's why the network can charge $250,000 for a 30-second commercial this year, up from $200,000 in 1983, the last time it had the Series.

If the Series goes the full seven games, the finale will be played on Oct. 27 in Kansas City, where it also will open tomorrow night. A rainout or two would have them playing on Halloween. Nights get pretty chilly in the Midwest that time of year, and those are mitts the fielders wear, not mittens.

The average nighttime temperatures in Kansas City and St. Louis hover around 42 degrees in late October, which isn't too bad. Still, you can drown in a lake that averages a foot deep, even if you have to fall through the ice to do it. I at least hope that Commissioner Peter Ueberroth has more sense than his predecessor, Bowie Kuhn, and wears an overcoat.

The players, of course, will show up no matter what the temperature, and of the two contestants, the presence of the Royals is the more surprising. This is a team that played in the weakest of the major league's divisions, the AL West, and had the fewest wins (91) of the four semifinalists. The Royals won the AL West last season, but were dropped summarily by the champs-to-be Detroit Tigers in the league playoffs, and got no respect for their effort. It wasn't wholly in jest that George Brett, their best player, said that when the Royals played an intrasquad game in spring training this year, they were favored to lose.

The Royals' batting order features one great hitter (third base-

man Brett), one very good hitter (centerfielder Willie Wilson), one
hitter who used to be very good (designated hitter Hal McRae) and
six guys named Joe. Brett batted .335 in the regular season, with 30
home runs and 112 runs batted in, and wore out the Jays' pitchers in
the playoff. Wilson hit .278. No one else topped the .260 mark from
the plate.

What the Royals do have are five very live young starting pitchers, baseball's best relief pitcher in veteran submariner Dan
Quisenberry, and a manager, Dick Howser, who is willing to use
them in ways that defy the game's hallowed percentages.

Howser's disdain for the verities showed through strongest in
game six of the Toronto series. The "book" on the Jays is that they
murder righties; they compiled a 75-win, 36-loss record against
them in the regular season. But when Howser found himself down
three games to two before a revved up Toronto crowd, he chose to
start a righthander, 23-year-old Mark Gubicza, in game six.

Gubicza did his utmost into the sixth inning and stepped out in
favor of lefty Bud Black, who usually starts. Twice during his turn,
Black faced the Jays' dangerous right-handed hitter, George Bell (28
homers and 95 rbis in the season), with men on base, and twice
Black got him out. It was only with two out in the ninth that Howser
called in Quisenberry to finish a 5-3 win.

Howser was questioned afterward about his unorthodox handling of his pitching. Wasn't he uncomfortable with Black facing
Bell? Yes, he said, but he'd have been uncomfortable with anyone
facing Bell. "The strategy worked because the people worked," he
said in a nice twist on Casey Stengel's old "I managed good but they
played bad" laugh line.

In game seven, Howser was at it again, starting righty Bret
Saberhagen, his 21-year-old, 20-game winner. Saberhagen went
three innings before departing with a bruised hand, whereupon lefty
Charley Leibrandt, another season-long starter, was called to duty.
Again, Trusty Quiz wasn't called until the ninth in a 6-2 victory. The
Royals' mound trio wasn't perfect, but it was good enough, leaving
nine Blue Jays stranded on base, six of them in scoring position. The
Jays could score only five of their 31 base runners in the series' last
three games.

"Our pitching was good. We stuck in there. They could never
put us away," said Howswer of his team's ability to overcome a 3-to-1

deficit in a seven-game post-season series, something accomplished only four other times in major-league annals.

Did Howser think his hurlers could do the same against the Cardinals, whose offensive horsepower rivals that of the Jays? "They had better," said he.

It must be noted that their initiation to playoff baseball, however unhappy its outcome, brought Toronto's fans firmly into the game's mainstream. Until this week the Jays' faithful had been models of decorum, regarding the "boo"—a standard expression in other towns—as beneath them.

In the stress of post-season play, however, Torontonians proved they could boo the opposition, the umpires, and TV broadcaster Tony Kubek, whom they accused of bias. And they managed to holler an eight-letter term for fertilizer as well as the fans at University of Michigan football games. Having real big-league fans surely will benefit the Jays in the seasons ahead.

● Oct. 18, 1985

A Royal Victory

KANSAS CITY

F or my money, the turning point in the baseball World Series came in the fourth inning of game five in St. Louis on Thursday night, when Frank White of the Kansas City Royals hit a foul ball into the stands behind third base and Avron Fogelman, the Royals' co-owner, caught it.

You figure it out. More than 53,000 people were there, and maybe 20 foul balls reached the stands. The odds against any one person getting one were about 2,650-to-1. If that could happen, anything could.

When I told the short, wet Mr. Fogelman my theory in the joyous Royals' locker room after they beat the St. Louis Cardinals, 11-0, here in the seventh and deciding game on Sunday, he exclaimed: "My opinion exactly! I've been going to games for 35 years, and I never came close to getting a foul ball before. I knew it had to mean something good."

On second thought, maybe the odds on what the Royals did were nearly as long. They came back from a three-games-to-one deficit to win the World Series after doing the same thing in the league championship play-off against the Toronto Blue Jays. That was after they'd entered post-season play with the worst record of the four division winners. "I guess coming back the way we did was unusual. But, then, that's the kind of season it was," said the Royals' ace relief pitcher, Dan Quisenberry.

Unusual may not be a strong enough term to describe a World Series in which the swift Cardinals, the National League's leading run producers, were held to 13 tallies in seven games and just two in the last three. Same goes for one in which the game-winning hits in the Royals' final three victories were struck by Buddy Biancalana, Dane Iorg and Darryl Motley, part-timers all.

Shortstop Biancalana's prowess at the plate was such that David Letterman, the late-night TV talk-show host, suggested counting down his career hits until they came within 4,000 of Pete Rose's.

The topper came in the last of the ninth inning of game six here on Saturday night. The inning before, the Cards had broken a 0-0 tie with a two-out pinch-hit single by Brian Harper, a utility outfielder who rivaled the least-known of the Royals for obscurity. Three more outs and they'd be the champs. The champagne, winners' trophy and ABC-TV cameras were at the ready in their locker room.

Instead, the Royals got the winning runs on an umpire's call, a catcher's passed ball and a foul that went thump in the night. Pinch-hitter Jorge Orta led off the home team's ninth by topping a grounder to first baseman Jack Clark, who flipped the ball to pitcher Todd Worrell covering the base. "Safe!" gestured American League umpire Don Denkinger. ABC must have rerun the play a dozen times, and Orta looked out on each.

The next hitter, Steve Balboni, lofted a foul pop up in front of the Royals' dugout. Clark took his eyes off it for a moment to gauge his position, and it dropped to the plastic turf behind him. Reprieved, Balboni singled Orta to second. Jim Sundberg tried to bunt the runners to second and third, but forced Orta instead. Catcher Darrell Porter gave the Royals runners those bases anyway, by letting a pitch to Hal McRae go past him to the screen.

McRae was walked intentionally to load the bases, and Iorg was sent up to bat for Quisenberry, who'd relieved starter Charley Leibrandt. "It was the kind of situation you dream about as a child," Iorg said later. His bat-handle single to right scored two to give the Royals the win.

Upstairs, the Royals faithful cheered and cheered some more. Downstairs, Cardinals manager Whitey Herzog was chewing nails. "That guy was out at first," he told reporters. "[Denkinger] said he beat the throw. Then how the hell could he step on Worrell's foot?"

"We're playin' them 24 men to 25 as it is," Herzog growled in reference to a baseball rule that didn't permit him to replace Vince Coleman, the speedster who missed the Series because his leg was caught beneath a rolling tarpaulin in the play-offs. "Now it looks like it's 24 to 28," the extra three being the American League umpires assigned to the Series. "Maybe we won't show up tomorrow."

The Cards did show up on Sunday, of course, but—their balloon burst—they might as well have stayed home. Lefty John Tudor, who had won games one and four for them in exemplary fashion, gave up a two-run home run to Motley in the second inning and three more runs in the third. The Royals added six runs in the fifth inning as some fans chanted "Outscore the Chiefs," KC's lagging pro football team, which had scored just 10 points in a loss that afternoon. Cards manager Herzog and pitcher Joaquin Andujar were tossed out of the game in the inning after run-ins with umpire Denkinger, who was now behind home plate.

What did Herzog say to Denkinger that got him ejected? "I told him we should have been home in St. Louis tonight," Herzog said later. He also told the umpire a few things it didn't take an expert lip-reader to discern.

The key to the Royals win in the Series was a pitching staff that held the Cardinals to a .185 batting average, a new Series low. Bret Saberhagen, a 21-year-old righty, started and won two games for the Royals, including a five-hit shutout finale, and was named the Series' Most Valuable Player. Leibrandt and Danny Jackson also performed nobly as starters, and Quisenberry won game six in relief.

According to Quiz, at age 32 the gray-beard of the staff, the Royals' hurlers did it partly by ignoring the report on the Cards that their scouts had meticulously prepared. "In the 1980 Series [which the Royals lost to Philadelphia] we stuck to the book and got burned. This time we pitched our own games," Quisenberry declared. "The book said we shouldn't throw inside to the Cardinals' big guys, but we like to pitch inside, so we did. I guess the fellows who wrote the book hadn't seen inside pitches like our guys threw."

● Oct. 29, 1985

OVALBALL

Part 2

Super Bowl Bets

A
•
s everyone who isn't in a coma knows, this Sunday is no ordinary Sunday. It is Pro Football Super Bowl Sunday, that annual culmination of the sport that has captured the American fancy like no other. Upwards of 80 million people—more than one-third of the population—will be tuned in to NBC to watch the Oakland Raiders have it out with the Minnesota Vikings.

Many reasons have been advanced to explain pro football's appeal; intellectuals are fond of saying that it fits our predilections for spectacle, technology and violence. But one reason certainly is its nice adaptability to gambling. Whatever other superlatives may attach to Sunday's contest, the surest is that it will be the largest single gambling event of the year, with several hundred million dollars riding on the outcome.

The vast majority of that money will be wagered illegally, but betting on team sports is so pervasive in this country that this has come to be regarded as a mere curiosity and no serious obstacle to the union of bettor and bettor, or, more to the point, bettor and underworld bookmaker. Equally curious is that just about everyone involved seems to prefer it that way.

The people who run big-time sports at once belittle and cater to gambling's hold on their fans. No small amount of juggling is required to keep these positions aloft, but through practice they have become skilled at

it. Better that, they believe, than legalizing the whole thing and per-
fecting a new act.

The truce with illegal gambling exists in all sports, of course,
but nowhere is it clearer than in pro football, which for a number of
reasons is admirably constituted to attract the widest possible betting interest.

National Football League teams usually play once a week, and
the league's regular-season schedule contains the fewest games of
any major U.S. spectator sport: 196, compared with 729 for the National Hockey League, 902 for pro basketball and 2,106 for major
league baseball. This gives bettors plenty of time to ponder the attri-
butes of the various contestants.

Every regular- and post-season pro football game (as well as
many pre-season ones) is televised widely, and the advent of nation-
wide Monday night games and weekend double and triple headers
means that fans everywhere get a chance to see just about every team
several times during a season.

The game is high-scoring enough so that individual contests
can be neatly equalized for betting purposes by requiring the team
that seems strongest to win by more than a certain number of
points in order to reward its supporters. In Sunday's game, for instance, Oakland has been made a 4½ point favorite, meaning that
it must beat Minnesota by five points or more for its backers to
prevail. Any other outcome will mean that people betting on Minnesota will collect. Point-spread betting has the additional
dimension of lending competitive spice to games that might otherwise be lopsided and dull.

By most calculations, between 25% and 50% of adult male
Americans (and some women, too) bet on pro football at least once
in a while. The NFL takes issue with such estimates, saying they are
far too high, but this hasn't kept it from supplying what can only be
called betting services. Among these are official, weekly injury reports (injuries to key players can affect point spreads) and an
in-house policing staff that sniffs out reports of collusion between
players and gamblers. The league says it does this to protect itself
against the suspicious, but the greatest beneficiaries are the book-
makers, who stand to lose the most if "inside information" on games
is allowed to circulate.

The link between pro football and gambling was made all the
more pronounced this season by the appearance of Jimmy "The Greek"

Snyder, the renowned oddsmaker, as a pre-game analyst on CBS's tele-casts of NFL games. In deference to the league, Mr. Snyder doesn't put his widely published point spreads on the air. But he obviously isn't there to tell the fans what the quarterbacks say in the huddle.

Going from there to supporting legalized gambling is another matter, however; the NFL opposes it in all forms, and has gone so far as to sue the State of Delaware to try to terminate its season-old ex-periment in football betting (a decision is pending).

The league argues that putting betting in the hands of the states—the most frequent proposal—wouldn't hurt the bookies much. It points out that the success of illegal gambling rests largely on its extending credit to bettors and conferring tax-free status on winnings, fringe benefits that states probably wouldn't offer. The league further asserts that legalizing wagering would complicate its security problems to the extent that government administration of sports would become a likelihood.

Mostly, though, the league bases its case on the assertion that legalized gambling would legitimize the practice and drastically alter the nature of fan interest in its games. The wholesome focus on the simple success or failure of the home team would be replaced by the effect of the team's performance on the winning or losing of bets.

The following hypothetical horror story comes from an NFL position-paper on the subject:

"Suppose the New York Jets were five-point favorites over the Buf-falo Bills in a game played at Shea Stadium in New York. The Jets lead 14-10 and have the ball at the Bills' 20 yard line with 20 seconds to go. Should the Jets try a field goal to win by seven points but risk giving the Bills another chance, or play it safe to be certain of victory by four?

"The Jets decide to play it safe and run out the clock. The fans who bet on the team to win by five points are losers. Shea Stadium resounds with the boos of disgruntled bettors."

That sort of thing happens now and then already, but as things stand most gamblers have the grace to suffer their private setbacks in silence. The NFL probably is right. Legalized gambling would make us even more mercenary than we are, and make our governments a party to further debasement of the emotional currency.

So before the kickoff on Super Bowl Sunday, lift a glass to the bookies, preservers of the integrity of our national games.

● *Jan. 7, 1977*

Colts Find
Another Stable

INDIANAPOLIS

A.
merica's professional football team opened its 1984 regular season here Sunday, losing to the New York Jets, 23-14. No, not the Dallas Cowboys; they've never had any home except Big D. I mean the Indianapolis Colts.

If you'll remember, the Colts were once the Dallas Texans, whose National Football League life began and ended with the 1952 season. Then they were shipped to Baltimore for a 31-year stand. Now they are here in the Heartland, ensconced in the conditioned air of the quilt-roofed Hoosierdome. West, East and Midwest. What other NFL team has lately claimed residence in so much of this great land of ours?

That not everyone is happy about the Colts' latest wandering is a trifle in the brave new world of sportsbiz. When owner Robery Irsay smuggled his chattel out of Baltimore in dead of night last March 29, a step ahead of the process servers, the moved was denounced in Crabtown as the biggest heist since the Brinks job.

The NFL isn't crazy about the switch, either. Its official 1984 schedule gives every other team a municipal designation, even when it's incorrect (the "New York" Giants actually play in East Rutherford, N.J., for example), but the Colts are listed as, simply, the Colts. League Commissioner Pete Rozelle was pointedly absent from Sunday's festivities here.

But since Al Davis packed the Raiders off to Los

Angeles in 1982, and won a $49 million lawsuit against the league for trying to stop him, the NFL is reduced to such empty gestures. Teams as well as players now enjoy free agency.

The wooing of Mr. Irsay best exemplifies this era of franchise freedom. The crusty Chicago construction company owner, who is fond of telling people how smart he is, entered the league in 1972 by buying the Los Angeles Rams and swapping them with Carroll Rosenbloom for the Colts. He apparently thought better of the deal early on, because he began shopping his team around as early as 1976. Over the years he received feelers from Phoenix, Memphis, Jacksonville, New York and L.A., along with Indianapolis.

When the Raiders' legal victory opened the door for Mr. Irsay to flee Baltimore without approval of his fellow owners, Indianapolis's offer was the juiciest. Its centerpiece was use of the 61,300-seat Hoosierdome, which local interests had built on spec for $80 million.

Indianapolis's city fathers sweetened the pot with the kind of freebies and guarantees that gladden the heart of any free-enterpriser. Among other things, the Colts received a 10-year, $12.5 million loan at 8% interest, a new training facility, and pledges that their annual ticket and local-broadcasting revenues won't fall below $7.8 million for the next 12 years.

Indianapolis also offered up a cityful of virgin NFL fans whose fervor for the Colts was unsullied by the team's six straight losing seasons. On April 2, about 20,000 of them turned out in the then-unfinished Hoosierdome to applaud speeches welcoming their heroes.

Mr. Irsay said he was delighted with the reception, but with typical charm he used the occasion to make one point crystal clear. "As I told the press, it's not your ball team or our ball team. It's my family's team. I paid for it, and I worked for it," he said.

In the months since, the Colts' Indianapolis honeymoon has curdled a bit. The team received 143,000 requests for 52,000 season tickets, and their lottery-style distribution left 91,000 people disappointed and, probably, created 52,000 eventual ingrates. Its cashing and keeping of all ticket-application checks for three months before issuing refunds to those who didn't get seats also put some noses out of joint.

Similarly, a proposal to put the Colts' new practice facility on public park land here hasn't met with universal applause.

But for the most part, the Colts have been greeted with the sort of fervor Indianapolis previously reserved for erecting war memorials. "Am I excited about the Colts coming here? You bet I am!" exclaimed Ovid Knick, a 47-year-old General Motors employee. He appeared at Sunday's opener wearing a Colts cap and T-shirt with dark-blue shorts to match. He said he'd also purchased about $75 worth of Colt-emblem gear for his home bar. "I've been a Colts fan since the Johnny Unitas days, so this couldn't be better for me," he explained.

"Having the Colts here is great. I do a lot of work in Baltimore, and I can rib my friends there about it," said Dick Webb, a Colts ticket holder who installs computers for a living. He said he feels "a little" pity for the bereft Baltimoreans, but noted, with some justice, that "if they really wanted to keep the team, more of them should have gone to see them play."

Inside the Hoosierdome, the locals showed that they have watched television, and know how to cheer their new favorites properly. They waved their dark-blue Colts towels, purchased outside for $2.95, a la Pittsburgh Steelers fans, and they arose from their seats sequentially in "human waves" just as the folks at Seattle's Kingdome do.

As for the game, well, you can't have everything. But even in defeat the Colts gave signs that those horseshoes on their helmets might again be the charms of the Unitas glory days. At the least, they were lucky. The Jets missed a field goal when the kick hit a goal-post upright. They had a touchdown nullified by a penalty and had to settle for a field goal instead. They missed an extra point, and gave the Colts a fourth-quarter touchdown by fumbling a punt on their own five-yard line.

The issue wasn't decided until the Colts' luck ran out with less than two minutes left: Quarterback Mike Pagel fumbled on his own four-yard line, and the Jets' Greg Buttle ran the ball into the end zone.

Pagel is a strong-armed young man with excellent scrambling ability (which is fortunate given his leaky blocking protection), but he also will go down as the first Indianapolis Colt to be booed at home.

In the third quarter Sunday, with the Colts trailing and their attack sputtering, some in the Hoosierdome went so far as to chant "We Want Art," Art being Art Schlichter, the team's No. 2 quarter-

back. In making a reserve quarterback their putative savior, they also
set a record for becoming full-fledged pro football fans the quickest.

● *Sept. 4, 1984*

The Sage of Ohio State

I
•

t had been a long week for Woody Hayes. Monday he'd been in Mansfield, Ohio, Tuesday in Pittsburgh, Wednesday in Coventry, Conn., and Thursday back in Pittsburgh, giving speeches at each stop. He's much in demand as a motivational speaker to business groups.

But Friday he was back in his office in the ROTC Building at Ohio State University, looking through his window at the university's huge, gray football stadium.

"You bet I'm here. Tomorrow is the big one," said Woody, glaring between the fat history books that line the front of his metal desk. "Us vs. Michigan. Best doggone rivalry there is! Competition is what makes you go, you know. You beat nobody, what have you got? You beat somebody and you've done something. Yessir."

For 28 years, beefy, bull-necked Woody Hayes led the Buckeyes of Ohio State against "that school up north" in the Midwest version of The Game, often with the Big 10 title at stake. He won that contest 15 times, and his overall won-lost mark at the school was 205 and 61, with 10 ties.

He might be leading them still if he hadn't punched a Clemson player on the sidelines in the heat of the 1978 Gator Bowl game. Referees, newspaper reporters, photographers and yardline markers had been previous targets of his wrath, but an opposing player was too much, and the university let him go at age 65.

Woody didn't go far, though; he's still a hero in Columbus, which had always forgiven his outbursts with an indulgent "There goes Ol' Woody again." He can't take a step outdoors here without being hailed, and the street on which the building that houses his office stands is named Woody Hayes Drive.

At a football game a few years back, he was asked to dot the "i" in the OSU marching band's famous "Script Ohio," a signal honor in Buckeyeland. The university later figured it lost about $30,000 in concession revenues because just about everybody in the crowd of 90,000 stayed put at half time to cheer him.

Woody is 71 years old now, and his fire still burns, albeit a bit lower than before. He returns the local affection in full measure. "Greatest city and university in America!" he declares. "We've always been winners here because we live right. Kids and adults both. Even back in the '60s, when the kids were acting up, we didn't have much trouble here. Our kids were always down to earth.

"I like to talk to students, and I do it every chance I get. Kids have changed lately—yes they have—and it's for the better. They're more practical and realistic than they used to be, and—Jesus—a lot of 'em are smart as hell. Did you see how many of them voted for Reagan a couple weeks ago? That's what I mean. They saw that the way the other fellow wanted to go wouldn't work. It's not a matter of left or right, it's up or down. We're going up again, and I couldn't be happier.

"Some people say it's tough being a kid today because the world is so competitive. Maybe they're right, but that's not bad," he goes on. "It was tough when I was a kid. My father was an educator—a town school superintendent—but he didn't get his college degree until he was 38 years old. I was there when he got it, and I knew what he'd put into it. He expected the same effort from us.

"I was going to be a teacher, too—probably history—until I got involved with football and saw what a wonderful game it was. And what an opportunity for teaching! Why, I spent more time with my players in a week than most professors spend with their students in a year.

"Football teaches things you don't learn elsewhere. A player learns to get up after he's been knocked down. He learns to run the play that's called, whether he's carrying the ball or not. And he learns that nothing in life comes easy.

"See this book here?" he says, holding up a volume of short stories by Irwin Shaw. "My favorite is the one about the guy who made an 80-yard run in school. Some people think it's a sad story, because that run was the best thing that fella ever did, but I look at it differently. If he hadn't made the run, he'd have had damned little to look back on with pride."

That afternoon, Woody expanded on that theme at the Senior Tackle, an annual pre-Michigan-game ceremony in the stadium in which OSU football seniors line up for a symbolic last tackle on a blocking sled. About 2,000 people showed up in the cold for the occasion, and they gave Woody standing ovations coming and going.

He told the Buckeye squad that what they did the next afternoon would stay with them as long as they lived. "I got a call today from a man named Fred Bruney," he said. "Fred said, 'Coach, remember what I did 32 years ago today?' I said I sure did. He intercepted three passes that helped us beat Michigan. He'll smile about that on his deathbed. You do the same thing and you'll have something to smile about, too."

Saturday's OSU-Michigan game had a strong Woody flavor. A lot of Big 10 games did this season, because five head coaches in the league were once his assistants.

Michigan's "Bo" Schembechler played under and coached with Hayes before becoming his archrival. Schembechler's demeanor and attitudes are so like his mentor's that he used to be called "Little Woody." Earle Bruce, who succeeded Woody at OSU, was a six-year aide.

Bruce has found Woody's a touch act to follow. Despite a 55-15 mark at OSU before Saturday, a columnist in the Columbus Dispatch wrote that if Bruce didn't beat the Wolverines, he'd be job hunting. It doesn't help Bruce that he looks like Boss Hogg on "The Dukes of Hazzard" and is platitudinous with the press, but as best as I could learn here, his main fault is that he isn't Woody.

Bruce's Buckeyes beat Michigan, 21-6, to earn another Big 10 title and Rose Bowl berth, but it wasn't vintage, grind-it-out OSU football. Underdog Michigan stopped Ohio State's Heisman Trophy candidate, running back Keith Byars, for three quarters, and might have won if flanker Mike Lanese hadn't made a diving catch for a 17-yard gain on a third-and-12 pass to set up the last-period touchdown that made the score 14-6. Woody was as fond of the pass as he was of dirty hair.

Woody watched from the press box, and while I didn't speak to him afterward, I'm sure the win pleased him. "Winning is the only reason you play. It's what the hard work is all about," he'd said earlier. "I heard it said that losing builds character, but I never tried to find out for myself."

• *November 21, 1984*

Hyping Super Sunday

F. irst off, it should be noted that the football Super Bowl isn't one game but two: The on-the-field contest, and the pre-game. The real game lasts about 3½ hours, the pre-game two weeks.

There's more action in the real game, but more is at stake in the preliminary bout: namely, the attention of the American public. The National Football League and the network televising the Super Bowl—this year ABC—want everybody's appetite nice and whet by late Sunday afternoon so we'll all tune in and watch the commercials, for which ABC is charging about $1 million a minute.

The NFL does it by depositing the participating teams and the nation's news media in a congenial setting like the City on the Bay, and having the latter go at the former. Sometimes, it's quite a show. Many observers rated last year's Los Angeles Raiders-Washington Redskins pre-game follies the best ever.

Fullback John Riggins carried the ball for the Skins. He showed up at a news conference wearing an Air National Guard jumpsuit and declared, Pattonlike, that the year before his team had run over the Miami Dolphins in the Big Game, but that this time it would fly over L.A.

The Raiders double-teamed Riggins with beefy lineman Lyle Alzado, who vowed to tear off some

Redskin lips, and end Todd Christensen, who distributed samples of his poetry and waxed intellectual about the geometrical beauty of football's pass patterns. Linebacker Matt Millen iced the Raiders' triumph when, informed that the Skins' Russ Grimm had said he'd run over his mother to win the game, said that he'd run over Grimm's mother to win, too.

Alas, nothing nearly so spirited has emerged from the pre-game here. Vanilla has replaced vitriol. From their head coach to their lowliest reserve, the San Francisco 49ers say the Miami Dolphins are great sportsmen and fine fellas, and the Fins return the compliments in full.

Attempts by troublemaking newsmen to provoke a squabble have been repulsed. We thought we had one Wednesday when Miami coach Don Shula said he doubted that his Frisco counterpart, Bill Walsh, really followed a script with his team's first 20 or so offensive plays, as some accounts maintained. "We all start with a plan, but I can't believe he doesn't deviate from his" if conditions dictate, Shula said.

Well, Bill, do you *deviate*? Walsh was asked at his news conference an hour later. "Oh sure. Everybody does," he replied mildly. Nuts.

Actually, this is a Super Bowl that might not need news hype to make it big in the living-room box office. It's the game that everyone seems to want to see. Most of us love offense, and this one matches Miami, the No. 1 passing team in NFL history, with a more balanced Frisco attack that may be better overall. On defense, we have a Niners unit that allowed the fewest points of any team this season, and the Dolphins' Killer Bees.

As for the opposing coaches, both Shula and Walsh have spent much of this week denying that they're geniuses. Still, the belief persists, and the adulators may have a point. Despite his Mount Rushmore profile, Shula has shown that he's one football prof who really can alter his style to suit his players, the rules and the times. In the defense-minded 1970s, he ground it out with Griese, Csonka and Kiick. In the nuclear '80s, his Marino, Clayton and Duper pose football's most formidable bomb threat.

Walsh has been a pro head coach only six seasons to Shula's 22, but he has already proved that a ball-control passing attack isn't a contradiction in terms. If it's variety you like, he lined up a guard at fullback and a wide receiver at quarterback in separate plays in the National Conference title game against Chicago.

In the Dolphins' Dan Marino and the Niners' Joe Montana, the game features not only football's two best quarterbacks, but ones with nicely contrasting styles. Marino, already turning fleshy at age 23, is the epitome of the cool, drop-back passer, the successor to Joe Namath as the man with the golden arm. Montana is slimmer and quicker afoot—a sort of latter-day Fran Tarkenton—and does some of his best work on the run. He's pretty swift off the field, also; his third marriage, to a gorgeous actress, is due soon.

Both men have been equally quick in adapting to the "I'm OK, you're OK" tenor of the pre-game. Says Marino of Montana: "He's a great quarterback. I admire him very much." Says Montana of Marino: "He's bigger and stronger than me, and has a better arm."

This, however, is not to say that the present pre-game has been no fun at all. A week of faithful quote-shagging by your correspondent has produced the following examples of humor in uniform:

Russ Francis, 49ers tight end and thrill seeker, on how it feels to fly upside-down in an open-cockpit plane: "Windy."

Mark Clayton, Dolphins wide receiver, on his most remarkable athletic feat: "When I was in college, I jumped across the width of a pingpong table, just because I felt like it. Somebody there said that was easy, so I jumped over the table lengthwise."

Ray Wersching, 49ers place kicker, on the Super Bowl-week diary column he's writing for the San Francisco Examiner: "I'm not going to read it until a week after the game. I may have misquoted myself, and I don't want to get upset."

Bob Baumhower, Dolphins defensive lineman, on the cerebral side of pro football: "Everybody talks about studying the other team's different keys and tendencies, but I try not to let it spoil my concentration on beating the guy I'm playing against."

Riki Ellison, 49er linebacker, on how people in his native New Zealand view America: "They think it's big and materialistic, like Disneyland or 'Dallas' on TV." Are they right? "Pretty much."

Renaldo Nehemiah, 49ers wide receiver and former world-champion hurdler, on how playing football has slowed him down: "I'm not as smooth as I used to be, and I'm carrying some excess weight. I used to run the 40-yard dash in 4.16 seconds. Now it takes me 4.22."

Bubba Paris, 49ers offensive tackle and a minister of the

"Church of Reconciliation," on how he reconciles his fundamen-talist-Christian beliefs with the roughness of his sport: "When someone hurts me, I don't strike back in anger. I pray that the Lord will give me strength to kill the guy on the next play—within the rules, of course."

Montana on the Niners' home-city advantage: "It keeps us off the streets at night."

- *Jan. 18, 1985*

Dolphin Sushi

T. he saving grace of football Super Bowl week is that, after the 10,000 or so news-media analysts and the President of the United States have had their say, the game is finally played. Then that which was hidden becomes revealed, as clearly as the headlights of a truck bearing down on you through the fog 'round Frisco Bay.

Thus it was here Sunday as the San Francisco 49ers were whupping the Miami Dolphins, 38-16, in SB XIX. Would the game be a shoot-out? we all had wondered. Yes, but the Niners did almost all the shooting. Are Niners coach Bill Walsh and Dolphins coach Don Shula both geniuses? No, just Walsh, at least until next year. Is well-roundedness still a virtue in America's most-popular sport? Most assuredly, yes.

In a game that bore more than a passing (and running) resemblance to the Los Angeles Raiders' slaughter of the Washington Redskins in last year's pro finale, the Niners triumphed on both the strategic and physical levels Sunday. A records search reminds that the same situation has obtained in most Super Bowls: 10 of the 19 have been decided by 14 points (two touchdowns and extra points) or more. Super Bowls are seldom super games mainly because one team usually is a lot better than the other.

On offense, the 49ers mixed it up with 40 runs and

35 passes, just like coach Walsh said they would. That those plays were correctly executed is attested by the fact that the Fins stopped just two of them for losses and that one of those, a five yard "sack" of quarterback Joe Montana by Doug Betters, looked more like a slip to me.

The graceful Montana showed up the inexperience and lack of speed in the Miami linebacker corps by passing repeatedly to his backs and tight ends after his wide receivers had cleared out the Dolphins' secondary. When he couldn't pass he ran himself, five times for 59 yards. That was 34 yards more than all the Dolphins gained rushing.

San Francisco's defense made Miami's one-dimensional passing offense look, well, one-dimensional. Beginning in the second quarter, the Niners abandoned their usual 3-4-4 defensive alignment, mostly in favor of four "down" linemen and six defensive backs. And at 6 feet 2 inches tall and 219 pounds, their lone true linebacker in the game, Keena Turner, was swift enough to be a defensive back himself.

Miami's record-setting passer, Dan Marino, found himself harassed by the 49ers' front four and unable to complete his beloved bombs against the six-back defensive umbrella. Did the Dolphins go to the run? Nope, they kept throwing—50 times against just nine ground plays in all. Marino afterward said that his team stuck with the pass in the second half because it was behind and wanted to catch up, but they ran just five times in half one, while they were still in contention.

The Niners sacked Marino four times, which was remarkable because he'd fallen just 14 times in 16 regular-season games. The Niners did it by using their nine defensive linemen in relays to wear down the Dolphin pass blockers. The pressure made Marino look like what he is: A second-year pro who hadn't seen it all yet. "I guess I didn't move away from trouble as well as I should have," he later admitted.

Ronnie Lott, one of four Pro Bowl selectees in the 49ers' defensive backfield, said that the pass-rush pressure on Marino is what allowed his mates to carry out their most important mission Sunday, which was to contain the Dolphins' speedy pass-catching duo of Mark Clayton and Mark Duper.

"We wanted to keep Duper and Clayton in front of us so that if they did catch the ball they couldn't go all the way," Lott said. In fact, he noted, the Mark Brothers managed to get free several times, but the pass rush kept Marino from finding them. "It's tough to complete a pass with four guys banging on you," he explained matter of factly.

As spelled out by Coach Walsh in his pre-game statements, a vital 49ers offensive objective was to control the ball, so that Marino and company wouldn't have time to run up the 33 points they'd averaged in their previous 18 games. Even when his team didn't score it had to get first downs before punting to deny the Dolphins close-in field position, Walsh said.

And, indeed, the Niners made at least one first down each of the 10 times they had the ball, no mean feat. They scored on six of those possessions and punted on three. On their tenth and final possession in the fourth quarter, they marched 78 yards on 13 plays before Roger Craig was stopped on fourth down at the Miami two yard line. The drive ate up eight minutes and doused any Miami hopes of a late comeback.

Mostly, the 49ers cut through the Dolphins like a freeloader through a Super Bowl party buffet. You probably saw it all on your TV screen, but let me rerun one play that I thought summed up their superiority.

In the third quarter, on the first play after a Miami punt, Montana stepped back to pass from his own 30. He sent his wide receivers deep, as was his wont all day, then flipped a short pass over the middle to running back Wendell Tyler, who'd been left to Dolphins rookie linebacker Jay Brophy to guard. A mismatch if ever there was one! Tyler spun and zipped 40 yards to the Miami 30. The touchdown four plays later made it 38-16. Turn out the lights, etc.

Coach Walsh later disclaimed any benefit from a hometown advantage, saying his team would have won the same way in Albuquerque, N.M., or Fargo, N.D., but SB XIX still retained a San Francisco stamp. On the Thursday before the game, a local radio station offered a pair of game tickets to the person who carried out the most outrageous stunt. One guy showed up wearing a Dolphins jersey and distributed eggs to the crowd to pelt him with. A fight nearly broke out when one fellow, who came dressed as an ice-cream sundae, squirted whipped cream on a man wearing pink ballet tights. Honestly!

A friend of mine, who watched from the stands, reports that the people sitting next to her smuggled in champagne—not Seagram's 7—to warm them against the early-evening chill, and that every time the Niners made a good play the guy behind her yelled, "Sushi! Sushi!" I guess he didn't know that Dolphins are mammals.

● *Jan. 22, 1985*

Slaughter at the Superdome

NEW ORLEANS

T he Chicago Bears upstaged everybody here Sunday, including NBC-TV. The network's cutest gimmick in its pre-Super Bowl show was a minute or so of silent airtime that was dubbed "the big flush." The Bears topped that by turning the entire second half of SB XX into flushtime in their 46-10 rout of the New England Patriots.

The Bears did about everything to the Patriots that they could have done without getting arrested. They held them to minus yardage in the first half and only seven yards rushing overall. They scored when they had the ball and when they didn't. They even got the referee to let them kick a first-half-ending field goal when he should have allowed the clock to run out.

The funny thing was that we should have expected such an outcome. Could less be expected of a team that convinced us that "trouble" rhymes with "shuffle"?

When it was over the Pats could only marvel at the neatness of their execution. "They connected with every punch," said Brian Holloway, the big New England defensive tackle. "They didn't confuse us—they just outplayed us," offered Steve Grogan, the veteran Pats quarterback who was called to duty when first-stringer Tony Eason was yanked for ineffectiveness in the second quarter.

The Bears' triumph stood out even in a series that

belies its "Super" title. Super Bowls seldom have been super games because one team usually turns out to be much better than the other; 11 of the 20 contests played to date have been decided by 14 points or more, and 14 by at least 10 points. Still, the Chicagoans' 46 points were a record, and so were their 20-point halftime lead and 36-point final winning margin.

They also were responsible for an unofficial mark for the earliest commercial exploitation of a Super Bowl win. At the end of the third quarter, with the Bears ahead 44-3, vendors already were in the stands selling pennants that proclaimed the team to be champions of the National Football League.

Given the outcome, the contest started peculiarly. New England recovered a fumble on the Bears' 19-yard line on the second play from scrimmage and kicked a field goal to lead, 3-0.

The "break" was double-edged, though, because several Bears later said that New England's behavior after capturing that turnover gave them a signal that the Pats could be had.

In their upset playoff wins over the New York Jets, Los Angeles Raiders and Miami Dolphins, the Patriots had relied offensively on a dogged running attack. But their first three plays against the Bears were passes, all of which fell incomplete and led to the field goal.

"When they passed instead of ran, they took away their own game," said Mike Singletary, the Bears' All-Pro middle linebacker and defensive "quarterback." Dan Hampton, the sterling defensive lineman, agreed. "After those passes, we [the Bears' defense] looked at each other and said, 'Hey, they're afraid to run on us! This is gonna be our day!' It really pumped us up."

The Bears' offense also received its confidence-builder early. On the second play after the Patriots' post-field-goal kickoff, quarterback Jim McMahon hit wide receiver Willie Gault with a 43-yard pass that set up a tying three-pointer.

"The Patriot cornerbacks are 'peekers.' They look into your backfield to try to see what the quarterback is doing," explained McMahon. "We figured we could go deep on them because while they were peeking, Willie'd run right by them. That play showed us that we were right."

McMahon had kept the press hopping all week with speculation about what headband he'd wear and the condition of his celebrated bruised left buttock. On Sunday, his stern apparently intact, he turned over his forehead space to such good causes as juvenile diabetes research and the plight of POWs and MIAs while keeping the Pats hopping. He completed 12 of 20 passes for 256 yards and scored touchdowns on runs of two yards and one yard.

Overall, the Bears netted 408 yards, divided nicely into 241 yards passing and 167 running. Not bad for an offense that Bears coach Mike Ditka hoped "wouldn't put too much pressure on our defense" in an SB-week jibe.

As was usual in Bear triumphs in an 18-win, one-loss season, however, most of the plaudits went to the defense, and rightly so. This is an outfit that attracts a lot of attention for craft as a result of the celebrated "46" alignment of defensive coach Buddy Ryan, the gnome o'Oklahoma. The "46" puts as many as eight defenders on the line and confounds foes with a wide variety of blitzes and pass coverages.

But Ryan himself is fond of saying that "it ain't how you line up that counts but what you do once the ball is snapped." What the Bear defenders did was smother the Patriots. The Pats' first 11 plays from scrimmage on Sunday went for either no gain or losses. They didn't record a first down until just over four minutes remained in the first half. They gained only 123 yards in toto.

The Bears sacked New England quarterbacks seven times, recovered two Pat fumbles and intercepted four passes. Reggie Phillips, a reserve cornerback, returned one interception for a touchdown. Henry Waechter, a reserve defensive lineman, tackled Grogan in the end zone for the game's final score.

The only blemish on the win was the Bears' field goal that ended the first half. Chicago was out of timeouts when a run by McMahon put the ball on the Pats' three-yard line. The Bears hurried the ball into play before the referee whistled them to begin and stopped the clock with an incomplete pass with three seconds left. They were penalized for illegal procedure, but the move got them the field-goal try, which was successful.

The league later ruled that the Bears shouldn't have been permitted the field-goal attempt, but it allowed the score to stand. Would a reversal have been made a difference? the Pats' Holloway was asked. "Yeah," he said, "They probably would have won 43-10."

• *Jan. 28, 1986*

ROUNDBALL

Part 3

John Drew Comes Clean

LAS VEGAS

J. ohn Drew joined the Atlanta Hawks of the National Basketball Association in 1974 after just two years of college. A quick, strong "small forward" standing 6-foot-6, he was a star from the first, averaging 18.5 points a game as a 20-year-old rookie. The next season he became the youngest player ever picked to appear in a league all-star game.

That same season he began using cocaine. He used it with increasing frequency until last year, all the while playing for the Hawks or his current team, the Utah Jazz. Then he got caught at it, went to a hospital and shook the habit.

He passed his first anniversary of coming clean on Nov. 23 and says he felt "real good" about it, "real, real good." He says he has a new habit now: "Living."

"Before, when I was on drugs, I was just existing," he says. "I felt bad a lot. Nothing was fun, not even the drugs.

"People ask me how I could take drugs and still play ball the way I did for eight years. I tell 'em I don't know. I was just lucky to be born strong, I guess. I do know that I never want to live that way again."

If you read the sports pages, you know that the phenomenon of the drug-taking athlete is neither new nor rare. What's unusual about John Drew is that he is willing to talk about it, even if he doesn't know all the answers.

Dr. Torrey C. Brown doesn't have all the answers,

either, and he ran a drug-rehabilitation clinic at Johns Hopkins University Medical School in Baltimore before becoming a Maryland state official. He's also an NBA consultant on drug abuse.

Dr. Brown says that people should be less surprised that athletes take drugs than that others do. "A lot of athletes are pretty sheltered, you know," he says. "They come out of school knowing about very little except their sports. Suddenly, they have money and find themselves mixing with people who are more sophisticated than they are. They can't handle it and turn to drugs, mostly to cocaine because it's so available, as a social crutch."

That rough profile seems to fit John Drew. He spent most of his youth with his grandparents in tiny Vredenburgh, Ala., population 433, and though he was a much-recruited basketball player, he chose to attend Gardner-Webb College in Boiling Springs, N.C., a not-much-bigger place. He majored in theater arts, which he says was fun and not too hard. Not that it mattered much; all he ever wanted to do was play professional basketball, and he says he knew he was so good that the scouts would find him anywhere.

They did, and his first contract with the Hawks paid him almost $200,000 a year for five years. That has since escalated to his current annual salary of $475,000. He has earned more than $3 million in his 10 NBA campaigns.

Drew talked about his cocaine addiction after an afternoon team practice last week at new Thomas and Mack Arena here, the Jazz's home for 11 games this season. He has discussed it publicly before, but it's a subject he's still not comfortable with. On court with his teammates, he is adept at the mock insults that are the staple of camaraderie among jocks. Talking later about drugs, he speaks in short, uneasy bursts punctuated by long silences.

He says he still doesn't know why he started taking cocaine. "It was curiosity, I guess . . . a social thing," he says finally. He can't pinpoint the time when it became more than a casual pleasure.

"I used it once in awhile, then more, then every day," he says. "I never thought about being hooked, even when I was. I told myself, I can handle this. I can stop when I want. But I always had a reason not to. I'd say I'd stop when the season ended, or when the next training camp would start. I always had an excuse."

Eventually, Drew started "free-basing" cocaine—cooking it down to highly concentrated form and then inhaling its potent vapors—and it stopped him. He missed a couple of practices and a game early last season with the Jazz. Pointed inquiries were made, and he confessed his addiction to team officials.

That was a moment he'd long dreaded, but he says that he felt relieved when it came. "The big thing that kept me from looking for help the last two, three years was fear," he says quietly. "I was afraid there'd be a penalty. I was ashamed that I could be, uh, defeated by drugs. But when I told somebody, I felt like a big load had been lifted off me. I didn't have to pretend anymore."

Drew was packed off to a drug-treatment hospital for a two-month stay. The Jazz kept him on the payroll while he was there. When he rejoined the team last Jan. 25, the fans at Salt Lake City's Salt Palace gave him a standing ovation. He finished the season well enough to boost his per-game scoring average to 21.2 points, his average for his first eight years in the league. He is again averaging better than 20 points a game this season.

"People have been great to me, and that's helped," he says. He believes that treatment and support—not condemnation and punishment—are what addicts need.

"They explained it to me in the hospital," he says. "They told me I was the kind of person who couldn't handle cocaine—that I was born that way. A lot of people are. I'm a good person. You can check with anybody who knows me. I never hurt anybody but myself. I just had a sickness, and I needed help."

Drew says that, yes, some other NBA players use drugs, and a few have approached him for advice on quitting since his return. "Some of 'em think I took a new kind of pill, and I was cured like that," he says, shaking his head. "I tell 'em, there's no pill, no shortcut. You have to admit you have a need to stop and then do it, one day at a time."

● *Dec. 9, 1983*

Note: John Drew later went back on drugs and was barred from playing in the NBA.

The Sweater Showdown

ho sez that successful college athletic teams don't redound to the benefit of the student body as a whole? The gaggle of ticket scalpers milling in front of Madison Square Garden here an hour before Wednesday night's basketball Big Game between top-rated St. John's and No. 2 Georgetown was largely composed of young people of a clean-cut and scholarly mien hoping to exchange their ducats for a down payment on next term's tuition.

The going rate for $4 student seats for the event, $50 to $75, was a disappointment to at least one fledgling entrepreneur from home-team St. John's "I read in the paper where they were going for $300," he groaned. But upon reflection he admitted that the 65 bucks he got wasn't bad for a game he could see on cable television at home on Long Island if he hurried.

That's the way it is when sophisticated New York gets hipped on a hype, and it certainly was this week. According to the Times, the game was the Big Apple's hottest ticket since a 1980 Bruce Springsteen concert. Early reports indicated that even New York Gov. Mario Cuomo, a St. John's grad, was having trouble getting in.

The strange thing was that the game wasn't all that important. Sure, it was erstwhile No. 1 against No. 2, but Georgetown's 85-69 win only meant that St. John's would have to beat weak-sister Providence on Saturday to clinch a Big East Conference regular-season crown. If form holds,

St. John's and G-Town will meet again next weekend in the Big East's post-season tournament in the self-same Madison Square Garden and, just maybe, at the March NCAA finals in Lexington, Ky.

Recall that in college basketball the tourney, not the polls, determines the national champ.

Still, Wednesday's game had a lot going for it. New York loves basketball and a winner, and with the pro Knicks lagging as usual, St. John's success has brought the college game back to the local prominence it enjoyed before the 1951 points-shaving scandal made the collegians allergic to MSG. (In a nice touch, the Garden matched old-time powers NYU and CCNY, now playing small-college schedules, in a preliminary to the main event.)

Towering, glowering Georgetown, last year's NCAA winner, made a swell villain for the show. St. John's upset 'em, 66-65, in Georgetown's Landover, Md., base in January to set up Wednesday's showdown.

And then there was Lou Carnesecca, St. John's 60-year-old coach, basking in the national spotlight after a long and honorable career on its fringes. His new eminence is popular here because he's a native son, readily accessible and—probably most important—a crackerjack stand-up comic in a town loaded with them.

The prop for his humor through most of this campaign has been a preposterous-looking brown, red and blue crew-neck sweater he donned at midseason to keep the winter chill from worsening a persistent cold. Going into Wednesday's contest, his Redmen had won 13 straight while he wore the thing, leading to speculation about its having supernatural powers.

What, Carnesecca was asked at a pre-game press luncheon, happens to the sweater between games?

"I never touch it," he deadpanned. "Two big guys—they go about 6-foot-4 or 6-5—take it from me right after the game and put it in a plastic bag. I don't get it back until the next game."

Do they keep it in a bank vault?

"Are you kidding? You know what happens in banks these days."

Even The Sweater couldn't save St. John's in The Game, though. The visiting Hoyas evened the score for their January embarrassment by beating St. John's at both ends of the court and in between. Unless something unexpected happens to them in their Sunday regular-season finale against Syracuse, they'll head into March favored to repeat in the NCAAs.

Georgetown won by exploiting two weaknesses that St. John's had heretofore overcome with excellent shooting: the Redmen's relative lack of depth and speed. The depth gap showed itself with about five minutes left in the first half, when the Redmen's 7-foot-tall center, Bill Wennington, was benched after committing his second personal foul. St. John's trailed 28-26 when he went out, but a stuff by the Hoyas' fearsome 7-footer, Pat Ewing, started a surge that gave G-Town a 44-33 half-time lead that it never gave back.

The speed deficit was revealed at the expense of Chris Mullin, St. John's all-everything guard and team leader. Mullin usually is an unflappable young man with the capacity to dribble and think at the same time, but he's no swifty. Georgetown coach John Thompson set about wearing him down by singling him out for special pursuit by his box-and-one defense, and by keying the Hoya attack on speedy forward Reggie Williams, whom Mullin was assigned to cover.

Mullin got his points all right, 21 of them. But Georgetown's unflagging defensive pressure forced him into some uncharacteristic errant passes, and at the other end of the court, Williams shot over or drove by him for most of his game-leading 25 points.

Another Thompson gambit was to allow his giant, Ewing, more room to roam against Wennington than he was given in the teams' first game, when Ewing stayed pretty much around the basket and was held to nine points. This time he shot from outside as well as in. Wennington couldn't handle him in either place, and Ewing hit 10 of his 13 shots to score 20. Overall, G-Town fired a dazzling 59.7% from the field while hustling St. John's to a poor 43.1%.

Thompson even unveiled a sweater of his own, a blue-and-red job that he wore under his sport coat. Carnesecca's had worked so well that he thought he would try one too.

Afterward, he strove to put the win in perspective: "It was good to play well from a confidence standpoint, but the real season is only beginning for us," he said.

Carnesecca bowed to Georgetown for playing a "marvelous" game, but he was unrelenting on the sweater front. Thompson's garment was but a "poor imitation" of his, he declared, adding, "I think I'll give mine one more shot. Maybe there's still some luck left in it."

● *Mar. 1, 1985*

Creative Harassment

DURHAM, N.C.

S
•

ending your kids away to college is expensive, but it's worth it. When they're that age, you don't want to know what they're up to.

The catch is that instead of being grateful and pursuing their vices quietly, the little savages stay awake nights thinking of ways to embarrass the home folks. Tune in any college basketball game these days and you'll see your offspring, their bodies painted in their school colors, hollering obscenities at the referees or waving their arms behind the opposing team's basket to distract free-throw shooters. It's almost enough to make you want to take away their Trans Ams.

The only consolation for most parents is that it could be worse. Their kids could be at Duke University.

Here at this educational monument to a bad habit, basketball-fan derisiveness has been honed (cured?) to an art. It's not enough merely to harass the refs, visiting teams and sundry others. They must be skewered.

If the methods aren't exactly tasteful, well, the view here seems to be that it's better to have bad taste than none at all. "Some people say we're mean to the opposition, but we like to think we're just clever," says Peter Lublin, a senior from West Hartford, Conn. "Anyway, it's a tradition here, and we have to carry it on."

Any highlight film of Duke-fan antics would begin with Charles "Lefty" Driesell, the Maryland coach, clumping onto the Cameron Indoor Stadium court here a few seasons back wearing a cast to protect an injured foot. Following him, single file, are a half-dozen Duke students who'd donned foot casts for the occasion. When the bald-headed Lefty sits down he's surrounded by Dukies wearing bald-head masks.

There'd also be these other scenes from seasons past:

—Spud Webb, North Carolina State's 5-foot-6-inch guard, being introduced to cries of "Hormones, Spud, Hormones."

—A banner proclaiming Mike O'Koren, a North Carolina player who suffered from acne, to be the "Oxy-1000 Poster Child."

—Detlef Schrempf, the German-born star of the University of Washington team, shooting a free throw while fans shout "*Fehlwurf!*" the German-language equivalent of "air ball."

—Television broadcaster Billy Packer going on the air at Duke to a background chant of "We Want McGuire," McGuire being Al, another broadcaster.

What wouldn't be on the film, because it was X-rated (or, at least, "R"), was the shower of condoms and women's underwear that greeted Maryland's Herman Veal when he played here in January 1984. Veal had been accused of sexually assaulting a Maryland coed. The charge was later dropped.

That display earned Duke students some bad press and a plea from Terry Sanford, then the university's president, that they spruce up their act. For the next home game, against North Carolina, some of them showed up wearing halos and presented a bouquet of flowers to UNC coach Dean Smith. When a ref's call went against them, the students shouted "We beg to differ." When a Carolina player shot a free throw, they held up signs reading "Please Miss."

"It was their finest hour," says Charley Scher, sports editor of The Chronicle, the school newspaper.

You never can tell when that might be topped, though, so I was on hand here last Saturday afternoon when Duke played North Carolina State. The match-up was promising. State, based just down I-40 in Raleigh, long has been a favorite Duke target ("When you can't go to college go to State" is the basic jeer), and this year's team included Chris Washburn, a 6-foot-11 sophomore center. Washburn last year was removed from the State team, and later served a

48-hour jail term, for stealing a stereo from a fellow student's room. The investigation into that incident also revealed that he had been admitted to State despite a very low combined SAT score of 470. In other words, the blood was in the water.

I arrived early at 8,500-seat Cameron Stadium to find a line of students stretching for blocks. It's first-come, first-served for the 3,000 or so student seats, and some had spent the night in line. The time isn't entirely wasted, though. "It gives us a chance to practice some things," noted Kris Evans, a junior from Rockville, Md.

The student sections were packed and rocking an hour before game time. "When you can't go to college go to JAIL," the kids sang, setting one theme for the afternoon. A sign reading "2+2=470" set the other.

When Washburn took the court for warm-ups, some Duke students waved stereo boxes at him. Five youths held aloft a sign that said "Chris Can You Read This?" followed by "Chris Kan You Spell S-T-E-R-E-O?" ("Harsh!" one Dukie said approvingly).

The band struck up the theme song from the old TV show "Hawaii Five-O," and a sign reading "Book 'Em, Dano" was unfurled. "Book 'Em!" yelled one student section in unison. "Dano!" yelled another.

Washburn's pre-game introduction was greeted by a shower of record-album covers and two records, which crashed and splintered on the court. Luckily, they didn't hit anyone.

When Washburn fouled during the game, the students stood, pointed at him and chanted "Guilty!" When he was called for walking with the ball, a sign went up that said "Chris Walks With The Ball But Runs With A Stereo." Harsh.

Afterward, however, everyone pretty much agreed that the fans were well-behaved, considering. "Ninety-eight percent of the kids were fine. The couple who threw the records were jerks," said Duke basketball coach Mike Krzyzewski, who has been critical of Duke fan behavior in the past.

"I expected the stuff they did. I was disappointed they didn't do anything special," young Mr. Washburn said quietly.

Jim Valvano, the State coach, was the most upbeat of all. "Hey, it's sports, and it's OK to have fun with it," he said. "Besides, I like the kids here. They all talk like they're from New Jersey, like me.

"You guys ever heard of Al Capp? I think he played some forward for Clemson," Valvano cracked to an assemblage of sportswriters. "Capp said that humor was about man's inhumanity to man. I think he had it right."

Oh, yeah. Duke won the game, 74-64.

● *Jan. 17, 1986*

Thoughts from Coach Bob

T• here are a lot of nice things about living in Indiana. For instance? Well, as Dwight Eisenhower said when asked to list Richard Nixon's accomplishments as his vice president, give me a week and I'll think of something.

But seriously, Indiana has a lovely state park in Brown County, some picturesque sand dunes along Lake Michigan, and a spiffy domed stadium in Indianapolis. Maybe best of all, Indianians get to watch the Bob Knight television show on Sunday afternoons in the winter months.

Now, you well may wonder what's so special about a TV show hosted by a basketball coach, the position Knight holds at Indiana University. Coaches' shows litter the Sunday airwaves coast to coast during football and basketball seasons. They're a convenient way that universities, with the help of sports-booster sponsors, can pad the "financial packages" they give coaches for heading their sports "programs." Coaches, of course, no longer are simply paid "salaries" to coach "teams."

To say that most coaches' TV shows are banal is to compliment them. The typical format has the coach, a tame announcer and a "guest" member of the team comment on films of the previous week's games and on next week's opponents. The coach babbles on about "real fine" efforts by his "real fine" players against "real fine" foes. The student-athlete is there to vary the pat-

71

tern a bit with phrases that begin with "like" and end with "you know."

The Bob Knight show stands out in this company like a jalapeno pepper among cucumbers. The cast consists only of Knight and Chuck Marlowe, the gray-haired "voice of Indiana basketball" on station WTTV in Indianapolis, which produces and syndicates the program.

Marlowe functions at Knight's questioner, pupil and foil. He approaches the coach with the good-natured wariness one reserves for the potentially dangerous pets of close friends. Guests have been dispensed with. So has all but a smidgen of game-action film. It's a half-hour, minus commercials, of the Thoughts of Coach Bob.

And as anyone familiar with Knight's career knows, those thoughts can range widely. Knight has taken time off from winning basketball trophies to express himself on topics as varied as the ethical state of college athletes (it's pretty poor, he thinks), the quality of U.S. sports journalism (also poor) and the shortcomings of law enforcement in Puerto Rico.

He has interspersed such verbalizing with physical assaults upon chairs, scorers' tables, his players' jerseys and cheerleaders' megaphones. People attending Indiana basketball games would be advised to select seats safely away from the Hoosiers' bench.

The above might lead one to classify Knight as an angry man, but his usual TV persona is better-humored. He brings along a chalkboard for diagramming plays, and is free with basketball advice "for you kids out there" in the audience. Sample: "Always put your passes away from the defensive man. It's more important to do that than to throw the ball to your teammate."

He also has a ready supply of folk wisdom with which to make his points. When, during a late-December show, Marlowe ventured that it would be nice if the Hoosiers could put together two good halves of basketball, Knight observed that "If a frog had wings, he wouldn't bump his butt on the ground when he hopped."

But just when you get to thinking that Ol' Bob has mellowed, he'll slip in a zinger. On the Feb. 9 show, poor Marlowe prefaced a question by saying that he might be "partial" to the Hoosiers, and Knight would let him go no further. "Why shouldn't you be partial? You're Indiana's basketball broadcaster!" the coach whooped. "If you weren't partial, we'd get another guy!"

Knight's TV shows have themes that run through one broadcast to the next. Last season, while the Hoosiers struggled to a 7-11 Big 10 won-lost record, their worst in many years, the coach regularly chided his players for the lack of attentiveness to his teachings. Things are looking up on-court this season (Indiana was tied for first place in the league this week), so he has turned his ire on the referees.

"Working the refs" is a time-honored coaching custom, the idea being that squawking loudly about adverse decisions early in a game might make the zebras pause before blowing a crucial whistle against you late. Coach Bob, however, works 'em early and late, on Sundays as well as on Saturdays.

Big 10 referees have three failings, Knight declared on his Jan. 5 show after a loss to Michigan. To wit: "They don't understand basketball. They don't know what to look for. And they don't know what to do out there."

This view was not softened by victory. On the Jan. 19 show, after Indiana had edged Ohio State, Knight declared the Big 10 to be "the most amazingly officiated league in the history of basketball." He noted that league refs are paid $350 a game and opined that "If we got that kind of popcorn at 25 cents a bag, we'd throw it away." He suggested that Marlowe put together a tape of officiating "highlights" and invite Wayne Duke, the Big 10 commissioner, to come on the show to narrate it.

By the following Sunday, the subject of officiating apparently had become too painful for Knight to address directly. When Marlowe suggested that Knight discuss a two-point win over Illinois in which he'd staged a chair-stomping sideline tantrum that was excessive even by Knightly standards, the coach talked instead of some fishing he'd done in the unseasonably warm weather earlier that week.

"I had a great, great fishing experience. You can't beat the tranquility of the outdoors," he said beatifically.

"I'll tell you something else," he went on. "In three days on the lake I didn't lose a single popper. No turnovers! Of course, a couple of 'em got chewed up pretty good. I named one 'Steve' for Steve Alford, our guard. The fish would hang on to 'Steve' and wouldn't let him go. It got so bad I whistled a foul on the fish 'cause I knew no one else was gonna."

Oh, that Bob. He's a card.

● *Feb. 28, 1986*

The Valhalla of College Hoops

DALLAS

There is much to be said, con and con, about the way the NCAA regulates the ethical side of intercollegiate sports, but one can only admire the way it puts on a basketball tournament.

Its Final Four, which commences in spiffy Reunion Arena here tomorrow afternoon, is my favorite. The reason is simple: I'm a semifinals freak.

As far as I'm concerned, the semifinals are the real main event of any tourney, and the Final Four is the only one that fixes its brightest spotlight there. Not only does the penultimate round give you a bargain—two games for the price of one—but it sometimes also elicits the best efforts from the contestants. Many an athlete has said that more pressure rides on getting *to* the finals of a major competition than winning them. There is distinction aplenty just in being in a World Series or Super Bowl. Out in the sem-eyes usually means out of sight and out of luck.

How the Final Four instead of the Terrific Two became the Valhalla of college hoops is a bit of a mystery. The NCAA has been gathering its national basketball tourney semifinalists for a weekend shootout since 1952, but the FF label, capitalized, didn't catch on until sometime later.

I give a lot of the credit for popularizing it to Al McGuire, the former Marquette coach and present

NBC-TV commentator. He speaks in capital letters, and his extolment of the event from bench and booth in the 1970s helped impress it upon the public mind. "When a coach gets his team in a Final Four, he gets a raise, his summer camp gets filled, and he gets a shoe contract!" McGuire explains. And when he retires from coaching, he may even get to go on TV.

Whatever the Final Four's nativity, the NCAA knows a good thing when he sees one. It copyrighted the name in 1981. That means you have to kick back to the organization if you want to use it on a T-shirt or something.

It is appropriate that four, not two, is the focus of college basketball, because so many teams are in the running. The NCAA's Division I in the sport numbers some 250 schools, a far larger number than compete for our other major team-sports titles.

As of last year, 64 teams are picked annually to try for the big prize, and they are distributed among four regional prelims without regard to origin. Thus, St. John's of New York played in the West earlier this month, Oklahoma was in the East and Fairfield, Conn., was in the Southeast. This means that players spend a lot of time out of school, but it's the show that counts, right?

And with all the basketball talent around these days, it's always quite a show. No teams in the present tournament exemplified this as much as Cleveland State and Navy.

Cleveland State is a commuter school with no great reputation outside of, well, Cleveland. Coach Kevin Mackey recruited his squad from various urban playgrounds. One starter never played in high school. Mackey's strategic model was the Chinese army: His charges attacked in human waves. He'd use 10 or 12 players during a game. Some foes claimed he got 'em all on the court at once.

Navy fielded a team of kids whose hair was a bit too long on top and a bit too short on the sides. It's rumored that they actually attend class and take courses like calculus. Navy's star, David Robinson, grew from a puny 6-foot-7 to a robust 7 feet while in the Academy. He was this year's "aircraft carrier" center. In a couple of years he may serve on one.

Cleveland State bumped favored Indiana and St. Joseph's from the tournament. Navy defeated Tulsa and mighty Syracuse. Then they played each other, and Navy won by a point. Then Duke beat Navy. Too bad.

The teams that made it to Dallas—Duke, Kansas, Louisville

and Louisiana State—have more-conventional elite pedigrees. All recruit blue-chip players from hither and yon, play before large and adoring home crowds, and almost always win. Who'll win on Saturday (and Monday night)? I dunno. You can cover the four with a postage stamp. Whom should you root for? Here are some things to help you decide.

Duke is coached by Mike Krzyzewski, whose name starts with a "K" but sounds like it starts with an "Sh." If you meet him, call him Mike. Duke's record is 36-2, the best in the field. That's not bad for a team that can't shoot very well. Duke students are known for the clever way they taunt opponents. They'll enliven the proceedings here if they can outscrap the alums for tickets.

Kansas has a guard, Calvin Thompson, whose right leg is 1¼ inches shorter than his left. His height is either 6-foot-6 or 6-4¾, depending on which foot he's standing on. The Kansas star is 6-11 Danny Manning. Kansas wanted him so bad it made his dad an assistant coach. The head coach is Larry Brown, who flits between jobs in the private (professional) and public sectors as frequently as Clark Clifford. He says he loves it in Lawrence, Kan., and the locals return the sentiment. They say if he wins in Dallas, they'll change the town's name to Larry.

Louisville will have a lot of fans in Camden, N.J., because three of its players are from there. Two of them, Billy Thompson and Milt Wagner, lead the team in scoring. It seems like Wagner, a cagey guard, has been playing college ball forever, and he almost has. He's a fifth-year performer who sat out 1984-85 with injuries. He appeared in the 1982 and '83 Final Fours. Give him the Barney Poole award for college athletic longevity.

Louisiana State goes farther afield than New Jersey for players. It has two from Yugoslavia, one from the Dominican Republic and one from an even weirder place—Los Angeles. The LSU coach is Dale Brown, a manic sort who is either stalking the globe in search of tall young men or wishing aloud that he was sipping wine in the Colorado mountains, far from the rat race. Chances are that if he ever got to Colorado, he'd be out measuring skiers after the first day.

• *Mar. 28, 1986*

Getting Down with Muggsy

CHARLOTTE, N.C.

ake Forest University's basketball representatives were having their way with those from Davidson College here last week until an eight-point Davidson spurt narrowed their lead to 10 points early in the second half. Said Wake Forest senior guard Tyrone "Muggsy" Bogues to himself, "Enough of that!" Or somesuch.

On the Deacons' next offensive sally, Bogues sank a 12-foot jump shot, and after a Davidson miss he scooped up a loose rebound and dashed the length of the floor for a layup. He was fouled on the play and added a free throw. Another Davidson miss, and Bogues fed teammate Tony Black for an open 15-footer. Turn out the lights, etc. Final score: Deacs 75, Wildcats 60.

It wasn't exactly an NCAA final, so who cares? you well may ask. Well, Muggsy stands 5-feet, 3-inches tall. If he's not the shortest male player in college hoops today, he wouldn't have to lower his eyes much to regard the fella who is. Most nights, he's the shortest person on the court, including ballboys and cheerleaders.

Young Mr. Bogues's presence in the Wake Forest lineup is no mere bid by the Winston-Salem institution to attract the patronage of the pint-sized. This kid can play. After three varsity seasons he holds the school career record for most steals and, given a modicum of good health, he'll gain that distinction for assists before long. Last season, on a team that won just eight of 29 games and was 0-14 in the tough Atlantic Coast Conference, he averaged 11.3 points a game, was third in the nation in steals and eighth in assists and minutes played.

Muggsy gilded his legend over the summer by not only making the U.S. team that won the World Championship in Spain, but also starring. He had 10 steals and five assists in the gold-medal game against the Soviet Union. The Spanish press nicknamed him *la chispa negra*, meaning "the black spark." The folks in Oviedo, one site of the tourney, were so taken with him that they invited him to be a guest of honor at their annual municipal feast in September. The mean old NCAA said no.

But, hey, Muggsy doesn't have to go abroad to be lionized. He probably holds the unofficial college mark for most standing ovations after games, and he receives a steady stream of letters from boys who want to be just like him if they don't grow up. He's even popular at archrival Duke, where the omnivorous student fans might be expected to pop him down like a shrimp hors d'oeuvre.

"Our band plays 'Short People' in his honor, but that's been about it. We really like him here," says John Roth, Duke's sports information director. Muggsy returns the sentiment because he enjoyed one of his best games at Duke, outplaying All-American Johnny Dawkins in an upset, 91-89, Deacon win two seasons back.

Little Big Man himself, a jaunty sort, vows that the basketball world ain't seen nothin' yet. "Being on the world championship team opened my eyes to my true potential. I'm playing better now than I ever did," he said before the Davidson fray. "People used to say I couldn't do this or that 'cause I was small. I don't hear that any more."

The sturdily built Bogues says that he never considered his height an obstacle to basketball success. "The ball's on the floor as much as it's in the air, and when it's down there, *I* have the edge," he says with perfect logic. His nickname, which he sports in large gold letters from a neck chain, derives from ball-stealing skills acquired in the playgrounds of his native Baltimore.

He starred for two years at Baltimore's Dunbar High, which was coached by Bob Wade, now the new head coach at Maryland. More than a dozen basketball bigtimers tried to recruit him. He says he picked Wake Forrest, with an undergraduate enrollment of 3,200, "because I thought going to a small school would be nice."

Once he was in Winston-Salem, the academic side of college nearly floored him. "Classes covered more in a week than we did all year in high school. I thought I'd never adjust," he admits. One up-shot of his classroom struggles was his being placed on school probation for a period for plagiarizing a paper in a literature course. He says that was really a "mixup" involving a student who tutored him.

He avers that he has righted his academic career and expects to graduate next summer with a degree in speech communications unless a professional basketball offer intervenes. Even if one does, he vows to finish his degree requirements sometime. "I'm proud of sticking it out in class," he says. "Getting a diploma is a big goal with me."

His basketball goals this season are to improve his shooting (his average from the floor going into this season was .456) and help get some more wins for his team. So far, he has done both. The Deacs are 2-0 in the young campaign, and Muggsy is their leading scorer with 39 points. His 23 shots have netted 15 baskets, four from three-point range.

Bogues scored 21 points against Davidson, but equally impressive were his game-leading seven assists and his defense against 6-foot-1 Derek Rucker, Davidson's All-Southern Conference guard. Rucker scored 20, but 12 of them came on three-point shots from the twilight zone that a 6-foot, 6-inch player couldn't have stopped, and he had only three assists. As usual, Muggsy handled the ball on just about every Wake Forrest possession, and "you can't steal the ball from him unless you're a ground hog," Temple coach John Chaney has remarked.

Wake Forest's coach, Bob Staak, is no less appreciative. "Muggsy's a great kid with a great work ethic, and you never have to tell him anything more than once," he says. "Having him around is like having another coach on the floor in practice. If another kid needs help, he's right there to give it to him."

"You mean the other players look up to him?" I asked.

"Oh, yeah. They really do," he answered. He didn't get the joke right away.

● *Dec. 12, 1986*

DIMPLED BALL

Part 4

Follow the Bouncing Ball

Mack Buck remembers the day well. "It was at Sunset Hills Golf Club in Edwardsville, Ill.," he says. "My partner and I were two down with three to go for a $1 Nassau, and I was teeing up at the 16th hole. It was a tough par 5 with an out-of-bounds all down the right, so, as usual, I switched to a cheap ball. My partner got sore at me. He said that using a cheap ball in that situation was chintzy.

"I said, 'Baloney, I'll use this ball and outdrive every turkey in the foursome.' Naturally, everybody pressed, and we hit four pretty indifferent tee shots, so it wasn't much of a test."

On the 19th hole, over beers, Mr. Buck and his golfing pals continued their argument over whether the extra driving distance expensive golf balls promise to deliver is worth the money to the average, weekend golfer. But being of a scientific bent (all were engineers for Shell Oil in nearby Wood River, Ill.), they weren't content to simply speculate on the question. Then and there, they devised the Average-Guy Golf Ball Driving Test to settle it once and for all.

"We figured, why not?" recalls Mr. Buck, now the owner of a consulting engineering firm in San Diego. "It would be our contribution to the game we loved."

The group first procured the raw material for its experiment: a batch of well-known "distance" balls that many touring pros use, and a batch of a drugstore brand advertised for durability. The name-brand balls sold for $1.25 each and were dubbed the E-balls, for expensive. The drugstore balls, at 69 cents each, were named the C-balls, for cheap.

Then the engineers conducted a series of bounce tests to determine if the E-balls really were livelier. They measured the rebounds of sample balls dropped on various surfaces from distances of five to 58 feet, the latter being the height of a distillation tower at the refinery where they worked. ("Just like Galileo at the Tower of Pisa," Mr. Buck chortles.) And, indeed, the E-balls consistently bounced about 15% higher than the C-balls.

For the experiment itself, the foursome enlisted six other Shell employees who frequented the Sunset Hills club. All 10 men were of ordinary golfing ability, as their average score of 89.9 strokes per round during the trial attested. Too, all shared the typical duffer's zest for showy slugging off the tee. "We were big, healthy guys who loved to hit," Mr. Buck recalls. "We'd take a 250-yard drive over a well-placed iron shot anytime."

The group centered its measurements on 11 of the holes at their home course, eliminating the par 3s and longer holes that put a premium on driving accuracy, not distance. Playing in randomly selected pairs, the golfers matched E against C balls on alternate holes. They paced off and noted the distance of their drives, then played out the holes and recorded their scores. After several weekends, they had data on 221 matched pairs of holes, a total they deemed sufficient.

The test had two main results. One was to irk the players who followed the golfer-scientists around the course; all that pacing and record-keeping slowed play considerably. The other was that, off the driver of an average-guy player, it didn't matter much whether the ball being used was expensive or cheap. The E-ball outdrove the C-ball on just 114, or 51.5%, of the 221 holes. The C-ball won out on 96 holes, or 43.4%, and 11 pairs of drives were judged virtually even.

Driving distance did matter in the outcome of the holes, and in the way you'd expect: the longer hitter won more often than he lost. Moreover, the average drive with an E-ball was almost five yards longer than those with a C-ball. But when the difference between drives was 25 yards or less, as were most in the test, the longer hitter won only 32% of the holes while tying 42% and losing 26%. Mr. Buck and his crew calculated that the average player's chance of winning a hole with a five-yards-longer drive—the "E-ball edge"—improved by about 3%, or about one hole every two rounds.

The analysis didn't end there, however. The engineers estimated that the chance of losing one's ball should be included, and they put that risk at about one lost ball every 20 holes, a conservative-enough guess, I think. At the price difference between the two kinds of balls, this negated the advantage of the E-ball's extra distance, they figured. Mr. Buck's final conclusion was a rule-of-thumb one: Expensive balls aren't "cost-effective" if you're playing for less than $1 a hole.

One would think that the Edwardsville group would have sought to rush this landmark study into print, but such was not the case. Its members got busy with one thing or another, and eventually they were separated by transfers or job changes. The data moldered for about a dozen years until Mr. Buck, looking for something to do while laid up with hepatitis, rediscovered the figures and tabulated the results.

He submitted them to a golf magazine, but received what he calls "the correspondence version of a stony stare." An engineering journal published a few paragraphs, but not enough to satisfy him. Knowing my fondness for the off-beat, he sent them to me on the condition that if I used them, I would pay him an "honorarium" that he could flash at his next reunion with his Illinois buddies. After brief negotiation, we decided that $1.25—the price of an E-Ball—would be appropriate.

• *July 19, 1983*

Tee Time at Oakmont

OAKMONT, PA.

T. he U.S. Open golf tournament is the sport's premier annual event, in large part because the course on which it is played is always one of the best.

For four days a year (seven including the three pre-tourney practice days), ordinary golf fans who are in the neighborhood with the requisite admission price can tread such hallowed courses as Merion, Pebble Beach, Oakland Hills, Winged Foot and Baltusrol. It's even a thrill for the folks at home in televisionland to ogle those pampered acres. That's the closest most of us will get to such places short of dying and being reincarnated as the heir to a soda cracker fortune.

The Open tees off again next week, and the treat will be bigger than usual. For the sixth time since 1927, its site will be the Oakmont Country Club in this suburb of Pittsburgh. Not only is Oakmont one of golf's reigning "monster" courses—an elegant stew of hills, huge sand traps, deep rough and slick, undulating greens—but it's also a self-conscious repository of the game's traditional virtues.

Usually, the U.S. Golf Association must lean on clubs that host the Open to toughen-up their courses for the tourney, but with Oakmont the situation is just the opposite. The most celebrated showdown between club and sponsor came before the 1953 event, when the USGA, after lengthy argument, persuaded Oakmont to end its 50-year practice of raking its sand traps into deep, V-shaped furrows. The furrows precluded anything but blast-outs by golfers caught therein, and made four-round scores of fewer than 300 strokes rare. Saved from their grip, Ben Hogan's winning 72-hole score of 283 that year trimmed 11 strokes from the previous course record.

This year, the USGA has had to *widen* some of Oakmont's fairways for the Open, and members boast that the course's greens, dubbed "the fastest in Christendom" by Nancy Jupp, the 62-year-old Scotswoman who oversees the event, are sometimes faster for regular play than they'll be next week. "If we wanted to play an ordinary course, we'd have joined one," sums up Jerry Hines, a retired manufacturer and long-time Oakmont member.

Oakmont's guiding spirit is the late William C. Fownes, who was the 1910 U.S. Amateur golf champion, the son of the club's founder, its greens' committee chairman for many years and, later, its president. His father, H.C. Fownes, a local steel magnate, designed the course on the premise that no errant shot should go unpunished, and his son implemented that philosophy by strewing 350 traps around the premises, about four times the number of the average course.

Mr. Fownes also had stern notions about how Oakmont should be run. Until his death in 1950, he led the opposition to building a swimming pool at the club and frowned on dances and other frivolity, stating "there should not be too much inclination toward the social." Oakmont didn't allow electric carts until the mid 1960s, and then limited their use to the infirm.

Oakmont has relaxed those strictures, and now has a pool, tennis courts and other country club amenities, but some members still make a point of refusing to use them. "Almost nobody plays tennis, and you rarely see anyone at the pool except wives and kids," notes Bob Cooper, a lawyer and second-generation member.

Not surprisingly, many Oakmonters cringe at the thought of thousands of heathens trampling their grounds and denying them the use of their course for a choice June week, but they permit it for the following reasons: The honor and related bragging rights, the money (no small matter for an institution with a payroll of about 200), and the fact that it's good for members' business.

No, make that great for business. "All my customers who play golf want to say that they played on the Open course, and I'm the guy who can arrange it for them," smiles member Larry Crissman, who heads a firm of manufacturers' representatives.

The course that the Open contestants will play next week is in some ways untypical of championship layouts. At 6,972 yards (members play it at 6,436 yards) it isn't especially long; and its trees, though numerous, rarely come into play. The only water on the place is in the ballwashers. Its difficulty lies mainly in its heavy trapping and rolling, speedy greens.

The 350 traps that existed in William Fownes' day have been reduced to 180, but that's still plenty. The most picturesque are the "church pew" variety—sand interspersed with ridges of grass—and some are humongous. The par 3, 240-yard, 8th hole is fronted by a comma-shaped job that measures 130 by 30 yards.

Some of Oakmont's greens are so large that different pin placements can alter club selection by a factor of two. On three holes— the 1st, 10th and 12th—the greens slope slightly away from the fairways, making them difficult to hold with a direct shot. Straight putts of longer than three feet will be rare on any green.

Even seemingly simple holes contain something extra for competitors. On two of the course's par 3s—the 201-yard 6th and the 185-yard 13th—there is no fairway, meaning that if a tee shot isn't on the green it will be in a trap or high rough. The 16th hole, a par 4, 322-yarder, would be cake for the pros if the green wasn't uphill and left of the tee and all but surrounded by traps so deep that the head of a player stuck in one is barely visible from the fairway.

How Oakmont will play next week will depend very much on the weather. Rain, if not accompanied by high winds, will mean lower scores because it will soften and slow the greens. The 72-hole course record of 276 strokes, set by John Mahaffey in the 1978 PGA championship, came on a rain-sodden course, and winner Johnny Miller's final round of 63 in the 1973 Open here, rated as one of the best ever played, also followed a downpour.

No matter how tough Oakmont is on the players, though, it will be tougher on spectators. The course is on a narrow residential street just uphill from a two-lane bridge over the Allegheny River. The bridge—on the main route from Pittsburgh—is a formidable traffic bottleneck at any time, and backups of two to three miles there have attended other major tournaments.

The course itself consists of 11- and 7-hole segments separated by the Pennsylvania Turnpike, and only a single footbridge, about eight feet wide, joins the two. If attendance averages the 25,000 a day that's expected, crossing the bridge will take a good 15 minutes, club officials say.

A one-day ticket to the Open proper will cost $24. Figure to add $5 to $10 a person for lunch. If you go, club members request that, for goodness sake, you deposit beverage-can pop-tops in your pockets or in trash baskets. They're still finding tops from the '78 PGA, and the club rule is that if your ball lands on one, you have to play it from there. Winter rules never apply at Oakmont unless there's snow on the ground.

- *June 10, 1983*

Up Against Winged Foot

MAMARONECK, N.Y.

nce a year, whether they need it or not, the touring golf pros do something difficult. They play the U.S. Open on a course selected by the U.S. Golf Association, the tourney's overseer and the game's rule maker, with an eye toward testing their souls as well as their swings.

The Open comes up again June 14, and this year's designated purgatory is the Winged Foot Golf Club's West Course, just 45 minutes from Times Square on a good day. Is Winged Foot tough? Does a golf ball get lost in the woods?

How tough is Winged Foot really? Well, three U.S. Opens have been played there—in 1929, 1959 and 1974—and no one managed to break par of 280 in any of them. The best 72-hole tournament score ever recorded on the course was the 282 that Billy Casper shot in winning the 1959 event. In the '74 Open, Hale Irwin won with 287, and only seven sub-par rounds were posted during the entire four days of play.

The above might lead you to believe that Winged Foot West is one of those "monster" courses: hilly, great of length and jammed with sand traps and water hazards. Not so. It will play at 6,930 yards for the Open, which is only a bit above average for the pro tour. It contains just 71 sand traps, fewer than the norm for any course. The only water on the place is a stream you can jump over that crosses the 15th and 16th fairways.

In fact, the course gives a first impression of an arboretum in which golf is secondary. Along its gently rolling fairways are more than 20,000 trees of 50-odd varieties, many of them flowering. The trees are there more for their beauty than as golfing hazards; most of Winged Foot's fairways are broad enough to accommodate even slightly errant drives.

The difficulty of Winged Foot is in the demands it places on approach shots. Its greens are smallish and tightly trapped, with narrow openings and slick and undulating surfaces. An approach that's not on target is in trouble. The Law of Winged Foot can be stated simply: "Miss a green, lose a shot."

"There are more penalizing courses, but few that require as much precision," says Tom Watson, winner of the 1982 Open, whose last-day 79 cost him the 1974 event here. He continues: "Even your misses have to be well placed. You can miss short on most holes, but you can't miss left, right or long. It makes for defensive golf, which is why par stands up so well."

"It's the kind of course that sneaks up on you," says Tom Nieporte, a one-time tour regular who has been Winged Foot's resident pro since 1978. "A pro will be playing along, enjoying the day and thinking he's doing OK. He doesn't have to worry about huge fairway traps, like at Oakmont, or losing a ball in the ocean, like at Pebble Beach. But he'll be picking up bogeys here and there, and before he knows it he's shot a 76 or 77. It's a hard course to score on—darned hard."

Jack Nicklaus, who has played Winged Foot many times, put it more succinctly. Asked a few years ago to rate the course for difficulty on a scale of one to 10, he answered "11, maybe 12."

Winged Foot gets its character from A.W. Tillinghast, the man who designed it. He was one of golf's first master architects. His other notable credits include Baltusrol in New Jersey, Oklahoma City Golf & Country Club and Baltimore Country Club's Five Farms course, all of which have hosted national championship events.

Mr. Tillinghast was hired in 1921 by the New York Athletic Club members who founded Winged Foot, and charged with building a "man-sized" course. He did them one better by putting two such courses on the Westchester County property. The East Course he designed is a good one, too. Two USGA Women's Opens (in

1957 and 1972) and the 1980 USGA Seniors' Championship were played there.

According to his biographers, "Tilly" was quite a sport—a gambler, boozer and backer of bad Broadway plays when he had the cash. He also was a golfer of modest accomplishment, which gave him a soft spot in his heart for others of his ilk. That's why his courses usually have generous fairways and aren't littered with fairway traps to bedevil short hitters.

But Tilly did believe that "a constricted shot to a closely guarded green is the surest test of any man's golf," and he designed Winged Foot with that in mind. And while average-guy players aren't penalized if they don't spray their tee shots too badly, the birdie-hunting pros must place their drives accurately for the best angles into the tight greens.

Within those limits, Winged Foot West's front nine is fairly straightforward. If there are birdies to be had on the course, this is the place to get them.

The fifth hole, a 515-yard par five, is reachable in two by most pros and is judged to be the easiest birdie hole. The 324-yard sixth hole is the course's shortest par four, and the 166-yard seventh is the shortest par three.

The fun starts in earnest on the 10th hole, Winged Foot's most celebrated. It's a 190-yard par three that requires a long iron shot to a trapped, steeply banked green surrounded by trees. Ben Hogan described the hole as "a three-iron into somebody's bedroom" because of the house that sits behind the putting surface. The hole was modified before the 1974 Open to make the green's incline less severe. It was too tough for the pros the old way, the USGA ruled.

Holes 11, 12 and 13 are standard Winged Foot toughies, and the last five—measuring, in order, 418 yards, 417, 452, 444 and 448—are a gantlet of long par fours that are to be survived, not attacked. "Psychologically, they're murder—you play the first part of the course knowing that they're there waiting to get you," says home-pro Nieporte of the final five. "Any player who isn't under par coming to 14 can pretty much write off his chances for doing it that day." In his winning effort in the '74 Open, Irwin was plus-five for four rounds over this stretch.

It's enough to make a pro ask for a mulligan, and while he won't get one he'll at least be in the right place to discuss the subject. Hotel executive David B. Mulligan, for whom the duffer's second-drive dispensation is named, was a Winged Foot member of 40 years ago. It's no wonder.

● *June 1, 1984*

North Wins at Oakland Hills

M
·

y high-school English teacher used to say that literature had three possible themes: man against man, man against nature and man against himself. That puts literature one up on golf.

Almost uniquely in sports, there isn't much man-against-man conflict in the links game, but there's plenty of the other two. Tall Andy North handled them well enough to win the U.S. Open, golf's most prestigious tournament, here Sunday.

Actually, to say that North won the tournament is somewhat misleading. Better to say that he didn't lose it. The real winner was Oakland Hills, the golf course on which the tournament was played. North was the only player to best par of 280 for 72 holes over the benign-looking but treacherous layout, and he did it by just one stroke.

The course had some help from another force of nature—the weather. Everything that could have happened here in June did between Thursday morning and early Sunday evening. It was, at various times, warm, cool, sunny, cloudy, windy and rainy. On Sunday it was all of the above, but some of golfing's greatest names, including Jack Nicklaus, Tom Watson and Lee Trevino, weren't around to experience it. They missed the 36-hole cut.

North's 74 on Sunday was one of the highest final-round scores ever posted by a winner of the venerable event, of which this was the 85th renewal. Interestingly, North also had a last-day 74 when he won the Open at Cherry Hills in Denver in 1978 with a score of 285. That was his last win. He's something of a U.S. Open specialist. He has won three professional tournaments, and two of them were Opens.

The 35-year-old North is a bit testy on the subject of his spotty record. After his 70 through the rain on Saturday put him within two strokes of the lead, he was asked if he was eager to dispel the notion that his '78 win was a fluke. "I don't think that was a fluke," he snapped. "Who labeled it that? I didn't. That answers that."

After his round on Sunday, his humor had improved markedly. Having lost as well as won (the meager $22,000 he earned last year didn't cover his bills), he found winning better. "It's nice not being asked why I fouled up," he allowed.

That much couldn't be said for the international trio of players who finished the four rounds at even-par 280, one stroke behind North. It's hard to say which of them had the saddest Open.

Denis Watson, who was born in Rhodesia and lives in Florida, was the most accomplished of the runner-up group by virtue of having won three tourneys in 1984. He might have won here if he hadn't been assessed a two-stroke penalty on Thursday for waiting more than the prescribed 10 seconds for a putt to drop from the lip of a cup. He had a chance to make things exciting on Sunday when he hit an iron shot to within 10 feet of the hole on the tough, 453-yard par four 18th, but he missed the putt.

Dave Barr, a husky Canadian with a choppy swing, played steadily through the tourney, and shoved his nose ahead of the pack briefly when a birdie on the par-five 12th hole Sunday left him at three under par. Then he reverted to the form that had relegated him to 81st on this year's moneywinning list by bogeying three of the last six holes. "I tried to tell myself that this was an ordinary tournament, but I guess I didn't believe it," he confessed afterward.

The fellow who may be remembered for this tourney after the winner is forgotten is Tze-Chung Chen, a 26-year-old from Taiwan. A golfer only since the age of 17, this pleasant, chopstick-thin young man, whose previous victories had come in an East that's farther than Boston, posted rounds of 65-69-69 to lead the field into Sunday.

Chen is, among other things, a former marine and one-time

basketball "power forward" back home, although having a 5-foot-10-inch, 140-pounder at that position explains his country's low estate in that sport. Going into the fifth hole on Sunday, he had a four-stroke edge over North and looked to be a winner.

Then he made a ghastly eight on the par four, 457-yard fifth that included a chip shot from just off the green that popped up straight and struck his club again before it touched the ground.

Not only could no one recall an Open leader suffering such a catastrophe, but no one quite knew what to call it. Quadruple-bogey was one candidate, "double-par" was another. One press-tent wit said that henceforth, a four-over-par score—a familiar enough feat for duffers—would be called a "T.C.," Chen's nick-name. So will a double-hit.

Whatever, Chen followed it with three-straight more bogeys, and they did him in. His final round score was 77. The eight upset him pretty badly, he later admitted. Man against himself again.

North was Chen's playing partner Sunday, and he almost couldn't take advantage of the latter's lapse. By my count, his drives found the rough or traps on 12 of the 18 holes on the final round, and he later complained about being "out of rhythm" all day. His 74 included five bogeys and just one birdie.

North, however, did putt well Sunday, as he had in posting previous rounds of 70, 65 and 70. He holds a putter the way Ron Hunt used to hold a baseball bat—about halfway down the handle. "I never was a good putter as a kid, and I fiddled with a lot of strokes," he explained. "I was putting cross-handed at age 14 or 15. That ought to tell you how messed up I was. This way feels pretty decent, so I've stuck with it."

He also played the sand well, and two trap shots keyed his victory. One was a booming five-iron from a fairway trap on the par-five 12th hole that saved his par and ended a three-bogey streak. The other was a deft short blast from a downhill lie to within inches of the cup on the par-three 17th.

As his foes staggered before him, North needed just a bogey five on 18 to win, and, playing safe, that was what he got. Did he back in? he was asked later. "I don't care what people call it," he said. "I beat the course, and no one else did."

● *June 18, 1985*

The Comeback of Darlin' Jack

AUGUSTA, GA.

Y•ou can't tell a book by its cover, but you can tell a lot about a golf tournament by its winners. The Masters always gets the best, thank you: Nelson, Hogan, Snead, Palmer, Watson, that kind of guy.

Jack Nicklaus, the best of the best, staged a vintage comeback to win the 50th Masters here Sunday. He did it by shooting a last-day 65 to beat a who's who (instead of the usual "who's he?") cast. It was his sixth win in the prestige-soaked tourney, and his 20th win in a golf "major." He also has won five PGAs, four U.S. Opens, three British Opens and two U.S. Amateurs. No one has won more. Maybe no one ever will.

It was the kind of tournament that people who saw it will tell their grandchildren about. The winner will do the same, and probably in not too many more years. He's 46 years old, and three of his five children are 20 or older.

Nicklaus's victory was as popular here as peaches and azaleas. The Masters gallery, made up mostly of middle-aged and early-elderly longtime ticket holders, usually considers polite applause the appropriate reward for shots well struck. On Sunday, as Darlin' Jack charged, his gallery carried on like college-basketball fans. "A couple of times today they got so loud you couldn't hear yourself think," said Tom Kite, a one-stroke runner-up, on Sunday. And Kite was playing two twosomes behind Nicklaus on the final round.

Nicklaus's 72-hole score was 279, nine strokes under par and, incidentally, seven better than his winning total here in 1963 when he was a beefy, crew-cutted 23-year-old (but eight strokes worse than his course-record 271 in 1965). At that rate, he noted afterward, he should be ready to break his '65 record when he's 60.

He didn't quarrel with assertions that he's past his prime. He said he had to ask his son, Jack Jr., who also was his caddy, where the four-iron second shot that set up an eagle-three on the 500-yard 15th hole landed. "I missed the pleasure of seeing where quite a few of my shots landed. I can't see that far anymore," he said.

"I kept reading that people 46 don't win Masters, and I'm afraid I agreed with that," he went on. "I'm not as good as I was 10 or 15 years ago. I don't play as much concentrated golf as I did then. But occasionally I'm as good as I used to be, and I guess it was good enough today."

In fact, his back-nine score of 30 on Sunday tied a Masters record, and might have been as good a nine as anyone has played under the circumstances. Nicklaus began the day at 214, four strokes in back of 54-hole leader Greg Norman, an Australian who was to tie Kite for second. Nicklaus was five under par at the 15th hole when Spaniard Steve Ballesteros, the man everyone thought would win, eagled the par-5 13th to go nine under and take a four-stroke lead.

Then Nicklaus smacked a four-iron to 12 feet of the pin and sank the putt to eagle the par-5 15th, put his five-iron shot just past the hole for a birdie on the par-3 16th, and punched a pitching wedge to within 10 feet of the pin and putted out for a birdie on 17. When he was on 17, he said, he heard "a roar that wasn't a cheer" come up behind him. It was the crowd's reaction to Ballesteros's skulling an iron shot in the water on 15 that led to the bogey that put Nicklaus ahead. (Ballesteros wound up fourth at 281.)

Nicklaus parred 18 and then waited in front of a TV set in Bobby Jones's old cabin on the grounds as Kite and Norman tried to catch or beat him. Kite, a short Texan who wears large eyeglasses, just missed a 15-foot putt at 18 that would have tied him for the lead. "I made that putt. It just didn't go in," Kite later said. "I putted from that same spot seven or eight times in practice, and the ball never broke left like it did today. It must have hit a spike mark."

The engaging Norman, whose light-blond hair and "Great White Shark" nickname make him a tour celeb, staged a charge of his own on the back nine Sunday. A double-bogey six on the par-four 11th had temporarily knocked him off stride, but he birdied 14, 15, 16 and 17 to go nine under and tie.

On the par-four 18th, though, he pushed his four-iron second shot to the right of the green, chipped long from a thin lie and two-putted for a bogey that gave Nicklaus the win. The gallery sound that followed Norman's misfortune sounded suspiciously like a cheer, although Masters galleries are asked not to engage in such negative displays.

Norman, who has come close in "majors" before, attributed his third-round lead to a new-found ability to control his ego and not be over-aggressive. On Sunday, he admitted that he let Mr. Ego get the best of him on his ill-fated iron shot on 18. "I tried to hit it too high and too hard," said he. Not to worry, though, he added. "I'm still young enough to get six wins here, like Jack." (He's 31.)

The final-round heroics were partly made possible by weather that turned benign for the weekend. In the tourney's first two rounds on Thursday and Friday, bright sun dried Augusta National's huge and treacherous greens and gusty winds made club selection difficult. Par was broken on only 35 of 176 rounds those two days.

But Saturday was overcast and windless, and Sunday was sunny but calm, and scores dropped. On Saturday, Nick Price, a South African-born Zimbabwean with a British passport who lives in Orlando, Fla., broke the single-round course record with a marvelous 63 that began with a first-hole bogey and ended with a putt that rimmed the cup full circle before staying out (someone called it a "victory lap"). On Sunday, six eagles were recorded, all on par-five holes. Kite and Ballesteros holed back-to-back wedge shots for eagles on the eighth hole Sunday. No one could recall anything like that happening before anywhere.

As usual at Augusta, good putting carried the day, especially Nicklaus's. His four-day scores were 74, 71, 69 and 65, and he said the only difference between the rounds was that he sank more putts on the better ones. "I don't understand putting," confessed the master of the Masters Sunday. "I felt so nervous today that I'm surprised I could pull my putter back, but I hit everything dead center."

● *Apr. 15, 1986*

FUZZY BALL

Part 5

Here's to Jimmy

A few years back, when Generalissimo Francisco Franco ruled Spain, one Spaniard asked another what he thought of the dictator.

The fellow to whom the question was addressed took his companion into his car, drove to an isolated lake, hopped into a rowboat and rowed out to the middle. Finally satisfied he couldn't be overheard, he nervously whispered, "I like him."

That's the way I feel about Jimmy Connors, the tennis player. I like him, but I somehow feel hesitant about admitting it.

Now, I have never met Mr. Connors, but I have seen him play many times, and I have read a lot about him. I'm fully aware that he's not an easy person to warm up to.

Most obviously, he is brash, cocky, given to displays of temperament and gamesmanship on the courts and quarrelsome with officials. I also read that he is careless with friends and occasionally disrespectful to his mother, who doubles as his manager.

Mr. Connors further suffers in comparison with his two leading rivals for the title of world's best tennis player—Bjorn Borg of Sweden and Guillermo Vilas of Argentina.

Mr. Borg's wan good looks and inoffensive demeanor have made him an idol of teenage girls everywhere, and some older ones, too. By contrast, Mr. Connors's impudent mug and manner make him look like a refugee from an "Our Gang" comedy.

Mr. Vilas is said to be a sensitive sort who spends his off-court hours reading and writing gloomy poetry, habits that endear him to newspaper and magazine writers who like their athletes intellectual. Mr. Connors's sole recorded brush with the world of the mind came during the one year he spent at UCLA. He won the NCAA singles title that year (1971), reasoned that academe had no more to offer him and left to seek his fortune.

Some of Mr. Connors's supposed deficiencies can be dismissed quickly, I think. It's not his fault he isn't better looking, and I have little regard for sportswriters who judge an athlete by the quality of interviews he gives. Indeed, the entire institution of the post-game interview could be eliminated with little loss to us fans. Winners always feel good, loser always feel bad, and a reporter should be a keen enough observer to tell us right out if the winning hit came off a fastball or a curve.

I am no more enamored with some of Mr. Connors's tennis-court antics than anyone else: I find especially irksome his interminable fiddling with his racquet strings. But his behavior isn't notably worse than that of some other tennis stars, female as well as male, and some of it undoubtedly can be traced to an overabundance of competitive spirit that would be applauded in a less-decorous sport. Anyway, I understand he has cleaned up his act some lately.

But I will continue to like Mr. Connors even if he never manages to earn an "A" for deportment. For my money, he's the only tennis player around who makes the game exciting to watch.

By and large, tennis players can be divided into two categories: the serve and volley boys and the baseline ralliers. In the former group are such as Roscoe Tanner, Brian Gottfried, John Newcombe and Vitas Gerulaitis. They serve, rush the net and either put the ball away or are passed. Wham, bam—it's all over, and not much fun.

The ralliers—including Messrs. Borg and Vilas, Manuel Orantes, Eddie Dibbs, Harold Solomon and all the top women players—mostly scurry around retrieving their opponents' shots. Theirs is a game of attrition that has become increasingly effective with the proliferation of clay-court tournaments. I find it about as interesting as watching a bricklayer put up a wall.

Mr. Connors is essentially a baseline player, but with a crucial difference: He does not temporize, he attacks, incessantly and from all parts of the court.

He has overcome an average physique (he's 5-foot-10 and 150 pounds) by being superbly conditioned, an all-out competitor and lightning fast; one TV commentator recently gushed that he possessed "excessive speed." Experts say his two-handed backhand is one of the best in the game, and his return of service from either side is *the* best, which is why he rarely loses to one of the big-serve boys.

When he does lose, it's usually to a skilled rallier whose patience (and, I suppose, maturity) exceeds his own; frustrated, he will try a too-fine shot, and err. But his errors are of commission rather than omission, and I find this admirable.

Mr. Connors doesn't dominate tennis the way Pancho Gonzales and Rod Laver did in their times; there are too many good players around now for that. But if he doesn't always win the big ones, he's almost always there. He has been a finalist at Forest Hills four years running, and at Wimbledon three of the last four years. When we think of the big matches of recent years, we think of Connors versus Borg, Connors versus Vilas, Connors versus Orantes. And win or lose, he always makes the match.

Farfetched as it sounds, there may even be hope that Mr. Connors will be a popular favorite one of these days. In sports, it seems, characteristics that are irritating in a young man become endearing in an older one. Who would have thought that Ted Williams would become a beloved figure in the later part of his career, or Muhammad Ali, for heaven's sake? Jimmy is only 26 years old. Give the kid a chance.

● *June 1, 1978*

Communist Plutocrat

There's a wire fence around the brick-and-wood house in the country outside this wealthy suburb of New York, and when a visitor rings at the electric gate his initial greeting comes from four noisy German shepherd dogs.

Ivan Lendl, who lives there, sticks his head out of the door and calls off the beasts in his native Czech. Another example of East Bloc secrecy? Apparently not. "Prowlers—you know how it is," he says apologetically.

Wearing a sweatshirt and jeans, the 24-year-old tennis star, currently ranked number three in the world, also apologizes for the trophies on the floor and the paintings stacked against the walls of the spacious abode. "I'm moving in a couple of weeks; same area, but a nicer house," he explains. "I saw it and liked it. I think that Connecticut is my first home now, so I might as well have the place I want."

Indeed, Ivan Lendl has become very much at home in uppercrust America. When he first came to this country at age 15 to brave the Florida winter junior circuit, about all he knew how to say in English was "Coca-Cola." Now he can discuss anti-burglary devices and video gear and play Trivial Pursuit with the rest of the Yuppies.

And, yes, he really can smile, although he professes not to understand why his stony-faced on-court demeanor is such an issue. "People who know me know I like to fool around. It's just that in matches I have no time for that," he says in fluent but accented English. "I have to be serious and concentrate. That is my style, just like getting mad is McEnroe's. I'll tell you what: When he starts being polite to linesmen, I'll start smiling."

Lendl will put his serious mien and abundant tennis skills on display again next week at the Volvo Masters in New York's Madison Square Garden. It's one of the biggest winter tournaments, with John McEnroe and Jimmy Connors, the two top rankers, also scheduled to compete. First prize is $100,000. Lendl won it in 1981 and '82, and was a finalist last year.

The tourney also is a fashion event of sorts, because it will mark the debut of a new "Lendl shirt" designed by Adidas, which pays him about $1 million a year to endorse its shoes, sportswear and tennis rackets. The garment features a series of diagonal stripes and boxes in place of the argyle pattern of the famous (infamous?) old Lendl shirt. Ivan says that he, like many of us, was getting tired of the old model.

His Adidas contract, coupled with his other endorsements and tournament winnings of about $6 million in the past six years, has made Lendl into a most unusual creature: a Communist plutocrat. The way he looks at it, it's not as contradictory as it sounds.

"Adidas likes it that I use their products; Czechoslovakia likes it that I am identified as Czech. It's really not that different," he says.

His relations with the Czech government haven't always been smooth. He was banned from Davis Cup play for a time for participating in a tourney in Bophuthatswana, South Africa, and didn't return to Czechoslovakia for three years before things were smoothed over last year.

He credits the example of Martina Navratilova, the Czech-born women's champion who is now a U.S. citizen, with easing the way for him to create a *modus vivendi* with his government.

"When Martina had problems, she felt she had to defect. In Czechoslavakia, they didn't like that," he says. "Then things changed so I don't have to do that. I must travel, so I can. I play in the U.S. mostly, so I live here mostly. I earn money, so I pay taxes everywhere I play and turn some of my winnings [about 20%, his advisers at ProServ Inc. say] back to my country. What I keep, I spend as I wish.

"If you want to know what I am, I am a Czech living in America.

Maybe some day I will ask to be American, but this is OK for now. Like they say, if it's not broken, don't fix it."

Lendl applies the same philosophy to the tennis game that has won him a score of Grand Prix tournaments and brought him tantalizingly close to the summit of the sport. Since 1981, he has never been ranked lower than third in the world, but never higher than second.

For a time, it appeared that 1984 would be his big break-through year. In June, his patented cannon forehand won him his first Grand Slam title at the French Open, where he defeated McEnroe in five sets after dropping the first two. But then he fell to Connors in the semis at Wimbledon and to McEnroe in hasty straight sets in the finals at the U.S. Open—one of his five final losses to the Long Island moaner over the season. Last month, bothered by a pulled stomach muscle, he exited the Australian Open in the quarterfinals.

Lendl won three tournaments last year against seven the year before, but he insists he was "quite happy" with his play. "Before last year, I said I'd exchange all my wins for one Grand Slam title. I won in France, so I shouldn't complain," he says.

"Some people say I should change my game to come to the net more, but I think I should work harder to improve what I do best," he continues. "Between McEnroe, Connors and me there is very little difference right now. I never walk on the court against them without thinking I can win. I am younger than them [McEnroe is almost 26, Connors is 32] and I know I will catch them. Maybe this year."

Meantime, he isn't sitting around worrying about it. He spent Christmas week playing golf in Curacao. He discovered the game a few years ago in Florida, and it has become a passion; self-taught, he can break 80 on a good day.

He has also discovered Porsche cars, and he vows that even an accident near his home here several weeks ago, in which he suffered a minor face cut, won't keep him away from the wheel. He has discovered Connecticut, and he has purchased a fair-sized chunk of it in addition to his homes.

"But don't expect Ivan to become an all-American boy—he is too Czech for that," says George Vborny, a Czech-born Canadian businessman who is the tennis player's longtime friend. "Yes, he drives Porsches. But he is East European-conservative, so they aren't the most expensive ones. When he invests, it is mostly in land, which he can see. And when there is work to do, he does it, on time, and with a working-day face. The tennis is always first with him. If he thought it could help him win more, he'd smile all day."

• Jan. 4, 1985

Wimbledon's Green

T
.

he words most often volleyed about in connection with the All England Lawn Tennis & Croquet Club (Wimbledon's real name) are "ancient" and "hallowed." Those who run it would have you believe it has been around forever, and even the most hardened tennis tourists say they get shaky in the knees at the thought of playing here.

Harrumph. The first Championships (yes, capital C) were sponsored by the club in 1877, one year after baseball's National League was formed. The present grounds for the tourney date to 1922. That makes them 12 years younger than Comiskey Park, and only beer vendors wax reverent about that place.

Wimbledon has maintained its cachet by ignoring almost everything that's happened in tennis over the past 30 years. The average tennis player today rarely sees, much less plays on, grass courts, but that's still the surface here. The All England is the last bastion of the white tennis ball and white tennis outfit. It's a wonder players don't have to use wood rackets.

Even currently accepted labels for women are ignored. Female players are referred to collectively as "ladies" and individually as Miss or Mrs., never Ms. Married ones must go by their husbands' names. Chris Evert Lloyd's *nom de Wimbledon* is Mrs. J.M. Lloyd. They put up with it for the $1 million-plus in prize money.

110

It is in matters financial that Wimbledon has kept up to date, and this largely accounts for its continuing pre-eminence in a sport that is as mercenary as any other these days. In 1968, Wimbledon became the first major tennis championship to submit to paying players with checks, thus ushering in the present "open" era. Its total prize purse of about $2.5 million is tennis's biggest, with the women's singles winner netting $152,000 and the men's $169,000.

Wimbledon raises that cash like any other sporting event. Ordinary admission tickets this week go for about $4 and a Centre Court seat costs between $16 and $22 more—if you can get one.

Tents where corporations entertain guests dot the grounds, just as at American golf tournaments. The club has sold its name to licensees that make everything from tennis rackets to neckties. Most of them are Japanese. "The original idea was to promote British industry, but it was dropped somewhere, I guess," a tourney official notes.

For all that, though, it's the biggest summer draw for Londoners. Daily crowds number about 35,000 people, many of whom stand in line for hours for the privilege of strolling the grounds and foraging among fastfood delicacies, among which the Dutch hot dogs stand out.

Seatless, these fans are limited to watching lesser players perform on outer courts. The big-cheese pros play almost exclusively in Centre Court and Court One, which are enclosed. The outer-courters do their bashing in a veritable pedestrian mall.

In fact, a dispute over courts involving John McEnroe was one of the things that enlivened the start of the final week of play here. When Jawin' John was assigned to Court Two, outside the stadium, to play young Christo Steyn of South Africa in a third-round match on Monday, he argued that that was beneath the dignity of a defending men's singles champion, which he is. After winning in straight sets, he allowed that the court really wasn't too bad, but noisier than he'd have liked.

In a way, it's fortunate that McEnroe is around to liven things up with his extracurricular antics, because the tennis side of Wimbledon has been pretty perfunctory to date. Seeds have fallen, to be sure, but some of them were bad seeds, ranked for their ability on softer surfaces.

McEnroe and the defending women's champ, Martina Navratilova, might be just OK on clay, but their supreme serve-and-volley skills make them the class of the grass, and they are odds-on choices to repeat. That has left the fans to pursue other interests until the two meet serious competition in this weekend's final rounds.

One perennial Wimbledon diversion is rooting for the home team, but after Monday's defeats of Virginia (Our Ginny) Wade and John (Mr. J.M.) Lloyd, only Jo (Our Jo) Durie was left to wave the Union Jack in singles. The popular Wade, whose 1977 singles crown was England's last big tennis thrill, gave a good account of herself, taking Pam Shriver to three sets before falling, 6-2, 5-7, 6-2.

The match marked the retirement from singles competition of Wade, who is gracefully graying at age 39. She said she leaves with bittersweet memories of playing on Centre Court before the home folks. "It's exciting, but it's also the type of court that makes you embarrassed if you're not playing well, and then you play worse," she said before sampling a farewell bottle of champagne.

Another Wimbledon amusement is finding the year's Great Young Hope. Usually, it's a kid with a big serve from Stanford or UCLA. This year it's a kid with a big serve from Leimen, West Germany. He's Boris Becker, who looks like Amy Carter from the neck up and a good college halfback the rest of the way. He had marked himself as a comer with a win in the Stella Artois grass-courts tuneup tourney before Wimbledon. With its usual gentle touch, the British sporting press took to labeling him things like "Der Bomber."

After the unseeded Becker beat seventh-seeded Joachim Nystrom of Sweden in a five-set rouser Monday, he told reporters he thought they'd gone overboard on the World War II stuff. "I don't think it's very good, the Blitzkrieg headlines about me. I'm a German, but I'm not a general or anything like that," said Becker, who is 17.

It was, however, left to McEnroe to give the drink its best stir, and he kind of snuck up on everybody with it. After his win over Steyn, he was telling newsmen how he thought his acceptance of the Court Two assignment marked his growing maturity.

"I like to take things easier now, and I feel a lot better about myself," he said. "I don't know if that's going to make me a better tennis player, but it's going to make me a better person, which is more important."

Did he think there was some room for improvement for himself in the "person" department then? a British voice asked.

"You know, if you people weren't such [unprintables], I'd answer that question honestly," he said, and stalked away.

That's Our John.

- *July 3, 1985*

A Star Is Born

oris Becker and Kevin Curren were going at it below, but the British journalists with whom I was sharing a side press booth at the Wimbledon men's tennis finals Sunday were engaged in England's real favorite sport: royalty watching.

The focus of their attention (literally, they had binoculars) was Princess Michael of Kent, whose alleged illicit liaison with a scion of the Texas Hunt family had tingled the tabloids mightily that morning.

"What's that she's doing?" chirped one.

"Putting on something," said another.

"I think it's a shawl."

"Looks more like a blanket."

"Now what's she doing?"

"Twisting her wedding ring."

"Oooh!"

"Is she watching the tennis?"

"Not a bit as far as I can see."

It's too bad the princess and the reporters had their attention elsewhere, because they missed a good match. Becker and Curren slugged it out for the heavyweight tennis championship of the earth (again literally: Centre Court was so stripped of grass it looked like an overused softball diamond), and the blond, bouncy, 6-foot-2 Becker won, 6-3, 6-7, 7-6, 6-4.

His triumph established a sizeable list of firsts. At

age 17, he became the youngest winner of what's usually considered tennis's most prestigious prize. He was the first German and the first unseeded player to win. He also set unofficial records for dirtying the most tennis togs with his hockey-goalie style, and for giving the most direct answers to reporters.

"Why did you win?" he was asked.

"I served better and was less nervous."

"Do you think you'll be the greatest player ever?"

"It's too early to tell."

Becker's victory rounded off a Wimbledon that was neatly two-sided. The women's half of the tourney went almost strictly according to form, with Martina Navratilova defeating her No. 1 co-seed, Chris Evert Lloyd, in the final on Saturday. Among the men, form was a myth. The top three seeds—John McEnroe, Ivan Lendl and Jimmy Connors—all bit the abundant dust of Centre Court and looked bad doing it.

Lendl went out first, losing to Frenchman Henri Leconte in the fourth round as his serve sputtered. But the chief seed-trampler was Curren, a South African reluctantly turned Yank because of the political difficulties athletes from that country face. Seeded eighth, he eliminated McEnroe and Connors on successive days last week with the loss of just 13 games.

McEnroe and Connors never got their guns out of their holsters against the University of Texas product. Curren's serve, a snappy job off a low throw, was so fierce that McEnroe described it as establishing a "different power level" after a 6-2, 6-2, 6-4 loss in the quarterfinals on Wednesday ended his hopes for a third straight Wimbledon title.

Becker's path to the finals was rougher. He lost the first set in four of his six pre-finals encounters, had to go into overtime to beat Joachim Nystrom of Sweden in a 9-7 fifth set in the third round, and was down two sets to one to Tim Mayotte before pulling out his fourth-round match.

Throughout it all, though, he followed one simple rule: Never temporize. If a hard shot didn't win him a point, he hit the ball harder the next time. He acted like he didn't know the meaning of the word "pressure." With a lucrative tennis career now launched, he'll probably skip college and not know the meanings of other words, too, but he probably won't need to.

Sunday's final was about as straightforward a match as you'll see. It was serve against serve, and Becker's was better by everyone's assessment, including the 27-year-old Curren's. There were just four service breaks in the 45 games, and Becker had three of them. Aside from the single game he won on Becker's service, Curren managed break points in just two others.

Becker's first service break came in the second game of set one. He didn't win it as much as Curren lost it. Curren hit a forehand kill shot long, netted as easy volley and double-faulted at game point. That game was "horrific," he later admitted. "It set me on the wrong path."

Curren won the second set by capturing the last five points of the tie-breaker, and in game seven of set three he went ahead, 4-3, on his only service break. But Becker curtly broke back the next game. He won the third-set tie-breaker, 7-3, broke Curren in the first game of set four, and chugged right on home. He had a match point on Curren's serve in the ninth game and lost it. He didn't make that mistake again in game 10.

Curren said he didn't serve as well against Becker as he did against McEnroe and Connors because Becker served better. "His power gave me more to worry about. It dictated the tempo of the match," he summed up. It made sense to me.

Saturday's final was the 66th meeting between Martina and Chris (Martina has won 34) in a rivalry that keeps improving. Each did what she does best superbly. But on grass, the best of Navratilova's serve-and-volley style was superior to Evert Lloyd's best base-line shots.

Evert Lloyd got off well and won the first set, 6-4, but as the match wore on, Navratilova's serves got sharper, her approach shots deeper and her volleys surer. Lloyd had to try for the lines with every ball, and couldn't always manage it. She lost the last two sets, 6-3 and 6-2, but they weren't as lopsided as the scores.

Neither Martina, 28 years old, nor Chris, 30, lost a set here before their meeting, and their reign over the women's game seems secure. One reporter, seeking a line on young women prospects, asked Martina after her win whom she saw as her main "future" rival. "Chris," said Martina, "I can't see farther ahead than that."

• *July 9, 1985*

A Cheer for Flushing Meadow

QUEENS, N.Y.

Y
·

ou know you are at the U.S. Open, not Wimbledon, when: 1) The noise overhead is from planes, not birds; 2) the orb overhead is as likely to be the moon as the sun; and 3) the fellow putting away the overheads is John McEnroe, not Boris Becker (this year, anyway).

And then there are the crowds. In England, they sit still during points and applaud politely after them. Here they move around, chat, cheer, question officials' calls and scratch when they feel like it. It's usually nothing atrocious, mind you, but at times it's untennislike.

If you are a player, your reaction to the fans who fill the big bowl at Flushing Meadow depends on whether you've just won or lost. Fifth-seeded Kevin Curren, a usually mild-mannered sort, opined after he was upset by Frenchman Guy Forget in the first round last week that an A-bomb should be dropped on the rabble. Winners tend to say that the crowd spurs them on, and Jimmy Connors, a spiritual New Yorker from Belleville, Ill., credits their support for his extraordinary success here over the years.

My own view is that there's no intrinsic reason why tennis fans shouldn't be able to cheer and boo at will the way people at baseball games do. I realize that's a position that flies in the face of custom, and has no chance of enactment anytime soon. Even the most vocal fans here are dubious about it. "It'd disturb the players," said one fellow who had been bellowing like crazy between points of the Heinz Gunthardt-Henri LeConte match ("C'mon Henree!"). Call it an idea whose time hasn't come.

A less disputable notion is that the U.S. Open is tennis's truest championship test. You've got to give it the clear nod over the French and Australian opens. French red clay is easy on the legs, but it gets all over everyone's socks, and a requisite for winning the June Paris test is the ability to stay awake through long baseline rallies. The Aussie Open is a December rumor in the rest of the world.

Wimbledon has history on its side, but its grass courts have become a tennis curiosity and they reward big servers disproportionately. The best player usually wins there, but one-dimensional blasters like Roscoe Tanner, Chris Lewis and, this year, Curren, keep popping up in the final.

The U.S. Open comes in late summer when promising, non-pro youngsters (yes, there still are some) have had time to hone their games. Two of them—Jay Berger, 18, of Florida, and Jaime Yzaga, 17, of Peru—made it to the round of 16 in singles.

Flushing Meadow's big edge is underfoot. The trade name for the courts here is DecoTurf II, but they are basically concrete, pretty much like the ones in your local park. They're slicker than clay but have more bite than grass. A big serve helps, of course, but it can't win without supporting artillery.

That fact came home strongest in the upset of Wimbledon champ Becker by Joakim Nystrom of Sweden on Monday. The two had met at the English tournament, with the 17-year-old Boris's boomers deciding the issue in five sets. Here, Nystrom had more room to parry, and he prevailed in four.

The premature defeat of the talented Becker disappointed ticket scalpers and ended Open Subplot One by forestalling a much awaited showdown between him and McEnroe in Wednesday's men's single quarterfinals. Boris's Wimbledon triumph was tainted in some eyes (not mine) because he defeated none of the men's Big Three of McEnroe, Ivan Lendl or Connors en route to the crown, and that blot could have been removed here. Not to worry, though; Becker's inevitable future clashes with the big boys should enliven many a tourney to come.

Subplot Two on the men's side involved the fate of the remarkable Swedish contingent of Nystrom, Mats Wilander, Anders Jarryd and Stefan Edberg, all of whom except Edberg made it to the quarterfinal round. Casual tennis fans may see the young Swedes as Bjorn-again Borgs, but that's not so. All of them shave and get haircuts regularly, and the unstoical Jarryd has been known to abuse his racket.

The best of the bunch ultimately may be Edberg. He's a big kid of 19 who, unlike Borg, enjoys coming to the net. In Tuesday's fourth round, however, Connors bounced a bunch of service returns off his shoes and bumped him.

Jarryd and Nystrom got the gate on Wednesday. Jarryd fell to hot and cold flashes that forced him to voice the Scandinavian version of *no mas* in a rare, third-set default to his countryman, Wilander. McEnroe, playing brilliantly, carved up Nystrom, 6-1, 6-0 and 7-5. Only a setback caused by a McEnroe tantrum about the conduct of a courtside TV microphone holder saved the match from being a total rout.

Wilander is the most accomplished of the Swedish group, with two French and two Aussie titles to his credit. McEnroe is next on his list in the semis tomorrow. Tune in. It could be a good one.

On the women's side, Martina Navratilova and Chris Evert Lloyd didn't lose a set on their way to the semifinals, as usual, and No. 3 Hana Mandlikova made it, too. But the march of the seeds was interrupted memorably by the appealing new face of Steffi Graf, a West German 16-year-old. She beat fourth-seeded Pam Shriver by the symmetrical score of 7-6, 6-7, 7-6.

The match was an arduous affair on a sticky afternoon that made you wish that the girls felt free to change shirts between games the way the boys do. Shriver later described some of the points as "violent." A bit overdramatic, perhaps, but close.

Graf was down four games to one in the final set, and four points to three in the last-set tie-breaker before running off four straight to win. A fine shot maker, she wore down the bigger Shriver and finally forced her to hit a backhand long at match point.

The win earned the gutsy blonde a shot at Martina in the semis, a prospect that didn't exactly thrill her. She said she thought it might be a year or two before her game was up to the defending champ's. But you never could tell, Graf said brightly, "She could break a leg."

Let's assume she meant it in the theatrical sense. And meantime, fans, "Quiet please . . . take your seats, please . . . quiet please. . . ."

● *Sept. 6, 1985*

Payday for the Bouncing Czechs

QUEENS, N.Y.

T
•

he U.S. received a bit of a balance-of-payments setback over the weekend when the U.S. Tennis Association wrote good-sized checks to a couple of Czechs. Hana Mandlikova got one for $187,500 for winning the U.S. Open women's singles title on Saturday. Ivan Lendl got the same for copping the men's crown the next day.

It's hard to say which of the victories was the more surprising. The swift, 23-year-old Mandlikova, from Prague and proud of it, entered the tourney with a No. 3 seeding and a reputation for inconsistency. She had won the French and Australian Opens as a teen-ager, showing that she could beat the big girls, but she also had a disconcerting habit of losing to lesser lights. This time, she defeated both Chris Evert Lloyd and Martina Navratilova en route to her title, and nobody has done *that* in quite a while.

Lendl, 25, a Greenwich, Conn., squire from Ostrava, had been all too consistent heretofore. He'd been dynamite in places like Tokyo, Brussels and Ft. Myers, Fla., but terrible at Flushing Meadow and Wimbledon. Despite a fat wallet, he had only one Grand Slam title—the 1984 French—to show for seven trips to the finals of such high-toned events.

Sunday, however, Ivan was wonderful in putting away top-seeded John McEnroe, the unhappy warrior, by scores of 7-6, 6-3 and 6-4. He smacked winners from both sides, outserved tennis's prime exponent of the serve-and-volley style, and, a few times, even outvolleyed him. "I felt like I was flying out there," he said afterward in a description of supreme athletic elation. "I felt there was no shot I couldn't get, no ball I couldn't hit."

The finals triumphs of the bouncing Czechs came at the expense of tennis's recognized best players and cast in doubt the No. 1 ranking among both genders. The two sides of the three Grand Slam events contested so far this year have produced six different champions. That hasn't happened in quite a while, either.

Despite his No. 2 seeding, nobody much expected Lendl to take the men's final. He'd been there the last three years with nothing to show for it, so why should this year be different? the reasoning went.

The star of the men's show before Sunday was McEnroe, suddenly erratic after four years as a solid *numero uno*. In the first round, Jawin' John had to go to five sets and a last-set tie-breaker to beat Shlomo Glickstein, a heavy-legged Israeli who carried a No. 175 world ranking. Against the more-skillful Joakim Nystrom of Sweden in the quarterfinals, he went from the sublime to the ridiculous. He played what many regarded as his best tennis ever in winning 14 of the first 15 games and then blew five straight in a silly snit over the conduct of a courtside TV soundman before recovering his aplomb and the match.

In Saturday's semifinal against Mats Wilander of Sweden on a steamy Gotham afternoon, McEnroe played lost-and-found with his game, variously sparkling and struggling. He hit on just 51% of his first serves and fumed and growled over a balky backhand before pulling out a five-set triumph. Wilander is the third-best player in the world behind McEnroe and Lendl, but the real match Saturday was McEnroe vs. McEnroe, not Mac vs. Wilander. That's getting to be a pattern with John.

Mac began Sunday's final as if he were going to extend his domination over Lendl that had earned him 13 wins in the last 16 matches between the two. He shot off to a five-games-to-two first set lead, winning his first four service games without the loss of a point. In game eight, on Lendl's serve, he came within a point of breaking to win the set.

But McEnroe said the effects of the four-hour duel with Wilander the previous day then began to tell. (Lendl beat Jimmy

Connors in straight sets in cooler temperatures in the Saturday-night semi.) Lendl held service in game eight, broke McEnroe at love in game nine, and sailed home from there. He won the first-set tie-breaker by a 7-1 score and broke Mac's service once in each of the last two sets while never facing a break point on his own service.

Lendl had been faulted previously for rooting himself on the baseline while McEnroe served-and-volleyed him into submission in tourney after tourney. On Sunday, McEnroe persisted in coming to the net even while Lendl rifled passing shots by him from all angles. Like Popeye, both players yam what they yam, and neither appears ready to change.

Mandlikova's wins over Evert Lloyd in Friday's semis and Navratilova in the Saturday final probably jolted women's tennis more than Lendl's roiled the men's. Martina and Chris had settled into what only can be described as a comfortable rivalry atop the women's game. It was Martina the puncher vs. Chris the boxer. Her occasional recent wins to the contrary notwithstanding, I suspect that even Chris had come to accept Martina's basic supremacy.

For all her shot-making skills, Evert Lloyd is an innately cautious player, and cautious means predictable. Mandlikova allowed as much after she beat Chris in two of three sets on Friday. "I knew where she would go," she said.

For herself, Hana said she thought her Czech upbringing made her a late boomer, er, bloomer. Back home, "your family does everything for you, and then I went out and had to be independent. It took time to realize that I had to do things on my own. Kids here do everything on their own from the beginning. They have shoulders and elbows and they just go like that. I think that's a great attitude."

Hana is the only woman player who can match Martina athletically, and on Saturday she sought to make the best of her gifts. She rushed the net at every opportunity, often taking Martina's fearsome service well inside the baseline. The result was a match of abrupt swings. Hana won the first five games and then had to hang on to win the set, seven games to six, with a 7-3 edge in the tie-breaker. Martina captured the next set easily, 6-1.

The third set seesawed to another tie-breaker, which Hana took, 7-2. Martina, the winner of four straight Wimbledon titles and the last two U.S. Open crowns, admitted afterward that playing the "new" Hana was unsettling. "She took chances when she was down and played safe when she was up," Martina said. "It was tough to get into any rhythm with her." Translated, that means that, unlike Chris, Hana was unpredictable. She—and women's tennis—seems likely to remain so now. It's overdue.

- *Sept. 10, 1985*

Stew without Pepper

T. he U.S. Open tennis tournament is arguably the most elegant international sports stew served up on these shores. This year, sadly, the pepper is missing.

Much of the vital condiment escaped on Day One of the tourney, when John McEnroe, the notable miscreant, was rudely upset by Paul Annacone, a player of little previous note. McEnroe was returning to the big-time tennis wars after a seven months' break for fatherhood and marriage, in that order, with actress Tatum O'Neal. He came back with his irascibility intact, but with eight pounds missing from his already scrawny frame due to an ill-advised diet.

Also missing was the steaming serve and deft volleying touch that had made McEnroe a four-time champion in this precinct. Annacone disposed of him in four sets and then was himself swallowed by Aaron Krickstein. Krickstein, in turn, was scarfed by Frenchman Henri Leconte. Thus was Big Mac reduced to the role of small fry in the tennis food chain.

Now, it well may be contended that McEnroe's absence is no detriment to tennis's truest and best test. To switch a line from a commercial he does for a safety razor, some people dislike John McEnroe and some aren't so sure. He regularly commits that most grievous of sins for a well-brought-up boy: losing his temper in public. Many consider it a daily blessing that he is neither their son nor close neighbor.

Without McEnroe around, though, and with 34-year-old Jimmy Connors also out of the fray as a result of a third-round, last-hurrah upset loss on Sunday, charisma has become as scarce as shade in the stark concrete bowl that is the centerpiece of the U.S. Tennis Center in Flushing Meadow. To be sure, the tennis has been good—even excellent. But though it may seem superficial, let's face it: One backhand looks pretty much like the next without some personal pizazz behind it.

McEnroe's exit leaves the men's side of the draw here with Ivan Lendl at its head; in fact, the Czech with the coat-hanger shoulders was there even before Mac got the boot. Lendl won the Open last year and had captured seven Grand Prix tournaments in 10 outings this year, including the French Open.

Nobody hits 'em better than Lendl from either side. His serve is a force, and he even ventures to the net now and again. His problem is that he ain't funny.

The No. 2 men's seed is Mats Wilander, a Swede. He hits the ball well, but so do all the other Swedes playing here. He seems amiable, but so do the other Swedes. He has light-colored hair, but so do . . . well, you get the idea.

No. 3 is Boris Becker. Now there's a kid with possibilities. He's a big, healthy freckle-face who hits every shot like it's his first—an all-American boy from Leimen, West Germany. The concrete courts at Flushing Meadow aren't as much to his liking as the grass ones at Wimbledon, where he's won twice. When he dives for a ball here, he gets bruises, not grass stains.

Still, you can't keep Boris from bouncing, and he's working on his post-game patter. On Sunday, at match point against Spaniard Sergio Casal, he stopped to say something to a courtside spectator. Asked later what happened, he replied: "Before the match the guy hollered that I should win because he had a big bet on me. At match point I asked him, 'For how much?'" Not bad for 18 years old.

The rap on the women playing here isn't so much that they are dull as that we know them too well. We refer to them by their first names, like members of our family. At the top there's Martina and Chris. Next come Pam, Steffi and Wendy. After that come the rest.

The march of the female seeds has come off about as predictably as ever, except for the defeat of defending champion Hana Mandlikova on Labor Day by 17th-ranked Wendy Turnbull. Fourteen of the 16 ranked players made it to the fourth round. Gabriela

Sabatini of Argentina and Mary Joe Fernandez of Miami, a couple of attractive newcomers, showed some early foot before being ousted by, yes, Martina and Chris, respectively.

Martina, a ripe old 29 years old, murmured a complaint or two about advancing age after she beat the 16-year-old Sabatini in a fourth-round match Monday. "I have a few gray hairs—that you don't see—and it takes me a little longer to get going than it used to," she said. You couldn't prove that by Gaby though, because Martina breezed through the first four games of their two-set contest.

In Miss Fernandez, aged 15, the 31-year-old Chris faced a studied mirror image of her own two-handed backhand, baseline game in the third round. Chris said she "felt flattered" by the imitation but was more gratified at the score, which was 6-4, 6-2 in her favor. "I wouldn't have liked it if she did *me* better than me," Chris allowed, sharply enough.

And just to show that even gray suits can have silver linings, the ouster of McEnroe and Connors has allowed the spotlight to fall on some Americans who had escaped previous notice. One is Tim Wilkison, who defeated France's Yannick Noah in a third-round five-setter that Noah later said "was what tennis is all about," and later roused a Labor Day grandstand full house with a straight-sets win over Andrei Chesnokov of the Soviet Union.

Wilkinson is a North Carolinian who was ranked 31st coming here. He's an acrobatic net rusher who wears a baseball cap on court, grunts when he hits, and talks to himself between points. Despite his aggressive demeanor, though, his strongest expletive after a miss is "fiddlesticks." No dummy he: In nine years on the pro circuit he's never been fined for cussing.

Wilkinson was up for questions on the international significance of his win over Chesnokov. Was it like Rocky IV? he was asked. "I'll leave the Russians to Caspar Weinberger. Personally, I preferred Rocky II," he said.

As to the tactics behind his victory, he opined that by alternating chipped and deep approach shots, he put Chesnokov off his rhythm. "It seemed to me that he was rushin'," he said. Honest.

● *Sept. 3, 1986*

WORLD BALL

Part 6

East Germany's Secret

A half-busload of foreign journalists heading for the College of Physical Culture here was given a list of experts who would be available for interviews later that day.

"Of course, you will want to talk to our Dr. Tittel. All visitors to the college do," said one of our guides, smiling slightly. "He is the one with the miracle drugs that make us strong."

The remark was meant as a joke, because no one in authority in this country will admit that drugs, miraculous or ordinary, play a role in the remarkable showing of East German athletes in international competition over the past decade. The talk about drugs was merely the result of Western envy over the achievements of East German sportsmen, our hosts declared. The only miracle was in the way socialism has organized the people's natural enthusiasm for sports to produce glory for the *Vaterland*.

As we were told seriously and repeatedly, the founders of the German Democratic Republic called the shot 35 years ago when they wrote in the nation's constitution that the right to participate in sports was necessary for the "complete expression of the socialist personality." As it is written, so it has been!

Well, something is up in the GDR because its athletes keep winning international medals and breaking records in numbers far out of proportion to the coun-

129

try's population of 16.5 million and its meager showings in other
fields.

In the 1976 Summer Olympics at Montreal, East Germany won
90 medals, just four fewer than those of the U.S. and 35 fewer than
the U.S.S.R., both of which had (and have) more than a dozen times
its population. In the 1980 Games at Moscow, it made its Soviet big
brothers sweat before finishing second to them in the medal count,
126 to 195. Based on its showings this year and last in its specialties
of women's swimming, women's track and field, rowing and canoeing, the GDR would have made another sizable haul in Los Angeles
this summer.

The GDR had planned the foreign-press tour as an occasion for
some pre-Olympic muscle flexing. The fact that it drew a fair-sized
turnout despite the GDR's withdrawal from the L.A. Games attested to the widespread curiosity about the country's sports activities.

The tour was launched formally in East Berlin last week with
speeches from GDR sports administrators and a look at the big,
police-sponsored Dynamo sports club. From there it was on to
Leipzig for a day at the sports college, and some reporters continued
on to Erfurt for the national track-and-field championships.

I had chosen instead to take in the GDR swimming championships the week before the press tour, because of the East German
women swimmers' incredible record in the past two Olympics (22 of
a possible 26 gold medals). As one of only about a half-dozen foreign reporters there I could move fairly freely and talk to whoever
could *sprechen* English with me.

What I learned at the championships about sports in the GDR
was this: The country systematically identifies promising athletes as
young as age six. It channels many of them into such out-of-the-way
sports as swimming and rowing, where relatively low world performance standards increase the opportunities for GDR victories. Kids
who show special promise are packed off to sports schools for training. Layers of local and national age-group meets winnow out the
losers. The best stay on and receive all the care that a high-priority
government program can provide. The medals and records follow.

That sounded straightforward (and coldblooded) enough, but
my hosts kept hinting that great things were to be seen in Berlin and
Leipzig. Nevertheless, their performances at both places seemed calculated to keep things *misterioso*.

At the Dynamo club in Berlin, for instance, TV cameramen in

our group were barred from taking pictures, although still photographers could shoot ahead. Most requests to see specific facilities were turned aside. Whenever I asked where the weight-training rooms were in the giant complex (several gyms, two swimming pools, an ice rink and many outdoor fields), I was told they were in other buildings. Could we visit an athletes' dining hall? Too early for lunch, said one guide. Too late, said another.

The drill at the College of Physical Culture here in Leipzig, where East Germany trains its coaches, was much the same. A quick tour of gyms and pools; no shining labs; no time for a lot of questions.

At last, I chanced upon a weight room. It consisted of some barbells and a battered weights-on-pulleys machine that was old hat in the U.S. 20 years ago. "We don't lay emphasis on equipment—the attitude of our athletes is what achieves good results," a guide told us lamely.

Finally, the press conference that was to clear up all our misconceptions was convened, and there, on a panel of nine faculty members of the college, was the eminent Dr. Kurt Tittel. The rest of the world may be impressed with him, but his colleagues apparently aren't. A short, stout man of about 60, he was seated at a far end of the speakers' table and was the only panelist without a Communist Party pin in his lapel.

I directed the first question to him, inquiring about the GDR's capacity to test athletes' blood-lactate levels. The test is an important way to measure fatigue. It's an up-to-date method that isn't widespread enough in the U.S. to suit many American coaches.

I guess the translation was faulty, because Dr. Tittel answered angrily, in German, that his country didn't go in for blood "doping," a controversial blood-oxygenation procedure that's supposed to enhance performance.

"No, I asked about blood-lactate testing," I repeated.
"Ah, yes," he smiled. His country had many places where such readings could be quickly obtained. A valuable tool, indeed.

Strangely, although many subsequent questions were about GDR sports medicine, Dr. Tittel wasn't called on to answer again. An official of the college did most of the talking. Skirting direct answers was his specialty.

Does the GDR use computers in biomechanical research? "We cooperate in international efforts in that area," he said. Why does the GDR lag in international team sports? "That's difficult to explain." Do young East German athletes ever experience a socialist variety of "Little League burnout"? "Our Spartakiad youth competition movement fosters great enthusiasm."

The press conference ended, but Dr. Tittel stuck around to chat in English with some American newsmen. He said he was nearing retirement after 25 years as a physician for GDR national teams and probably wouldn't have gone to this Olympics even if he could have. He said he'd rather stay home and do research into athletic performance, "a very, very big complex we don't know much about."

What did he think was the secret of the GDR's playing-field success? "First is to look for talent very early," he said. "Second is to be patient with athletes, not to expect too much improvement too soon. Third is to gain friendly cooperation between coach and athlete. I think that last is the biggest thing.

"It's no secret, and it's an art, not a science," he concluded. "If it were a science, we'd know more about it."

● *June 8, 1984*

Olympic Preview

LOS ANGELES

efinition No. 1 of "venue" in my Webster's New World Dictionary reads as follows: "The county or locality in which a cause of action occurs or a crime is committed." There are other definitions, but none identifies the word as the site of an Olympics athletic event.

I've asked around, but no one seems to know how that last usage obtained currency. It may have to do with venue's Frenchy tang, which goes with things Olympic. But perhaps—given the memory of the 1972 Munich massacre—an element of prescience was involved.

The organizers of the present Games, whose opening parade steps off Saturday afternoon, are doing their best to make sure the word isn't prophetic again. They have hired about 17,000 guards of various sorts to patrol the Olympic installations. That works out to more than two cops for every athlete, and it's a bigger army than a lot of nations represented here maintain.

Security here is tighter than your high school graduation suit. Last Sunday, I took a press tour through the Olympic Village at the University of Southern California, the largest of the three official living quarters for athletes. We had to show our press credentials to be admitted to what our guide called the "twilight zone," a fenced-in area *outside* the village.

To get into the village itself we had to receive a separate pass, go through a baggage- and personal-search setup like the ones at airports, and exchange our regular credentials for a magenta card the size of a license plate that we had to wear around our necks at all times within the area. Four escorts accompanied our group of eight. We could speak with athletes only inside a separate fenced compound on the grounds.

The USC village, done up to resemble an amusement park, seemed pleasant enough, but some of the residents admitted to feeling more like inmates than guests. "I like it, except there is too much police," said Soren Ostberg, a swimmer from Denmark. He said that even as we spoke he was tangled in security red tape. "I left my identity card in my dormitory room, but they say I can't get back into the dorm without it," he said with a shrug.

Even if security manages to be effective and relatively unobtrusive, there are other things that could bollix up the 23rd Olympiad. Here are some of them:

LOGISTICS. The decision to make the L.A. Games Spartan, utilizing existing facilities wherever possible, has spread competition over a 200-mile stretch from Santa Barbara on the north to San Diego on the south. Transporting athletes and officials (not to mention spectators and reporters) around this vast area, where traffic congestion is a way of life in the best of times, promises to be a major headache.

Olympic history is replete with examples of athletes who lost their medal chances because they didn't make it to their races on time. This could be the first Games in which whole busloads of them suffer that fate.

Many competitors will spend more time in transit than at their venues. Wrestlers living at USC, for instance, will face a daily round trip of about three hours between the village and the Anaheim arena where their bouts will be held.

SMOG. Let's define the basic terms. A Stage 1 smog alert is when strenuous outdoor activity is discouraged and people with respiratory problems should stay indoors. During Stage 2 alerts, which have been rare, everybody is advised to stay in. There never has been a Stage 3 alert, but Johnny Carson joked that the only people allowed out during one would be those assigned to pick up the bodies.

Stage 1 alerts occur about a dozen days a year in Los Angeles proper, where track and field will be held. In Pasadena, the soccer site, the average is about 60 days a year. Equestrian endurance events were moved to San Diego to save horses from the smog, but human Olympians will have to tough it out.

Distance runners who can will follow the plan made for U.S. marathoner Joan Benoit by her coach, Bob Sevene. "We'll arrive in Los Angeles on Friday, rest on Saturday, run on Sunday and leave," Sevene said.

DRUG TESTING. Improved drug-testing facilities were unveiled at the Pan-American Games last year, and 15 athletes from 10 countries were disqualified when their urine samples came up positive for steroids. A dozen other athletes withdrew from that meet rather than submit to the tests.

That debacle probably got a lot of athletes off steroids, but the full Olympics proscribed list is much longer, encompassing 160 muscle builders, uppers, painkillers and decongestants, and some athletes probably will run afoul of it. Last week, Alexi Grewal, a U.S. bicyclist, was suspended from the Games when a banned substance was found in his urine after a race in Denver. He said he thought it came from a Chinese tea a friend had given him.

NEWS COVERAGE. Here, overkill is a certainty. ABC-TV has set the pace by scheduling 180 hours of Olympics coverage over 18 days starting Friday. The network will have to televise every moving object in town with a number on it to fill that time.

ABC's newspaper equivalent is the Los Angeles Times. Last Sunday, six days before the start of competition, it began publishing a daily Olympics supplement in addition to its regular sports pages. The supplements will continue until two or three days after the Games end. The first issue devoted 11 of its 40 pages to marathon running. On Tuesday, 14 of 32 pages were given over to swimmers and swimming. What will be left to say when the Games begin? Not much, but it will be said anyway.

THE COMPETITION. This will be a bright spot for lovers of "The Star Spangled Banner." American athletes could well win more than the 80 gold medals the Soviets captured in 1980 when we boycotted their Games.

In 1976, the last Olympics at which Big East met Big West, athletes from nations who won't be at L.A. won 13 of 14 golds in women's track, 12 of 13 in women's swimming, all eight in weight lifting and six of 10 in boxing and freestyle-wrestling. U.S. athletes should be the main beneficiaries of their absence.

With the Soviets and their associates at home, the U.S. figures to win about 20 of 41 golds in men's and women's track, 25 of 33 in swimming and diving, and 15 or so in the 22 boxing and freestyle-wrestling events. That would leave 125 events in the 19 other sports from which to pick up the 21 golds to top the Russians' 1980 haul. It's doable.

"It's a shame about the boycott, but all we can do is try to beat whoever shows up," says Don Gambril, the U.S. swimming coach. "The U.S. used to be the New York Yankees of international competition. We looked 10 feet tall to everybody else. I think we'll have that image again this year. Who knows? Maybe it'll stick past the Games."

• *July 27, 1984*

The Nine-Minute Olympics

LOS ANGELES

A ndrew Seymour's Olympics lasted just nine minutes here Tuesday. The 17-year-old, 112-pound boxer from the Bahamas had traded punches with Oppe Pinto of Paraguay for three rounds, and when the bout was over the judges said they thought Pinto had gotten the better of the transaction. The referee raised the Paraguayan's arm in victory, the two fighters embraced and the ring was cleared for the next match.

Afterward, at the first news conference of his life, a sweat-drenched Seymour looked at his hands and told the two newspaper reporters who were present that the decision surprised him. "I felt I won the first and second rounds," he mumbled. "Maybe he was better in the third—I don't know. I thought I was even with him at least."

Then it was off for a quick shower and back out into the arena, where he watched the afternoon's remaining card. There, he was able to look on the bright side. "The food in the Olympic Village really looks good, you know, but before the fight I couldn't eat too much because I had to make my weight. Now, maybe I can pig out some."

Andrew Seymour's condition as an Olympic loser is a common one; of the 7,800 or so athletes here, only a few hundred will emerge from competition unscathed and begolded. That's the way it is in sports generally; losers always far outnumber winners.

Graciousness in defeat is *de rigueur* at the Games, where the taking part is supposed to be supreme, but in reality losers' styles vary greatly. On Monday, a defeated Thai boxer reacted to the referee's stopping of his fight by taking two, kangaroo-style jumps across the ring in frustration, and the coach of a loser from Barbados had to hold a towel in front of his fighter's mouth to keep him from denouncing his opponent, the ref and goodness knows who else at a post-fight news conference.

Boxing losers might be excused some bitter feelings. Theirs, after all, is a sport in which losers typically suffer more than bruised egos, but most manage at least to put a good face on things. That's probably partly because even in an elite competition such as the Olympics, fighters who have never tasted defeat themselves are very rare.

That was true of Seymour, a tiny (5-foot-1) hard-bodied young man with quick brown eyes and the singsong voice of the Caribbean. He had lost three times in his 23 bouts going into Tuesday. That record was good enough to make him the best fly-weight boxer in the Bahamas, but he admits that he had some doubts about his standing in the rest of the world. "I hoped I would win, but I didn't really know," he said. "I guess I would have been surprised to be the champion."

Indeed, for Seymour, as for most athletes here, just getting to the Olympics was achievement enough. The high-school student is one of 10 children of William and Clementina Seymour who live in the town of Matthew on the island of Inagua, the third largest in the Bahamian chain, and most of the family have never been off the islands.

Seymour's father is a plumber who works for Morton Salt Co. in Matthew, population about 900. Extracting salt from the briny sea there is the sole industry of the town, and almost every adult who lives there works for the company.

Andrew's oldest brother, Harold, now 29 years old, was the amateur light-heavyweight boxing champion of the islands, and Andrew started boxing with gloves Harold had brought home.

He entered his first competition at 14. "I like all sports, but boxing was best," he says. "You can be good even if you are small."

He says his parents welcomed his taking up the sport. "They are glad I am at the gym training instead of running on the streets doing nothing with the other boys."

Andrew brings an intrepid, wade-in-swinging style to his fights. His boxing idol—from watching televised fights—is Ray "Boom-Boom" Mancini, a former professional lightweight champion, who does the same thing in a more refined way. His success locally brought him trips to tournaments in Santo Domingo and Miami. Wins in those fights, plus his victory in a six-man flyweight elimination tournament in Nassau in June, made him one of three fighters his country selected to send to the Games.

Andrew's neighbors in Matthew helped out by holding a cookout at his high school to help finance his training and trip to Los Angeles. Here, he lives with four other Bahamian athletes in a room in the Olympic Village at the University of Southern California. Other athletes have complained that the accommodations at USC are too crowded, but they suit Andrew fine. "All we do is sleep there, so it is not bad," he smiles. "It is less crowded for me than at home."

Andrew marched in last Saturday's Olympic parade in his team's standard get-up of blue blazer, white slacks and yellow hat. He gets to keep those items, along with the memory of an occasion he describes as "exciting, man." He says his favorite part of the ceremony was "when they let all those birds loose to fly around the stadium." He also like the part when the audience flipped cards to reproduce the flags of the attending nations.

Even better were the chartreuse-colored Adidas boxing shoes that came with his yellow-and-blue ring uniform. "They're very fine," says he.

Andrew paid for his new outfits in his bout Tuesday. He came out smoking, and probably threw more punches than his foe. But at 21, Pinto was an older and more experienced fighter who eventually met Andrew's rushes with effective counterpunches, and was a clear, though close, victor. He got the nod from all five judges.

Andrew emerged from the fray with a purple bruise under his left eye and a badly swollen nose. He couldn't remember how he got them, and maintained that they didn't hurt.

He said that the defeat didn't hurt much, either, because he is young and would keep boxing "for sure." He predicted that he'd be at the 1988 Games.

He took further solace in the fact that the crowd of about 5,000 cheered his efforts, and that the fight was close. "It will be on television at home in Matthew, and everyone I know will watch," he said. "It would not have been good to have lost badly, or be knocked down."

● *Aug. 2, 1984*

Gypsy on the Balance Beam

LOS ANGELES

Ronnie and Lois Retton are happy that the 1984 Olympics are in the U.S. It gives them a chance to get together with their 16-year-old daughter, Mary Lou.

"We might have gone if the Olympics were in another country, but it couldn't have been one that's too far away," says Lois, a small, dark, lively woman. "Ronnie hates the thought of flying long distances over water. He hasn't done it yet."

As it is, the Rettons are having a reunion of sorts here while Mary Lou, America's premier female gymnast and a prime gold-medal prospect, spins and bounces her way through her routines at Pauley Pavilion on the UCLA campus. "We've seen her a couple of times—between her events, of course," says Lois. "She's a very busy girl."

Mr. and Mrs. Retton are used to hurry-up meetings with Mary Lou, the youngest of their five children. Since they packed her off on New Year's Day, 1983, to train in Houston under Bela Karolyi, the famous Romanian-born coach, Mary Lou has been at home in Fairmont, W. Va., for exactly four days, last October. She was supposed to have stayed for seven days, but ABC-TV wanted to film her in action, and she had to hurry back early. Their other visits have been at gymnastics meets or between practices in Houston, where she boards with the family of another gymnast while her parents look after their other offspring.

"I'm sure it's wonderful for her, the competition and the travel and all the attention she's getting, but it's tough on her folks," Lois sighs. "It seems like forever since we've all been together and normal."

That's the way it has been for the families of other top female gymnasts in the dozen years since 17-year-old Olga Korbut wowed the world at Munich and made the sport the province of tiny, elastic-bodied girls. Kathy Johnson, the Billie Jean King of women's gymnastics, is 24, but the other seven members and alternates of the U.S. team here average 16 years old, and most of them train away from home.

Mary Lou Retton joined that gypsy caravan out of necessity. When she left home at age 14, six years after she took up the sport, she was the only "elite" gymnast in West Virginia, and had gone as far as she could with the coaching available there.

"At every meet we went to, we were told she'd be world-class with the polish an experienced coach could give her," says Ronnie Retton. "We checked around, and we always came back to Karolyi. We figured that if he trained Nadia Comaneci [the 1976 Olympic all-around champ at age 14], he must know something. He's tough on the girls, but Mary Lou is no little violet, and she can handle that. We're satisfied with how he's done for her."

Karolyi might have supplied the polish that made the 4-foot-10-inch, 95 pound Mary Lou a star of world gymnastics, but she came by her athleticism and Atom Ant physique naturally. Despite standing just 5-foot-7, Ronnie Retton played basketball and baseball at the University of West Virginia and spent six years as a shortstop in the New York Yankees' minor-league chain before hanging up his spikes to raise a family and go into the coal-mine-equipment repair business in Fairmont.

Her brothers Ronnie, 23, Donnie, 18 and Jerry, 17—chunky fellows all—play varsity baseball in college or high school. Sister Shari, 21, is a varsity gymnast at the University of West Virginia.

The Retton home, a colonial affair on a winding road above Fairmont, has a swimming pool and a baseball pitching machine that the Retton boys and local Little League teams keep busy. "I think it's safe to call this an athletic family," Ronnie smiles. "Mary Lou and Shari had to take up some sport in self defense."

In American track and field, shoe companies pay most of the training bills, and in basketball and swimming, colleges do. In gymnastics, daddy pays. Mr. Retton says that Mary Lou's first year of training in Houston, including gym fees, living expenses and travel to meets, set him back almost $15,000.

This year's bills won't be as high because the Karolyi gym received some outside help, the U.S. Gymnastics Federation began financing Mary Lou's training when she made the national team in May, and a tag day in Fairmont netted $3,000 for her. But Mr. Retton still writes some checks. "I'll say this: A poor person couldn't afford it," he says.

There also have been costs that checks won't cover. The need for Mary Lou to be away from school to attend gym meets precluded her enrollment in a Houston public school, and she had to leave a private school there because of too-frequent absences. She has been taking correspondence courses, but has fallen about a year behind her high school class.

She has had injuries, too. In June, she underwent arthroscopic surgery to remove bone chips from a knee, and she'll probably need another operation after the Games to repair the joint fully. Last year she suffered a wrist stress fracture, and she has had numerous sprains and bruises. "I swear her poor little body is so beat up, it's a shame," Mrs. Retton says quietly.

The Rettons expect that Mary Lou will get some lucrative financial offers if she captures gold here, but they aren't sure how they would handle them. They wonder if their daughter would forfeit a chance at a college athletic scholarship if she cashed in on her fame by making commercial endorsements. Mr. Retton fears that she may have already jeopardized her amateur standing in college eyes by appearing in an ad for a Texas bank. "It's something a lawyer will have to look into," he says.

Uncertain, too, is what Mary Lou will do after the Games are over. The Rettons say that she isn't sure if or how she'll continue training. Mrs. Retton, though, knows how *she* feels about the matter. "I want her home!" she says. "A girl of 16 needs to have some normal years. The Olympics is the ultimate. What point is there to go on after that?

"But it might not be easy for her," she goes on. "Can she be happy in high school in Fairmont after working day and night on gymnastics the way she has these last two years? We'll have to all sit down and talk it over, and, honestly, I don't know when that will be. They're going to take the medal winners on a tour of the White

House and some other places after the Games. After that, there'll probably be something else. Sometimes I think it's a conspiracy to keep her away from home."

• Aug. 3, 1984

Chewing the Fat with a Fan

LOS ANGELES

I like this city a lot better since I found Canter's Restaurant on Fairfax Street. It's off my usual track here, but it's worth the detour. The chicken soup is terrific, and the sandwiches are piled so high you have to jump on them before you can bite.

Every time I go there, the same thing happens. I sit down at the counter and the waitress, a heavyset woman, comes over to take my order. She always acts surprised when I ask to see a menu. I guess everybody else who comes there knows what to order without one.

It's certainly true that some of the Canter's patrons have unusual ordering styles. They don't so much order as negotiate. The last time I was there, a woman down the counter told the waitress she wanted "something soft" because her gums hurt. She suggested a muffin. The waitress countered with toast. They settled on a cherry sweet roll, which the lady ate with knife and fork.

I was there the other day, eating a corned beef on rye, and a man of about 60 years sat down next to me. Sans menu, he ordered the barley soup and a roll. We chewed in silence for a few minutes when, to be friendly, I asked him how he was enjoying the Olympics.

"Wonderful!" he said. "We're winning all the medals."

"That's partly because the Russians and their friends stayed home," I noted.

"They should stay home permanently!" he explained.

145

"Actually," he went on, "I don't know much about a lot of these Olympic sports. I grew up in the East. We played baseball. Is baseball in the Olympics?"

I told him that it was, but as a "demonstration sport" whose medals didn't count.

"What are they trying to demonstrate? We've been playing baseball for a hundred years, and it works," he said. I had to admit that I didn't know.

We chewed for a while more, and I asked him if he had been to any Olympic events. Yes, he said, he'd spent an afternoon at the Coliseum watching the track and field: "My son-in-law bought some tickets, but he couldn't go, so I went."

"How did you like it?" I asked.

"Not much," he said. "Too dull. Too much sitting around in the hot sun between events. It wasn't snappy, like on TV."

I explained that television showed just the action parts of track and field, editing around the boring stuff. He said he understood that, but it didn't make it any better, especially at $60 a ticket.

He asked me what I did for a living, and I told him. He brightened visibly. "Hey," he said, "maybe you can explain some things for me. Those guys who swept up and raked the broad-jump pit between jumps, how come they were all dressed up in ties and yellow blazers?"

"They're officials," I said.

"And all they do is sweep? How much do they get paid?"

"Nothing," I said. "They paid their own way to come here. It's an honor to be an Olympic official."

"I bet they don't sweep up much around their own houses," he opined. I said I thought he was probably right.

"And swimming," he continued. "It's a nice, clean sport and everything, but it isn't on TV much except for the Olympics. Once those kids get in the water, they all look the same, don't you think?"

Once again, I had to agree. "Do you know what they call people who go to swimming meets that aren't part of the Olympics?" I volunteered.

"What?"

"Parents."

"Ha-ha."

"Tell me one more thing," he said. "The gymnastics, it was very exciting, but why was there always so much arguing about the scores?"

"The scoring is subjective," I said. "What looks good to one judge doesn't always look so good to another. So the judges argue until they can agree on what the score should be."

"From what I gather, the judges think that gymnasts from their own countries do great, and the ones from other countries are not so great, right?" he said.

"That's about it."

"Well, just so long as nobody breaks his neck. The gymnasts, I mean."

As we were about to leave, I asked him how long he had lived in Los Angeles. He said 26 years. "Then let me ask you something," I said. "A lot of the events I've been going to are sold out, but there usually are a lot of empty seats when they begin, and sometimes people leave early, even when the contests are close. Why is that?"

"People here figure nothing much happens in the first few minutes of a game, so they come late, and they want to beat the traffic going home, so they leave early," he said.

"Why do they bother to come at all?" I inquired.

"Because they love sports," he said, laughing.

● *Aug. 7, 1984*

The Best Race of the Games

A. high-school track coach once told me that he always had more candidates for the half-mile than for any other event. "It's a race for kids without enough speed for the dashes, and not enough endurance for the distances," he said.

Maybe that's true of high school, but here at track's uppermost level it's a race for athletes with plenty of both those runnerly virtues. They ran the 800 meters in the Coliseum late Monday afternoon, and although much of the Olympic track card remains, it may go down as the best footrace in these Games.

The winner was Joaquim Cruz, a 21-year-old University of Oregon student by way of Brazil. His time of one minute, 43 seconds, was an Olympic record, the third-fastest ever in the event, and the fastest time posted in a major international meet.

The long-striding Cruz won decisively over a field that Britain's Sebastian Coe, Monday's second-place finisher and holder of the world mark of 1:41.73 at the distance, called the best ever assembled. "This is one race that the East Bloc boycott didn't affect," Coe said on Sunday after he had qualified for the eight-man final. "Anyone who wins a medal should be pleased. I know I would be."

After the race, Coe repeated that assessment and called Cruz a "supreme champion." Donato Sabia of Italy, a former European titleholder who placed fifth, said the winner was *"terrible,"* which sounds like "terrible" but means "terrific" in context.

What made Cruz's time especially impressive was that the 800 wasn't one race but four, three qualifying heats and a final run on four consecutive days. The grueling heat system, dictated by the large Olympic starting fields, operates in all the middle-distance and distance events here. It's the reason that few world records are broken in those races at the Games.

It's a system that rewards youth and vigor, and, indeed, three of the four top finishers Monday were relative youngsters: Cruz at 21, third-place Earl Jones of the U.S. at age 20, and fourth-place Billy Konchella of Kenya, 22. That none of those runners brought significant international reputations to the games signals a changing of the guard in the event.

That change took place in the U.S. at the Olympic Trials here in June, when Jones, 24-year-old Johnny Gray, and John Marshall, 20, grabbed the Olympic berths away from veteran campaigners James Robinson and Don Paige. The race in which they did it was memorable because it was the only one in history in which the four top finishers all broke one minute, 44 seconds.

Jones, a chesty young man who attends Eastern Michigan University, stood out in that race not only because he won it in a photo-finish with Gray, but also for his all-out, front-running style. A newcomer to the event (he formerly was a miler), his disdain of tactics was a tactic in itself.

"Me and Bob Parks, my coach at Eastern Michigan, had it figured: The other runners in the Trials didn't like to be pushed, so I'd push them," Jones said. His plan for the Olympics was the same. "If the pace in any race I'm in is too slow, I'll take control and speed it up."

The Old Guard was represented by Coe and Steve Ovett, who together have dominated the 800 for a half-dozen years. Coe, 27, is known in press circles as "The Good Brit" because he is pleasant, articulate, and unfailingly sportsmanlike. A smooth, seemingly effortless runner, he hadn't trained much in 1982 or '83 because of a mysterious glandular ailment, but that had cleared up this year and he came to Los Angeles proclaiming himself "90% fit."

Ovett, 28, is called "The Bad Brit" because he treats newsmen like skunks at a garden party and he's handy with his elbows on the track. He had been hampered by leg injuries of late, and it turned out that he had come into the Games with a bronchial infection as well. He barely qualified for the 800 final, and finished it last and staggering. He spent Monday night in a hospital, and probably will miss the 1,500-meter run, in which he holds the world's record.

The other main contenders were Cruz, Konchella and Gray, Marshall having been eliminated in a heat. Cruz, who stands 6-foot-2 and weighs 170 pounds, is the 1984 American collegiate champion at 800 and 1,500 meters. He steamed through his heats here in the eye-popping times of 1:45.66, 1:44.84 and 1:43.82, causing Coe to remark that "anyone who can do that is in wonderful physical condition, or foolhardy, or both."

Jones's plan to push the pace seemingly insured that this would be no slow, "tactical" race like the 1980 final in Moscow, won by Ovett in 1:45.4. But the American started in lane one, on the far inside, and was beaten to the lead and boxed in by little Edwin Koech of Kenya, who started in lane eight. Later, Jones said he never could get free to follow his front-running plan even though the time for the first 400 meters, a brisk 51 seconds, was a full second slower than he would have liked.

Koech held his lead until about the 650-meter mark, when he was passed by Cruz, Jones and Coe. Coe passed Jones with 70 meters to go, but Cruz was a good 10 feet ahead by that point, and he finished that way. Koech would up sixth and Gray, who never got started, was seventh.

Cruz hadn't spoken with U.S. reporters before the final, and his victory sent them scurrying to their Brazilian colleagues for biographical information about the winner. These facts emerged:

He lives in Taguatinga, a city of about 40,000 near Brasilia. His father died several years ago, and his mother takes in washing. As a youngster, he played mostly basketball, but turned to running at 14 and quickly outdistanced the local competition.

He came to the U.S. in 1981 with his coach, Luiz Olivera. They stopped for a term at Brigham Young University in Utah, but found the weather there too cold and moved to the university at Eugene, Ore., where Olivera does graduate work and Cruz runs track. He's the quiet youth who likes to read. He ate a bean salad for lunch the day of the final.

Cruz showed up for his news conference about an hour after his win, and flashed wit as well as a brilliant smile. Surveying the mostly

American gathering, he asked "Who here doesn't speak Portuguese?" When a chorus of grunts arose, he said "Too bad."

Just joking. "I wanted the pace to be hard, so I pushed the first 200 meters to see if anyone would take the lead," he said in good English. "When the guy from Kenya did, I thought that was great. I just stayed behind him until there were about 150 meters left, and made my kick."

How fast did he think he could run eventually? "If I had to run just one race, against a good field, I think that maybe I might break the world record."

Coe might have finished second, but he had the last word. When one of his countrymen asked him what he had said to the exhausted Ovett on the track after the race, he replied: "I told him we were too old to be playing with fire like this."

● *Aug. 9, 1984*

Playing Games in Moscow

MOSCOW

Athletic attendance at the inaugural Goodwill Games here isn't what its sponsors had advertised, and a number of factors are involved. Conflict with next month's world championships deprived the swimming competition of both the top U.S. swimmers and those of East Germany, the major power on the women's side of the sport. The best part of the Cuban boxing team, which dominated the world championships in Reno in May, is also staying home, pleading fatigue and previous commitments.

Fallout from the nuclear-power accident at Chernobyl, some 500 miles distant from Moscow, claimed the participation of Danny Harris, who won the 400-meter hurdles title at last month's U.S. national championships. "I don't wanna breathe no radiation," Harris explained. Another American track star, sprinter Valerie Brisco-Hooks, reportedly won't come because her agent and the Goodwill Games people couldn't agree on money.

But the one reason that no one gave for not coming is security. Soviet athletes may, indeed, have refused to come to the 1984 Olympics in Los Angeles because the U.S. couldn't guarantee they'd be snug there. Compared with Moscow, the fenced-in Olympic compound at L.A. was Gap City.

You know that a country is serious about security

when airline passengers are frisked and their luggage is X-rayed when they *leave* the Moscow airport. Every games participant and auxiliary was issued a pass to wear around his neck with his photograph and hotel's name on it. That's the only hotel he can enter here, and passage from floor to floor in the same hotel ain't easy.

American distance runner Cindy Bremser and her husband, Kim Whitmore, arrived here separately last week and were assigned different rooms in the Hotel Rossiya. Whitmore says it took him three hours to learn his wife's room number and three more to persuade hotel officials to allow him on her floor for a visit.

Vigilance is maintained inside the games' press center and sports facilities. Guys in uniform or suits and sneakers stand in every doorway, either checking passes or, simply, denying entrance. They are polite but firm. "I had my pass in my shirt once, and a guard asked me to take it out," says Darrell Robinson, a U.S. quarter-miler from UCLA. "I wanted to kid around some, so I put on a big smile. The guard shook his head like I should stop smiling so I'd look like my picture. Then he let me through."

The overall impression isn't unpleasant, however. "We are *safe* here—no two ways about it!" exclaims Robinson. "If you're traveling abroad this year, I guess this is the place to go," smiles Claudette Groenendall, a U.S. half-miler.

The official vibes are more upbeat. The games' co-chiefs, Marat Gramov, chairman of the state sports committee of the U.S.S.R., and Ted Turner, the head of Turner Broadcasting Co., held a news conference here on Friday, the morning before competition began, and tried to outdo one another in the goodwill department. The games, said Gramov, "are proceeding in an atmosphere of enthusiasm and elation, and are a real and tangible reflection of the Soviet-American dialogue begun in the 1985 summit meeting in Geneva."

Turner took things more personally. "I'm so happy with the way things are going I'm having a hard time keeping from jumping out of my skin," he said.

Turner did allow, however, that he was more than a bit put out by a U.S. Defense Department announcement that day that 11 members of the 24-member U.S. boxing team for the games, who are in the armed forces, wouldn't be allowed to compete in the U.S.S.R. in a sporting event with commercial overtones.

The reasons for the edict were strange in light of the fact that all public sporting events are commercial these days, and the numerous trips that American athletes, including servicemen, have taken to the U.S.S.R. You'd at least think that the D of D would be grateful for the opportunity for some on-site reconnaissance here. Whatever, taking the Americans out of the boxing along with the better Cubans would just about scratch that competition.

It wouldn't be international sports without such tempests, though, and we Yanks quickly and thoughtfully provided a second one. The U.S. swimming team protested the outcome of the men's 50-meters on Friday—the games' second event. Curiously, it had been won by an American, John Sauerland of Shaker Heights, Ohio, but the U.S. thought a rerun might also produce silver and bronze medals as well.

"I know that a protest won't look good, this being the Goodwill Games, but the race was started before all the swimmers were set, and fair is fair," said Selden Fritscher, chief of the U.S. swimming delegation.

Sauerland played the good soldier in the affair but admitted he was upset because he'd have to go to bed Friday without knowing whether he'd keep his medal. It was ruled, on Saturday, that he could.

Otherwise, the swimming races that opened the games went swimmingly if you don't count the processions and anthems that stretched 20 or so minutes of action into two hours. Before an orderly and not-quite-full house at the handsome Olympic pool, a young U.S. team won six gold medals in 18 races through Saturday, and Soviet veteran Vladimir Salnikov, the fastest distance swimmer ever, gave the home fans a thrill Friday by setting a world's record of 7:50.64 in the 800-yard freestyle. Not much was expected of the U.S. team because the first- and second-place finishers in the recent U.S. national meet were tabbed for the August world championships in Spain, leaving this competition to lower placers. Still, Angel Myers, a pug-nosed blonde of 19 from Americus, Ga., won the games' first gold in the 50-free and her mates took it from there.

Salnikov has held a flock of records, but Friday's was notable if only because it alone got a rise out of a Soviet crowd whose most boisterous response otherwise was staccato applause. Actually, it wasn't the swimmer who got the biggest hand, but his wife, Marina. She jumped into the pool, sweatsuit and all, to give her hubby a big, wet kiss.

• *July 8, 1986*

Back in the U.S.S.R.

MOSCOW

For most American visitors to the Goodwill Games here, Moscow is a jolt. The Cyrillic alphabet, the strange food and the cops every 50 feet along the streets take some getting used to.

For Alla Svirsky, it's all too familiar. "I look at the people on the streets, with their sad faces. If you go up to them and smile and say hello, they think you're crazy," she sighs. "I have to remind myself that it's not them, it's their situation. That was me not too long ago."

Mrs. Svirsky is a short blonde of 45 years who wears bright-colored dresses and large earrings. She is the coach of the U.S. rhythmic gymnastics team in these games.

A native of Odessa, she left the U.S.S.R. for the U.S. in 1974. Two of the four girls on her team also were born in this country. So was the woman who plays the piano during their routines. All are Jewish. All are now U.S. citizens. All are making their first return visits to their homeland.

Three of the four gymnasts originally picked for the team would have been Soviet-born, but the parents of 15-year-old Shura Feldman, now of Los Angeles, wouldn't let her make the trip.

The coach and her charges are back in the country that had been inhospitable to them because they think it will help promote their sport in the U.S. In rhythmic gymnastics, women (usually girls, really) do acrobatic ballet exercises while manipulating a ball, a ribbon, a jump rope or two Indian clubs. It's a relatively new sport that became part of the Olympics only in 1984. It caught on strongest in the U.S.S.R. and Eastern Europe, which is why many top American participants have their roots there.

The Goodwill Games offer American rhythmic gymnasts a welcome crack at top-notch competition and a rare opportunity for national television exposure. Bulgaria and the Soviet Union, the one-two finishers in the last world championships, have strong entries here, and WTBS has scheduled prime-time airings of the event for tonight and tomorrow. Watch it. You'll like it.

The U.S. has yet to claim a major international medal in this most feminine of sports. Its best current hope for one is Marina Kunyavsky, a tiny, large-eyed 21-year-old who was born in Leningrad and emigrated with her parents in 1979. She won the past two American championships and led the U.S. team with a 26th-place all-around finish in the 1985 worlds in Spain.

Other team members are Irina Rubenshtein, 16, who was born in Odessa and now lives in Agoura, Calif.; Diane Simpson, 17 of Evanston, Ill.; and Elizabeth Cull, 20, of Los Angeles.

Kunyavsky and Rubenshtein are reticent about their Soviet memories. "I was a gymnast here, but I was not allowed to compete because I was Jewish," Kunyavsky says quietly. "It was not a rule, but it was a fact." The pert, ponytailed Rubenshtein, who came to the U.S. in 1976 at the age of six, says she doesn't recall much about her life in the U.S.S.R. "I can still speak and read Russian, so I must have learned it. But now I use only English. Especially here," she says.

Mrs. Svirsky, a former gymnastics coach at the University of Southern California, whose Los Angeles School of Gymnastics turns out top performers in both the rhythmic and artistic (Mary Lou Retton) arms of the sport, is more expansive. "It was Valentin, my husband, who mostly wanted to emigrate," she says. "He wasn't comfortable being Jewish here. This was even before things got as bad for Jews as we hear they are now.

"I had a nice job as a gymnastics coach and I could travel, which means a lot here. But I tell you: It wasn't that good. I didn't always bend when I should, and I had trouble.

"Once I trained 2,000 children two months for a May Day show. On the day, the director said he wanted the kids out at 6 a.m. for one more rehearsal. I told him no. I'd come, but not the kids. They didn't need to be standing around all day to perform at 4 p.m. For that, I lost half my salary for a year.

"And when I got to the U.S., I found a thousand reasons to like it the first week, and more every day since; now I wonder how I could have lived like I did before."

Mrs. Svirsky jokes that having four Russian speakers in her group is a benefit here, because "we're the only Americans who know what these guys are saying." But there also have been drawbacks.

"We didn't get our visas until two hours before we were supposed to leave, and when we got here there were no tickets for us for the opening ceremony. I think all the other teams got them. The girls were very disappointed," she says. "And we always have lots of company when we go out.

"See that guy?" she says, pointing to a man wearing sunglasses and leaning against a bridge railing near where we spoke outside the Hotel Rossiya here on a sunny morning this week. "I think he's one of our escorts. Yesterday some of us took a walk in Red Square and the same seven faces followed us the whole two hours. Seven guys—can you imagine? When I talked to my aunt who lives here on my hotel phone, I heard clicks. Maybe somebody was listening. I hung up and called her back from outside.

"My husband was worried about my coming to the Soviet Union," she goes on. "He thought it would get me upset. I wondered, too. But you know something? I'm here and I feel fine; I'm doing something for my sport, and I'm liking it. If it helps the U.S. and Soviet people get along better, that's fine, too.

"And if they want to look at me, let them look. They'll see I'm happy and successful. They'll see I'm well dressed and have money to spend. I'm a bad example for them. Maybe they'll get some ideas."

● *July 9, 1986*

King Carl's Royal Visit

MOSCOW

ladimir Salnikov, the greatest swimmer the Soviet Union has produced, walked through a crowded Red Square here the other day, hand in hand with his blond wife, a knockout in a pink jump suit. I followed for a few minutes to watch how the Russians responded to their sports heroes. They didn't respond much. Some people turned and a few smiled. He wasn't stopped for autographs. Maybe it was politeness.

I have it on good authority that when the American sprinter Carl Lewis took the same stroll two days later, he got a quite different reception, including plenty of long stares and lots of autograph requests. "Maybe I stood out because I'm black," Lewis offers.

Maybe, but he also stood out because he's Carl. Tall, bright-eyed and tightly wound, the Olympic multichamp has been the nearest thing these Goodwill Games have to a star. On Wednesday night in Lenin Central Stadium, on the last night of the track-and-field competition, he proved it by doing something no other athlete here has yet managed: putting fannies in the seats. Upward of 60,000 people, by far the biggest turnout of the games, watched him finish third in the 100-meter dash and anchor a U.S. team to victory in the 4 X 100-meter relay.

Until Wednesday night, these exercises might better have been called the No-Show Games. Among the missing from the fields of play have been East German swimmers, Cuban boxers and a host of international track-and-field celebs. Just as noticeable has been the absence of Ivan Fan. Near-empty houses have been the rule in every competition except, strangely, swimming. Lots of parents came to that one, I guess.

One reason that turnouts have been slim is that the security-conscious government hasn't encouraged them. Moscow has been "closed" during the games, which means that non-Muscovite Soviets can't visit without official permission.

Even folks already here have had a tough time getting a peek. My press pass got me through several lines of police to the finish line of the women's marathon last Saturday in the park outside Lenin Stadium, but non-passholders (i.e., ordinary folks) were turned away. One Soviet official explained the action to me by claiming they didn't want the race disturbed by a finish-line throng. The hustling promoter-sponsors of all those U.S. city marathons will find that interesting.

Another explanation—that extensive local television coverage of the games is holding down ticket sales—sounded more convincing generally. The disinclination to pay cash for what comes free is universal.

Whatever the reason, the small crowds have raised the ire of Turner Broadcasting, which is co-sponsoring the games and televising them in the U.S. The word here is that the empty seats aren't playing well in Peoria.

"I've been banging on those turkeys all week to get some people out, but all I get is blank stares," said Robert Wussler, a Turner Broadcasting executive vice president. "Those turkeys" are Turner's Soviet partners in this enterprise.

It thus is no wonder that the presence of Lewis, a genuine international drawing card, has been cherished here. While other U.S. athletes are accorded tidy but hardly sumptuous digs, Lewis and his entourage are housed at the Mezhdunaro Dnaya Hotel, the last word in luxury in the people's republic. While others are bused to and from events, he has a private car.

In case you hadn't heard, amateur track ain't amateur anymore, and all U.S. track-and-field participants here pocketed $3,000 appearance fees. Lewis's stumpy manager, Joe Douglas, avers that's all Lewis got to run, too, even though his usual fees for gracing big-time meets start at $10,000. But Douglas notes that other considerations were involved, including pay for some TV commentary Lewis is doing for TBS, here and at other events.

For their money, the games got Lewis on the track for about 20 seconds, which is what it took him to run his two 100s. He also had qualified for the long jump here by winning that event at the U.S. national championships, but he passed it to calm a sore left knee, he said.

That was a shame, because watching Carl Lewis long-jump is a transcendent sports experience. In the dashes, he lines up with a bunch of other guys who look pretty much like him. In the jump, he is alone, running free and routinely soaring lengths exceeded by a child of man only once, and then probably by accident, in the fine air of the 1968 Olympics at Mexico City.

But even in the dashes the 25-year-old Lewis stands out. At 6-foot-2, he is taller than most of his fellow sprinters, and his flattop haircut is distinctive. His running style also is eye-catching. A notoriously poor starter because of his height, his habit is to overtake his foes at about the 50-meter mark and pull away through the finish.

On Wednesday night, Lewis's late surge was too late to catch Ben Johnson of Canada, who has the build of a weight lifter. Johnson's win was no great surprise to track buffs. He had already beaten Lewis twice this season, and his time Wednesday of 9.95 seconds was just .02 second off the world's record. Still, when the race was done, the photographer horde followed Lewis, and it was his comments that were solicited for television.

Lewis gave the fans what they came to see in his relay leg. He took the baton about a stride behind his Soviet foe, passed him on the curve, and finished, languidly, two steps ahead.

Lewis then displayed his clout by breaking precedent and leading his relay mates to the waiting press before their medals ceremony. All the questions save a couple were him.

The Soviet running the press room was visibly annoyed that medal-awarding big shots were outside cooling their heels, and after about 10 minutes decreed that questioning would cease. King Carl raised five fingers. "We'll be done here pretty soon," said he. The Soviet shrugged helplessly, and the questions continued. A star is a star, even in the U.S.S.R.

● *July 11, 1986*

COLLEGE BALL

Part 7

Building a Bigger Husker

sually, coed hostesses escort visitors around the University of Nebraska's West Stadium Strength Complex here, but Boyd Epley, the head man, was my guide.

"We've got 13,300 square feet of floor space here," he said, gesturing proudly at the gleaming facility. "There are 125 workout stations, so 250 athletes can use it at one time. We've got 20,000 pounds of iron for lifting. I designed a lot of the equipment myself.

"That platform in the center of the room is for record-setting attempts only. We don't let players walk or sit on it unless they can press 400 pounds, lift 900 pounds on our hip sled or clean 325 pounds. It gives them something to shoot for.

"Those certificates on the wall are for our All-American Strength Team members. Every year the national strength coaches' group picks the strongest college football players at every position. We always have somebody on it. For two straight years we had four kids on the team, but then they made a rule saying no school could have more than one. I liked the old way better.

"Our coaches recruit football players for height, speed and athletic ability, and we supply the weight and strength," he went on. "Meet Neil Smith here. He's a freshman from New Orleans. Defensive tackle. Stands about 6-foot-6. Great prospect. He runs the 40-yard dash in 4.8 seconds. That's electronically timed, so it's like a 4.6 hand-timed.

"Spread your arms, Neil." The player does so, smiling broadly. "Ever see anything like that? He measures 85½ inches, fingertip to fingertip. Longest armspan we ever had.

"How much do you weigh, Neil?" Epley asked.

"225."

"How much did you weigh when you got here in August?"

"215."

"How much will you weigh when you're a senior?"

"260."

"Remember this kid," Epley said to me. "You'll be reading about him in the sports pages in two or three years."

Epley can predict such future events with confidence, because he has worked plenty of similar transformations. A businesslike 37-year-old whose broad shoulders attest that he practices what he preaches, he has been Nebraska fooball's strength coach since 1969, when weight lifting was in its infancy as an athletic training technique. He's a founder and past president of the National Strength and Conditioning Coaches' Association, and his former assistants run football strength programs for more than a dozen major-college and professional teams.

His facility here, dubbed the Taj Mahal of Iron, produces the massive linemen who have been the trademark of the Nebraska teams that have been voted into the nation's top 10 for each of the past 14 years. Weight gains of more than 50 pounds, with strength increases to match, have been common for this breed, and the walls of the huge complex are lined with their photos. There's Dave Rimington, the 1982 collegiate lineman of the year. He came to Nebraska weighing 235 pounds, and left it at 297. There's Dean Steinkuhler, last year's top lineman. He went from 220 pounds to 275 under Epley's tutelage.

"Football players today are superior to any in the past, and strength training is the reason," Epley declares. "In 1970, we had one player who could bench-press 350 pounds; today we have 20. Johnny Rodgers was a great back for us, and in 1972 everybody was amazed that he could run the 40 in 4.6 seconds. Today we have a dozen kids who can do that. The time is past when players can complete at our level at their natural sizes and strengths."

Not everyone is convinced that the effects of Nebraska's strength program, and others like it, are entirely beneficial. Despite their prodigious collegiate feats, most Nebraska products in the National Football League haven't made great pros, and Sports Illustrated magazine recently suggested one reason may be that "the intensive, five-year weight program there burns them out." (About 75% of Nebraska football seniors are fifth-year students.)

Some physicians say that players who gain a lot of weight on the high-calorie, high-protein diets that go with weight training run risks of high blood pressure and kidney ailments that increase with age. There's also the suspicion that steroid drugs are sometimes part of the "bigger-stronger-faster" mix.

"It's possible to turn out those huge linemen without steroids, but it's not possible, if you know what I mean," contends Frank Katch, chairman of the department of exercise sciences at the University of Massachusetts and a fitness consultant to several NFL teams. "I couldn't prove that in court, but I know it's true. Everyone in sports does."

Epley answers that he considers the "NFL burnout" charge a compliment of sorts "because it means we've made pros out of some players who might not have made it on natural ability." He flatly rejects the notion that his programs have a negative short-term impact on players' health, saying "everything we see shows that they're sick less than other students, and have lower resting heart rates."

He's a bit less adamant on the steroids question. "We don't approve of steroids, and we believe our players can accomplish their goals without them. But I couldn't tell you with certainty that no kid here ever took them on his own," he says.

He can tell you, though, what every Nebraska footballer—and there are about 200 of them—can lift, run, throw and jump; it's all on the strength center's computer, which prints out a personal workout schedule for every player every week.

Student assistants are on hand afternoons to make sure the players lift every pound they're supposed to. Add in Epley's aides, other full-time staffers and the 10 coed volunteers who help out around the office and conduct tours, and the unit's work force numbers about 25. The center puts out its own athlete-recruiting magazine, called "Husker Power," and sells shirts, caps and posters carrying that motto. Says Epley: "If there's a finer strength program anywhere, I haven't seen it."

It's a far cry from the days when the former pole-vaulter first schooled a handful of Nebraska footballers in weight-lifting techniques in a tiny, dank weight room under Memorial Stadium here.

That room contained a battered weights-on-pulleys machine, an exercise bike and a few old barbells. He remembers it well, because he keeps it in a small corner of the giant West Stadium center, surrounded by a red-velvet rope and topped by a sign that reads "Strength Museum."

- Oct. 19, 1984

Playing with Numbers

J
•

ohn Swinton isn't the most popular guy in State College, Pa. He's a nice enough fellow, but he has a habit that some of his neighbors and colleagues at Pennsylvania State University find irritating. Whenever he reads the claim that Penn State graduates more than 90% of its varsity football players—an assertion made in university publications as well as in newspaper articles quoting its coaches and officials—he takes pen in hand to contest it.

"It makes me angry for a lot of reasons, only one of which is that it's not true," says Mr. Swinton, an instructor and editor in the university's hotel, restaurant and institutional management school and a Nittany Lions season-ticket holder.

He continues: "It's not the sort of thing a university should be saying; if our English department did it, we'd be labeled a diploma mill and lose our accreditation. It suggests that coaches control the academic process. It invites one to confuse diplomas with education.

"Worst, its intention is to mask reality, which is precisely the opposite of what good teachers and researchers try to do. It's athletics department P.R. that's supposed to leave the impression that we're purer than the schools we play. The fact is that we're a good university, and we probably do better by our athletes than many. But we shouldn't have to play with numbers to make that point."

167

Over at the Penn State athletics department, information director Dave Baker insists that the 90% graduation figure is "pretty accurate"—if you count only players who reach their senior years at the school. "Actually," he hedges, "the figure used to be 90%. We think it's dropped a shade the last few years, but we don't know. We haven't calculated it lately."

From there the picture gets fuzzier still. Mr. Baker says that Penn State "never" kept track of football recruits who left the university before their four-year athletic eligibility expired. Yet he says that a Pittsburgh Post-Gazette story of a few years back, which put the Penn State all-recruits football graduation rate at 67%, was inaccurate because it miscounted some drop-outs.

He takes similar issue with the National Football League Players Association, which says that 61% of the Penn State products in the NFL last year (24 of 39)—all of whom completed their college eligibility—were degree-holders. "That study was based on reports by the NFL teams and players, and they don't always report correctly. The actual total is higher," he maintains.

College-athlete graduation rates are something a lot of people talk about—especially when the recruiting of high-school players is hot and heavy—but it's hard to get a serious handle on the subject. Coaches who can tell you what play an opponent is likely to run on third-and-four from his own 38 say they haven't the foggiest notion how many of their charges complete their educations.

The most obvious reason for this ignorance is that, for the vast majority of big-time sports schools, the answer wouldn't comfort alums or dazzle the moms and pops of lads they wish to recruit.

The National Collegiate Athletic Association has taken a couple of stabs at clarifying the issue. In 1980, it reported that 43% of the football lettermen and 42% of the basketball lettermen who had entered 46 member schools five years before had graduated, about the same rate as male "nonathletes" at those schools. This year it looked at 8,371 athletic-scholarship holders, male and female, at 206 big-school members, who had begun college in 1977. It found that five years later, 50% had graduated from those institutions, against an all-student rate of 55%.

Neither study was all it should have been. The first looked just at lettermen and was too small to be of much use. The second lumped golfers with football players, ignoring the fact that nonacademic pressures on the latter are great. Still, the message of both seems clear enough: Jocks do OK in the classroom (perhaps better than we should expect), but nothing to brag about.

But that's intolerable for some schools, and claims of 90%-plus graduation rates have a way of getting into print around recruiting time. In February 1980, for instance, under the headline "Bryant's Players Excel," the New York Times ran a story quoting Alabama football coach Paul "Bear" Bryant saying that 96% of his players in his 22 seasons of coaching had got their degrees. (Mr. Bryant retired in 1982 and died last year.)

Jimmy Carroll, director of academics for 'Bama's athletics department, says that while he doesn't know for sure, he thinks that "a bit more" than half of his school's football recruits have graduated in recent years. "Bear was my coach, and I loved the guy. But I don't know where he got his figures," Mr. Carroll says.

The University of Nebraska claims a 92% graduate rate for its four-year footballers, but academic counselor Ursula Walsh says she doesn't know how many players leave school before that time, and wonders aloud if dropouts are her responsibility. And she doesn't quarrel with NFL Players Association figures showing that just six of 22 Nebraska products in the NFL last year, or 27%, earned degrees, against the all-league average of 33%.

The picture is much the same elsewhere in the upper reaches of college football. I contacted the other schools in last year's Associated Press Top 10 about their graduation rates, with the following results:

Officials at the universities of Texas and Georgia didn't return my calls. Ohio State said it did a study six years ago, and found that its athletes graduated at a "much higher" rate than other students, but it could cite no figures. Auburn said it's just now doing a study.

Florida offered that of its 22 football recruits in 1976, 18 played out their eligibility and 12 graduated. Brigham Young said that of the 81 players on its 1979 team, 59% graduated after five years.

Michigan said that 63% of its scholarship football players between 1967 and 1976 won degrees, but said the figures hadn't been updated. Illinois said 57% of its football and basketball lettermen between 1972 and 1981 graduated. It didn't know that happened to the non-lettermen.

Keeping accurate graduation rates for athletes isn't a major point, but the way the schools handle this question says a lot about their attitudes toward their athletes. They think that what the kids don't know won't hurt them. That's the biggest problem with college sports generally.

● *Nov. 9, 1984*

Designated Villains

T
•

he National Collegiate Athletic Association is nothing if not consistent. When it identifies an enemy, you can be sure it will be a "them."

To hear the NCAA's minions tell it, the ills of intercollegiate sports can be traced to such pernicious outsiders as drug pushers, gamblers, player-agents and high schools that don't adequately prepare their students for careers as "student-athletes." If those guys could be shaped up, slapped down, or whatever, the games could proceed in tranquility, the organization holds.

The NCAA is well along in dealing with its designated villains. It has informed high schools that, beginning next fall, member colleges no longer will welcome as freshman varsity athletes graduates who don't attain a "C" average or better in a core of college-prep courses. Why have most of these same colleges been scrambling to recruit prospects who don't meet those standards? Don't ask.

Prospective player-agents also have been brought under the NCAA's purview. They now are asked to fill out a form detailing their qualifications and to notify a school's athletics director before they solicit young jocks on campus. That way, I guess, the ADs can learn if the agents are offering the kids more than they're already being paid.

The NCAA's current targets are gambling and

drugs, which it has linked as a result of this past spring's allegations that drugs were used as inducements to basketball players at Tulane University to shave points on games.

The organization wants Congress to pass laws banning gambling on intercollegiate sporting events and making it a crime to use interstate wires to transmit betting odds and point-spreads to newspapers. On the drug front, it is putting together a program of random testing of athletes starting in 1987 at football bowl games and national championships in other sports. In the meantime, between 50 and 60 schools have begun testing their own athletes for drug use.

The NCAA's gambling and drug efforts seem most noteworthy for what they won't accomplish. What the anti-betting push won't stop is betting. Gambling on college sports—and professional ones, too, for that matter—already is illegal in every state of the U.S. save Nevada, but that is only a minor obstacle between the union of gambler and bookmaker. Sports betting predates the NCAA and newspaper betting lines, and, undoubtedly, will postdate them, laws to the contrary notwithstanding.

The colleges' drug stance is more complex. Testing for drug use is one of those ideas that's great as long as someone else is being tested. Civil-rights issues are involved, and, even though college jocks have no unions (yet), they will be raised once the testing programs draw blood or other fluids.

Further, when it comes to drugs, the colleges' hands are far from clean. They are quick to denounce their athletes' use of such "recreational" substances as cocaine and marijuana, but less vocal on the subject of anabolic steroids, which have been linked to liver, heart and prostate problems and psychological ills. Steroid use—often with the tacit approval of coaches—is college sports' worst-kept secret. A good many of the behemoths who entertain us on Saturdays didn't get their 19-inch necks just from drinking milkshakes.

Schools that have begun their own drug-testing programs "have been quicker to test for the so-called recreational drugs than for the performance enhancers," confirms John Toner, director of athletics at the University of Connecticut and head of the NCAA drug-testing policy committee. He says that while anabolic steroids are on the NCAA's proposed prohibited list, problems of detection could arise and others relating to the use of results and punishment of offenders remain to be worked out.

The NCAA's zeal for attacking the enemies without stems from its reluctance to tackle the tougher task of eliminating those within. As I and, I think, more and more others have come to conclude, the real problem of intercollegiate sports isn't the occasional point-shaving headline, or cocaine use by a few athletes, or even the alum or would-be agent who slips money to a player, distressing as those things are. It's that colleges are violating their educational and parental missions in their lust for sports cash and glory.

Young athletes (we're talking about teen-agers here), some with meager academic credentials, are enticed to campuses with the promise of an education, and then tied to team-practice schedules that don't give them time to pursue one. Many are placed in Mickey Mouse courses, awarded grades they don't earn, or both. When their eligibility for sports expires, they are cast adrift.

Such practices aren't limited to a handful of "outlaw" schools. Ask professors or college students of your acquaintance what goes on at their institutions. I have.

A cry has gone up to tie the number of athletic scholarships a school can award to the number of recruited jocks it graduates. That's a bad idea. A school that will admit anyone will graduate anyone. Playing with athlete-graduation rates already is a popular campus sport. Ask some athletic departments about the proportion of jocks they graduate and they'll give you figures for seniors or lettermen, or they'll lump basketball players with golfers.

College sports need to be scaled down and placed in an educational context, and athletes' rights need to be protected. At the risk of being unoriginal and repetitious, here are some proposals:

—Colleges should stop admitting athletes in higher proportion than other students to programs that have lower-than-normal entrance requirements.

—Athletic scholarships should be for five years, not one as at present, and rescindable only if the holder quits his team or violates rules of conduct governing all students.

—Practice time should be limited to three hours a day in season, with one day off a week.

—Intercollegiate schedules and post-season bowl games and tournaments should be cut back, reversing present trends.

—Athletes should be required to make steady progress toward a degree and maintain a "C" average.

—Academic counseling for athletes should be taken out of the hands of athletics departments.

—The use of anabolic steroids should be condemned in no un-certain terms and athletes should be informed of their hazards.

Putting these things into practice might be something of a strain at first, especially on the cash drawers, but I'm sure they'd make everyone involved—including us alums—feel better about college sports pronto. It'd be a real upper. I'd bet on it.

● *Oct. 16, 1985*

Winners That Fail

T his is early-signing week for high-school-senior basketball players who have been the objects of colleges' attentions. The inducement for kids to commit themselves now is a final prep season free of recruiter pestering. Given the nature of the activity, that's no small benefit.

Signing week is a time of beginnings and optimism. Every kid who scrawls his name on the dotted line is hailed as a future All-American and first-round professional draft pick. Every team's tomorrow looks brighter than its today.

The queer thing is that just about everybody, including some of the kids, knows that it doesn't work that way. Some teams will be losers and some of the high-school aces won't be players in college, much less stars. And sure as anything, the majority of this week's young athletic-scholarship winners will leave their chosen halls of ivy with no pro contract in sight or any education worth the name.

Too often, discussions of how colleges treat their jocks come down to comparisons of schools' asserted athlete-graduation rates, with heroes cheered and villains booed. This equates a diploma with an education and overlooks the face that a school that recruits anyone can graduate anyone.

Also, it encourages schools to play games with their

numbers, counting only athletes who complete their four years of sports eligibility or mixing football players with golfers. Even after all the controversy of recent years, solid statistics are hard to come by. About all that can be said with assurance is that roughly 40% of the football and basketball players recruited by big-time sports schools graduate after five years.

The fuss over figures obscures the more important point that the pressures and time demands of the major-college "revenue sports" make a classroom education hard to get even for the well motivated. In this, like other, "real" worlds, good guys and bad guys sometimes are hard to identify.

"I know I tried to get my degree, and I think the coaches and the school wanted it for me. It was just that too many things were going on to get it done," says Norman "Skip" Dillard.

Basketball fans will remember Dillard as a starting guard on the DePaul University teams of 1980, '81 and '82 that won 79 of 85 games and ended their regular seasons ranked first or second in the news-wire national polls. He averaged 12.6 points a game those seasons, and was co-captain as a senior.

The Chicago-born Dillard, who is black, soft-spoken and smiles easily, left DePaul some 20 hours short of a degree in physical education. He was picked by the Chicago Bulls in the ninth round of the 1982 National Basketball Association draft, but was cut from the team after rookie camp. A season in the Continental Basketball Association, a minor league, led nowhere. Back home in Chicago for the past three years, he has worked in construction, as a sewer-pipe repairman for the city and as an instructor in a health club, among other things. He's out of work now, and wondering what to do next.

He could go back to school, and says that DePaul has promised to extend his scholarship another year to allow him to earn his degree. The school is proud of having graduated 23 of the 29 scholarship basketball players who completed their eligibility between 1976 and last June, the period it held sway as a national power in the sport.

The rub is that most of DePaul's better players during those years didn't get diplomas. They include Mark Aguirre and Terry Cummings, who quit school after their junior years to join the pros (and thus aren't included in the graduation figures), as well as Dillard, Gary Garland, Clyde Bradshaw, Bernard Randolph and

Kenny Patterson. "The guys who played had other things on their minds besides school," Dillard says quietly.

DePaul's head basketball coach during most of those years was Ray Meyer, a respected figure in the sport. He retired in 1984 after 42 years in the post. Dillard remembers him fondly. "Coach was great. You could talk to him like your father. He cared how you were doing," he says. "He'd hold up practice to chew you out if he heard you missed a class. He even knew when you were *late* for one."

Then he pauses and continues: "But Coach was from the old school, you know? He thought a pat on the back would get you through. I don't think he really understood what it is to play college basketball today.

"Like, we'd have practice every day, November through March, and informal practice the other times. During the season we played teams coast to coast, so we'd be traveling a lot. We'd miss two-three days of school here and a whole week there, and when I'd get back to class I'd be totally lost sometimes. We'd take our books on the road and all, but it was hard to get into them.

"Then there was the news media. There'd be people at every practice, interviewing us. My head'd be buzzing all day wondering how I'd look on TV or how my quotes'd come out in the papers. I've talked to Coach about that since. He agrees he should have protected us more."

Academic quarters during the season "were pretty much a lost cause," Dillard goes on. He says he was a "C" student, but he kept that average only because DePaul allowed a grade of "incomplete" for classes taken but not finished. "If you owed a paper or missed a test, you'd get the 'incomplete' instead of a fail, and you could go back in the summer and make it up," he explains. "If it wasn't for summer school, I'd have never stayed eligible."

Dillard left DePaul with high hopes for a pro-basketball career even though his height (6-foot-2) and ninth-round draft status worked against it. His being cut early by the Bulls in 1982 still rankles; he believes he outperformed several players who made the team that year. He still plays in night leagues around Chicago, hoping to be "discovered" by a scout from the NBA or a European pro league. "I still have the dream. What can I say?" he shrugs.

He has given thought to going back to school. "My mom is a teacher and I can't go home without her bringing it up," he says.

"The trouble is, I've been out four years and I don't know if I could pick up the books again. It's funny, you know. I have a lot of time now, and I don't know what to do with it. When I was at DePaul and I needed more time, I didn't have it."

● *Nov. 14, 1986*

SPEED BALLS

Part 8

Devil's Bag in Repose

MIAMI

There are two things to be learned from the unexpected defeat of Devil's Bag in last Saturday's Flamingo Stakes at historic old Hialeah Park here, neither of them startling.

The first is that betting on 3-to-10 shots is not the road to financial security. The second is that a losing horse cannot be expected to share its backers' chagrin.

On Monday morning, the celebrated three-year-old colt was in Barn M, Stall 48, as usual, munching on oats and showing no displeasure. A scrawny stray feline called Devil's Cat, who sometimes shares his living quarters, was held up to him by a handler, and the horse nuzzled and licked her. The cat suffered the affection, but it wasn't her idea of proper hygiene. As soon as she was put down she re-licked the affected area.

After Saturday's race, about 30 reporters had gathered at the barn to inquire why Devil's Bag—unbeaten and unchallenged in six previous starts—had finished a distant and fading fourth to the prophetically named Time for a Change in the 1⅛-mile Flamingo. Trainer W.C. "Woody" Stephens mostly shook his head and said "I don't know." On Monday morning, only one reporter was there to disrupt the stable routine, and the answer was pretty much the same.

The 70-year-old Mr. Stephens wasn't at his barn Monday morning; he was at a hospital having his side checked. On the Thursday before the race, he had slipped in the shower and banged it, and it still hurt. A bad week all around.

Phil Gleaves, his young English assistant, was in charge in the boss's absence. "We wish we knew why Devil's Bag lost," he said. "We thought he was ready for the race, and he came out of it fit, as far as we can see. We're having his blood chemistry tested, but we don't think anything bad will turn up. I guess he just threw in a bad one."

Mr. Stephens spent about an hour in the hospital being told that he had a cracked rib but that there was no point in taping it. The doctor prescribed Tylenol and guessed that the pain would go away in a few days. The diagnosis cheered the veteran horseman. "At my age, it's good news to be told that any pain will go away," he said at his home.

A short, wiry man (an ex-jockey) with a deeply lined face, Mr. Stephens confirmed his assistant's assessment of Devil's Bag's health. "The vet and I checked him real good, and every bone was as solid and cold as can be," he said.

He allowed that while he was disappointed at his horse's defeat, he wouldn't say the thought had never occurred to him. "I've been in the game a long time, and I've lost a lot and won a few," said he. "I'm well past being shocked when a horse doesn't run the way I think he should."

Mr. Stephens was being overly modest in his description of his career. The "few" races he has won over the past 43 years include more than 200 stakes events and just about every so-called classic. He took the Kentucky Derby in 1974 with Cannonade, the Preakness way back in 1952 with Blue Man, and back-to-back Belmonts with Caveat last year and Conquistador Cielo in 1982.

His horses have won four Bluegrass Stakes, four Kentucky Oaks and four Ashlands. He's in Thoroughbred racing's Hall of Fame in Saratoga. Henry de Kwiatkowski, owner of Conquistador Cielo (the horse was syndicated for breeding for $36 million after his racing days), called the trainer "a gift to me from God."

Even so, Devil's Bag was special. He won his five two-year-old starts (and $355,000) by a total of 27 lengths and was never headed. The only time he had run behind another horse was in a seven-furlong prep for the Flamingo Feb. 20—his only race since last October—and that was because his jockey, Eddie Maple, had been instructed to restrain him for a bit to see if he could run from off the lead. He won that one by seven lengths.

Before his three-year-old season, he was syndicated for breeding for $36 million, the most ever paid for a horse that young and more than 100 times his yearling-sale purchase price of $325,000. "Super horse" went before his name like "oil-rich" precedes Saudi Arabia.

His defeat in the Flamingo was a particular stunner because he had twice beaten Dr. Carter, his supposed main rival. He had never faced Time for a Change, but his stablemate, Dancing Crown, had run a respectable second to the horse in January, and "Dancing Crown can't even warm up Devil's Bag," Mr. Gleaves asserts.

On Saturday, though, it was Dr. Carter who battled Time for a Change down the Hialeah homestretch, while Devil's Bag was being passed for third by outsider Rexson's Hope.

Everyone in racing has excellent hindsight, and Mr. Stephens is no exception. He said that if he had it to do over, he would have given Devil's Bag another prep race before the Flamingo. He also said that he probably spent too much time training his speedy charge to pace himself for the longer distances instead of letting him "go about his business." He doesn't think he'll make that mistake again.

It is whispered around Hialeah that Devil's Bag may not run again because members of his breeding syndicate, having already plunked down their $1 million a share, don't want to see their investment further battered by another loss. Mr. Stephens said that if that's true, no one has told him. "A sound horse like Devil's Bag—you got to run him," he said. He plans to do that in the Gotham Stakes and Wood Memorial in New York this spring, and then in the Kentucky Derby.

Meantime, over at Barn D at Hialeah, Angel Penna Sr., trainer of Time for a Change, was still accepting congratulations for the victory of his horse. No, he said, he wasn't surprised by the race's outcome, and he merely smiled at the suggestion that he may have liked the 7-to-1 odds on his horse enough to hazard a bet. Time for a Change had won at 1⅛ miles in excellent time twice before in 1984, and had merely repeated himself Saturday, he noted.

"The horse was ready to run at that distance. It was right there in the Racing Form for anyone to read," said the soft-spoken, 60-

year-old native of Argentina. "Of course," he added, "everything always is clearer when you win."

● *Mar. 9, 1984*

Note: Devil's Bag was retired to stud after winning the 1984 Derby Trial at Churchill Downs.

Rooting for
Spend A Buck

T he Kentucky Derby is nigh (neigh?) again, and while it's a lovely event it always presents the sports fan with a rooting problem. What I mean is that everyone has a favorite team, but who has a favorite horse?

Some of us solve this difficulty by paying for the privilege of picking the name of one of the entrants from a hat in an office pool, but that's a cop-out. Conscientious rooting should involve a mesh between contestant and spectator based on an appreciation by the latter of the background and qualities of the former.

With that in mind, I propose Spend A Buck as a suitable object of your support come Saturday afternoon. He can be recommended on looks alone; one female colleague of mine says the bay colt looks "cute" and "shy" off the track, and I can only agree. Further, I have it on good authority that he's a sweet-tempered beast, unlike a lot of race horses who'd sooner bite you than look at you.

And from there the story gets better. Everybody loves a bargain, and Spend A Buck certainly is one. Purchased at a going-out-of-business sale for $12,500, he has earned $919,000 to date. If his health holds, he will add to that and have a pleasurable and lucrative career as a poppa besides.

Like medical drama? There's that, too. Spend A Buck survived knee surgery after his two-year-old season. Beginners' luck? His owner, 42-year-old Dennis Diaz, of Tampa, Fla., has been in racing just 3½ years, and his trainer, Cam Gambolati, 35, has had his own stable only a year and a half.

But wait. We get ahead of ourselves. Here's Mr. Diaz, starting from the beginning:

"I was in real estate and insurance until I was 38 years old. I made money, all right, but I got tired of the grind. You might say I burned out. I sold out and looked for something else to do.

"There are some successful horse farms around Tampa, and I always liked the sport. I grew up on a dairy and cattle farm, and while I never raced horses I knew how to take care of them. I like being out in the country, and when my wife, Linda, and I heard about a farm being available, we bought it.

"We wanted to start small, buying fillies, racing them some and then breeding them. In the summer of 1983, Irish Hill, a horse farm near Lexington, Ky., was liquidating its stock, and I came up to look. It had a mare named Belle de Jour I liked. She was by Speak John, who'd sired some fine runners. The price was right, so I bought her.

"The fellow running the sale said that as long as I was there I should look at a Belle de Jour yearling on the place. The yearling was small and not muscular, but nicely balanced and with no obvious confirmation problems. His sire was Buckaroo, a Buckpasser horse. I loved Buckpasser.

"The colt was smart, too. I went to look at him in the paddock, and I guess he didn't want to be looked at, 'cause he kept putting this great big colt between him and me. That's bright for a horse. At $12,500, I thought I'd take a chance.

"We got him home, named him Spend A Buck, and put him in training. He looked good. Took him to Florida last summer and raced him at Calder. He had four firsts and a second in five races; won his last race by 9½ lengths. It was in Florida I knew I had something special, because some smart people were asking to buy him. I figured that if he was worth something to them he was worth it to me, so I kept him.

"We put him in a two-year-old stakes at River Downs in Cincinnati, and he won by 15 lengths. Took him to the Arlington Washington Futurity in Chicago, and he won that, too, and $355,000. He was leading the Young America at the Meadowlands in New Jersey against a top field until he jumped some tire tracks in the homestretch where they'd pulled the starting gate away, and finished second.

"In November, he was in the Breeders' Cup race in California. He finished third by 1½ lengths behind Chief's Crown and Tank's Prospect, a couple of Derby horses. He didn't run right, though, and came out with bone chips in his knee. Our guess is that he got 'em jumping those tire marks in Jersey. We were worried, I'll tell you."

Not long ago such an injury would have ended Spend A Buck's career, but arthroscopic surgery saved it. It's a routine operation for humans, but riskier for a horse because it requires a sizable general anesthetic. Spend A Buck's handlers say it's a tribute to his horse sense that he didn't injure himself while recuperating, as horses are apt to do.

Back on the track this spring as a three-year-old, Spend A Buck placed third in the Bayshore Stakes at Aqueduct in New York. Then he won the Cherry Hill Mile at Garden State Park in New Jersey in track-record time, and, two weeks ago, the 1⅛-mile Garden State Stakes in a blazing 1:45 4/5, just 2/5-second off Secretariat's world record in the often-raced distance. That performance marked him as a serious Derby contender.

Horses, however, run against other horses, not the clock, and that's what worries trainer Gambolati as the band tunes up for "My Old Kentucky Home." Trainers are professional nail-biters, and these things have Gambolati chewing:

—Spend A Buck likes to run on the lead, but so do Chief's Crown and Eternal Prince, the probable betting favorites Saturday. A too-fast-pace could tire the leaders and give the 1¼-mile race to a late runner like Stephan's Odyssey.

—The Churchill Downs track is deeper and heavier than ones on which Spend A Buck has done his best.

—There's bound to be some bumping in the 19-horse field that's expected, and little Spend A Buck could be a bumpee.

Gambolati takes solace from the fact that veteran jockey Angel Cordero Jr. will ride his horse Saturday. "Cordero will keep him out of trouble," he states with more conviction than he might feel.

And he already counts himself as blessed for the animal's success so far. "If you'd have told me a couple years ago that one of my first runners would have a shot at the Derby, I'd have said you were dreaming," says he.

Owner Diaz feels the same way. He says that his only regret

about Spend A Buck is that he named him wrong. He notes that Belle de Jour has delivered another colt, and that he hopes to name it Make A Buck. "Better late than never," he declares.

● *May 3, 1985*

Note: Spend A Buck won the 1985 Kentucky Derby.

Betting in the Press Box

ARCADIA, CALIF.

t may come as a surprise to you that there are rules for sportswriters just as there are rules for the games we cover. In the team sports, it's frowned upon to cheer in the press box. Partisan outbursts not only disturb the concentration of us professionals, but are considered bush to boot.

In horse racing, however, this rule is not observed. It's OK to root, as long as you don't get carried away and clobber the person next to you. It's even expected.

It's also OK to bet in the racing press boxes, and track managements typically set up windows for the exclusive use of the inhabitants. It's a service, to be sure, but I suspect it also serves a business interest. I've heard it said that anyone who could get the betting concession in the jockeys' quarters at a track could retire in comfort after a year. We writers are probably a bit smarter than that. It might take two or three years to get to Rio on our wagers.

All that is apropos of my day at the Breeders' Cup at Santa Anita Park here Saturday. Did I bet? Are you kidding? The seven featured races offered purses of $1 million, $2 million or $3 million, and matched the best horses in the world, not just the little old USA. Not betting would have been like working for the water company and never taking a drink.

Now, I fancy myself a decent handicapper. By that I

mean I am close to breaking even over my lifetime. Like Joe E. Lewis said, that's fortunate, because I need the money. I attribute my record mostly to the fact that my luck has never been good enough to encourage me to be unwise.

Breeders' Cup Day, though, was enough to tempt Sister Sarah Brown to risk a few bucks. The richness of the fields was almost painful to contemplate, like a seven-course meal with hot-fudge sundaes for every course. In every race, you would "throw out" (that is, exclude from your betting calculations) horses with lifetime earnings of several hundred thousand dollars. That seemed a shame when bettors on the wooden-grandstand circuit are starved for a glimpse of such horseflesh.

Nature cooperated by providing sunny skies and temperatures in the 70s. On such a day, racing could forget its declining national attendance and aging clientele, and the fans at Santa Anita could look past the parking lot in the foreground and enjoy the San Gabriel Mountains beyond. Some 69,000 people turned out. They felt so good they bet $15.4 million, a North American record.

A few of those dollars—70 to be exact—were mine, and an account of what I did with them might give more sense of the affair than a bald recitation of the winners, or even a hairy one. Open the Daily Racing Form with me for the first race, a 1 1/16-miler for two-year-old males with a purse of $1 million. Here's Polish Navy, winner of all four of his starts and $364,000. Here's Gulch, winner of five of six starts and $387,000. Here's Bet Twice, winner of five of six and $620,000. Sensory overload threatens. What's a bettor to do?

Look for bargains, I decide, taking hold of myself. Gulch and Capote, winner of two very fast races, go off as 2½-to-1 co-favorites. Late-running Bet Twice, the richest animal in the field, is 9-to-1 in a race where the speed might burn itself out. Knowing I may never see such a price again, I put $10 on his nose. He runs late—too late. He's fourth and Capote wins, wire to wire. I'm out $10 but undismayed.

A search of the Form for the second race, a 1 1/16-miler for two-year-old fillies also worth $1 million, reveals Zero Minus, the nicest 30-to-1 shot you'll ever see. She's been out of the money only once in seven starts. I bet her $5 to win and $5 to show. She's seventh to Brave Raj, who was purchased for $24,000. Her $450,000 first prize comes on top of the $461,000 she's already won. So what's $10?

Next is the three-quarter-mile sprint. The crowd goes nuts and makes Groovy a 2-to-5 favorite. If he wins, he pays $2.80 on a $2 bet.

That's a bond yield, not a racetrack price. Smile, who has won 12 of 22 and almost $1.2 million, goes off at 11-to-1. So does Taylor's Special, who has taken home $837,000. I take 'em both for $5 each. Smile wins, and I get $60. "He don't go when I say," says Jose Santos, the Chilean-born jockey of Groovy, who winds up fourth. Smile's people just smile. Me, too. I'm up $30.

The fourth, at a mile, is a puzzle, with no clear favorite. I put my $10 on Glow, who has won six of his last seven but still goes off at 10-to-1. The winner is Irish-bred Last Tycoon, who never has won at more than five furlongs and hasn't been on a track since August. At 36-to-1, he turns out to be the bargain of the day, and no wonder.

The fifth is the 1¼-mile Distaff featuring Lady's Secret, the best female runner extant. She goes off at 1-to-2 and seems to deserve it. I hold my peace and my $10. Lady's Secret wins by 2½ lengths, a bit tight for the risk.

The sixth race, 1½ miles on the turf for $2 million, brings us Dancing Brave, the English hero. He has won eight of nine and $1.4 million in Europe. The Form calls him "the star of stars." Angelenos feel lucky to have him and bet him down to 1-to-2. But hey! Manila, who's won his last six, is 9-to-1, and Duty Dance, who's won seven of 17 and $432,000, is 95-to-1! That's the kind of day it is.

I put $5 to win on each. Manila's jockey, Mr. Santos, makes a big-league move by steering him around two horses in the stretch and winning by a neck. Dancing Brave is fourth. He didn't like Santa Anita's "tight" turns, his jockey shrugs. My $5 turns into $49.

No. 7 is the main event, the $3 million Classic at 1¼ miles. I'm $59 ahead. I break a weakly held rule and bet $20 to win on a favorite, late-running Turkoman at 8-to-5. Again, my late runner runs too late. He's second and Skywalker, at 10-to-1, wins it, and $1,350,000. I'm up $39 on the day.

A bigger winner was Eugene Klein, whom I will call Uncle Gene from now on. He owns Capote and Lady's Secret, and collected $900,000 in purse money Saturday.

Feeling his oats, he used the occasion of Lady's Secret's victory to declare the animal horse of the year. "She's not just the horse of the year, she's the horse of the century," he enthused.

Until next year's horse of the century. Like I'm up $39. Until my next trip to the track.

● *Nov. 3, 1986*

SQUARED CIRCLES

•
Part 9

Ali's Legacy

Muhammad Ali says he has retired from boxing. He has said this before, but this time most people believe him. Anyone who has watched his last few fights knows that his skills have deteriorated as alarmingly as his waistline has expanded. As much as he is admired as a fighter, the consensus about this recent announcement is that it's about time.

Mr. Ali is certain not to play the old soldier and fade away; he isn't that sort. He is one of those rare athletes whose influence has extended far beyond his principal field of endeavor. He is probably correct when he boasts that he's better known around the world than the President of the United States. At the very least, he has been prominent much longer, his career having spanned six national administrations. He is likely to remain in the public eye for some years to come.

Yet Mr. Ali's retirement from the ring is an important milestone, and it offers an appropriate opportunity to assess this remarkable person. The easy part of this assessment is its pugilistic component: As a boxer, he fully lived up to his self-proclaimed title of "The Greatest." He might not have punched as hard as some heavyweights, present or past, but most experts agree that his grace, speed, resilience and ring acumen have been unsurpassed in his weight class.

His three fights with Joe Frazier (especially, I thought,

the first, which he lost) rank among the greatest in boxing history. His eighth-round knockout of the massive George Foreman in 1974 is one of sports' most notable examples of mind over matter. His 15-year domination of boxing's most widely followed division was a stupendous feat of physical conditioning that may never be repeated.

Mr. Ali was only slightly less conspicuous outside the ring: He has been an active, though peripheral, participant in some of the great movements of his time. His outspokenness and refusal to be patronized set a standard of behavior for many blacks both in and out of sports. His refusal to be inducted into the military during the war in Vietnam, on the grounds of his "Black Muslim" religious beliefs, must be regarded as courageous if only because it cost him far more than it did others who followed that course. As a result, he was stripped of his championship at his fighting peak and couldn't get a match for three years.

But I think that Mr. Ali's influence has been strongest—and least fortunate—on our notions of sportsmanship, or on how we regard winning, losing and competing. Sportsmanship always has been partly sham because no one enjoys losing, and hard feelings frequently arise between competitors. But the willingness of athletes to treat their opponents with respect—which is at the root of the concept—long cushioned them in the comforting knowledge that they someday would receive solace in defeat, and it helps the rest of us keep sports in proper perspective.

Mr. Ali, with his superior abilities, would have none of this. For him, boxing wasn't merely a test of skills with an opponent within a confined area under agreed-upon rules. It was psychological warfare that knew few bounds.

His preparation for his fights typically included hanging unflattering nicknames on his opponents, composing doggerel poems about them and mimicking their characteristics. Inside the ring he taunted them verbally, showed them up and even tortured them physically; recall if you will his cruel beatings of Floyd Patterson and Ernie Terrell.

His goal often seemed to be to not only defeat his foes, but also to destroy them professionally, and in a number of cases he succeeded.

With Mr. Ali's example to recommend it, such behavior spread: The football spiked in the end zone, the gratuitous slam dunk in basketball and the baseball batter standing at home plate to admire a homerun might be regarded as the "Ali shuffle" of those sports. I find them all tough to take.

Mr. Ali toned down his act some in recent years, and it has become fashionable to excuse his excesses by theorizing that he was "just kidding" or trying to hype the gate of his fights. It has been enough to win for him the popular acceptance that eluded him earlier. Among other things, he's the star of a Saturday morning television cartoon show aimed at children, and he appears in commercials for no less a mainstream American concern than Ford Motor Co.

This undoubtedly also reflects our appreciation of some of his better qualities, which include generosity and occasional displays of true (nondestructive) humor. But it also might indicate that some of us have bought his approach to the business of playing games.

In the coming months it frequently will be asked if boxing will survive in the U.S. without Mr. Ali. Almost certainly, it will. Joe Louis succeeded Jack Dempsey as a popular heavyweight champion, Rocky Marciano succeeded Mr. Louis and Mr. Ali succeeded Mr. Marciano. Someone will succeed Mr. Ali.

A better question might be to ask if sports in general will survive Mr. Ali's conduct as heavyweight champ. As comedian Mort Sahl said of Richard Nixon about 20 years ago: "His chances look good, but I'm not so sure about the rest of us."

• *June 29, 1979*

Note: Ali returned to fight again, finally retiring in 1981.

No-Show Gerry

he wind had come up on the desert, and the weather had turned chilly, so when Gerry Cooney arrived for his afternoon training session in the big tent behind the Americana Canyon Hotel here, only about a dozen people had gathered to watch. The boxer was disappointed.

"Where are all the people? This place is usually full," he said to no one in particular. But then he brightened and commenced his workout—skipping rope, punching the light bag, and dodging or blocking the slaps of his trainer, Victor Valle, in a prolonged game of "hit me if you can." The game ended with the 6-foot-7-inch-Cooney taking the offensive against his short, gray-haired handler, pummeling him with mock punches until both men broke up laughing.

Afterward, a smiling, sweating Cooney signed autographs and posed for snapshots with members of his audience, which had swelled to about 20. He shook hands with the men, kissed the women, and generally seemed to be enjoying himself greatly.

"That's the old Gerry—having fun with the people," said Dennis Rappaport, his co-manager. "I tell you, I've never seen him so happy. And look at the way the people react to him! They love him! This kid is destined to be the most popular heavyweight champion of all time. Just wait until he gets back in the ring—you'll see."

When this return to action will come, Mr. Rappaport isn't saying. He hopes it will be in April or May, but he isn't sure, because the injured knuckle and middle finger of the fighter's left hand, operated on last June, is still tender. The Cooney camp is trying to have a glove fashioned that will protect the delicate digit. Meantime, the light bag is the hardest thing the 27-year-old boxer is hitting these days.

Boxing folks might be pardoned if they take the news of Gerry Cooney's imminent return with a mine of salt, because they've heard it before. It has been 20 months since Cooney was stopped in 13 rounds by champion Larry Holmes in the June 1982 version of the Fight of the Century, and Cooney hasn't fought since, pleading a variety of psychic and physical ills.

He didn't fight very often before that, either. In the two years before the Holmes bout, he entered the ring in earnest but three times, and never hung around for long. In 1980, he kayoed Jimmy Young in four rounds and Ron Lyle in one. His sole 1981 appearance was a one-round pummeling of Ken Norton. The finality of those wins tended to obscure the fact that the combined age of those three gentlemen when he fought them was 104 years.

Nonetheless, few doubt that if he fights again with even a modicum of success, Cooney quickly will be back near the top of his profession. He has everything it takes to make it big in U.S. boxing: He is large, good-natured, white and American, and he possesses a left hook that has registered 22 KOs in 26 fights and takes away the breath of both foes and commentators. "If you're in there for three minutes with Cooney, you look like you've been in there three hours," says Gil Clancy, a noted former fight manager.

He also has the kind of nervy management that gets the most out of his infrequent showings. Before the Cooney fight, managers Rappaport and Mike Jones, a couple of New York real estate brokers, coolly defied tradition by holding out for financial parity with the champ, reasoning that it was Holmes who needed Cooney for a big payday, not vice versa. Holmes and his advisers squawked, but they later gulped and signed. The two each received a reported $10 million from the fight's $50 million television and live gate.

But even the likelihood of lifelong security didn't dull for Cooney the pain of defeat. Unused to adversity, he went into a six-month funk, during which time he abandoned his beloved discos as well as the ring.

"It was real, real tough for me," he recalls. "So many people wanted me to win, and I wanted so bad to win for them. It wasn't a celebrity-fan sort of thing. Those people really touched me. Maybe I shouldn't have reacted that way, but I did."

He says he felt especially bad because he thought he didn't fight as well as he should have. He says that an earlier shoulder injury he suffered, which had forced a three-month postponement of the match, hadn't healed completely, and 10 days prior to the fight he first bruised the left-hand knuckle and finger that were later to sideline him.

Then, too, he says he shouldn't have listened to the sportswriters and others who questioned his ability to go 15 rounds with the more experienced champion. "It got so that going the distance became more important to me than winning," he avers. "Early in the fight, when I should have been aggressive, I held back, and then I didn't have it when I needed it. I was dumb to let myself get screwed up."

Cooney returned to training in January 1983 for a scheduled April fight with young Phil Brown, but the following month he hit a sparring partner on the point of his elbow and reinjured the knuckle and finger. Surgery in June revealed bone chips and extensive ligament and tendon damage. He tried to spar last November, but the area swelled again. He has been working out in Palm Springs since early last month, feels good, and hopes he can fight soon.

Cooney's long layoff has earned him a "reluctant dragon" label that disturbs manager Rappaport, an animated 38-year-old. "This kid is dying to fight! Only real pain kept him away!" he contends.

Still, he feels that some amends must be made for his tiger's absence, and he is planning to make them by staging Cooney's comeback fight—against a "respectable" opponent yet unnamed—for charity. "We'll call it the 'Fight for Life,' and it'll be for the benefit of the families of the Marines who were killed in Lebanon and Grenada," the manager says. "Maybe we'll have it at Camp LeJeune [a Marine base]. The whole place'll be done up in red, white and blue. Gerry will come in behind the biggest marching band we can find. It'll be great!"

Mr. Rappaport says that once the initial opponent has been dispatched by a Gerry Cooney who is stronger and wiser than he was when he fought Holmes, he'll match Cooney with a heavyweight contender. That fight will be on network television, "where everybody can see it free," he says. The inevitable Cooney victory there will trigger an irresistible public demand for a fight against Holmes or South African Gerry Coetzee, holder of the World Boxing Association version of the heavyweight crown, he believes.

And when it comes, Mr. Rappaport says, it will make the gate of the 1982 Holmes fight look like peanuts. "I think I know how much we can make, but you'll laugh, so I won't tell you. But I'll be right.

"Listen, there is no fighter in the world more popular than Gerry. He's been out of action nearly two years, but he's still tops with the fans. We can't go anywhere in Las Vegas because people keep stopping him to talk. We were in the Palm Springs airport the other day, and you'd have thought there was an accident the way people ran to get his autograph. Former President Ford was there, too, but nobody paid any attention to him. Gerry went over to him to say hello, and you should have seen Ford's face light up. It made his whole day."

● *Feb. 24, 1984*

The Fight Behind the Fight

I n Hollywood, they sometimes say they should have forgotten about the movie and filmed the deal. They say something like that in the fight game, too.

"Oh, yeah, boxing can be a weird business," says Morris Goldings, lawyer for Mr. Marvelous Marvin Hagler, of Brockton, Mass., middleweight champion of the world. "Take what happened after Marvin knocked out Mustafa Hamsho in three rounds last year. The World Boxing Council wanted to take away his crown because the bout had been scheduled for 15 rounds, not 12 like they wanted, and we had a heckuva legal fight to keep it.

"Can you beat that? The fight goes three, and they're sore it wasn't scheduled for 12. It's like the joke about the guy who goes into a restaurant and orders coffee without cream. The waiter tells him: 'We don't use cream. Will you take it without milk?'"

But now Hagler is here in the polyester capital of the Free World to defend his title against Mr. Thomas Hearns of Detroit on Monday night, and Mr. Goldings couldn't be happier about the deal. Negotiations for the match went smoothly, he declares, and the results were fair for all concerned, "very fair."

The other afternoon, poking at his salad in the coffee shop at Caesars Palace, the hostelry in whose parking-lot stadium the fisticuffs will take place, promoter Bob Arum allows that he can see Mr. Goldings's point of view. Says Mr. Arum: "For him the deal is fair. His client will get rich from it. Hearns, too. Me? As we sit here, I'm breaking even, but I'm sure I'll make out all right.

"If you're talking 'smooth' I'd have to disagree," he goes on. "Each fighter had an exaggerated idea of his own box-office appeal, and neither wanted to take less than the other. But we worked things out, like I knew we would. This is one fight everybody wants, including the fighters."

Mr. Arum is not one to count his customers before they are seated, or their dollars before his accountants have examined them under strong light, but he is talking in terms of a $40 million gross for the bout, about 75% of which would come from 700-odd closed-circuit television outlets around the U.S. and Canada. The fighters and Mr. Arum would get 55% of those revenues, or about $22 million, to divide.

Hagler's guarantee under the fight's contract is $5,340,000 and Hearns's is about $4.8 million, Hearns having swallowed his pride and taken the short end because it is Hagler's title they will contest. Training expenses ($100,000 to each camp), sanctioning fees to the alphabet agencies that keep boxing confused, and a $265,000 payoff to a promoter who had signed Hearns for a match that was pre-empted by the present one, bring the guarantees to $11 million. Expenses should come to about $3 million. Once that $14 million nut is cracked—and Mr. Arum is confident it will be because closed-circuit advance ticket sales have been strong—proceeds will be split 45% to Hagler, 35% to Hearns and 20% to the promoter. A $22 million take would leave Hagler and entourage about $8.7 million, Hearns & Co. about $7.5 million and Mr. Arum about $2 million. That's not bad for a fight that can't exceed, yes, 12 rounds.

It's also not bad considering that neither fighter packs the charisma of Muhammad Ali, Sugar Ray Leonard, or, even, Gerry Cooney, the major drawing cards of previous megabuck ring battles. "This is one case where the whole looks to be greater than the sum of its parts," muses the bespectacled Mr. Arum. "We have two excellent fighters, in the same weight class, at their peaks at the same time. I'd hate to have to depend on circumstances like that to stay in business."

The fight is especially intriguing because it raises more than the usual number of burning issues that hover over ballyhooed bouts.

Hearns is the younger (26 years old), taller and swifter of the combatants, and he is believed to possess the harder punch. But he is moving up in weight from superwelterweight, whatever that is, and that has proved difficult for fighters of greater accomplishment. Also, men with narrow builds like his have been known to be discouraged by the sort of bumps to the breadbasket that Hagler can deliver.

Hagler is an experienced, durable brawler with a good wallop of his own (50 KOs in 60 career wins). Because he's tough and a left-hander, higher-ranked fighters ducked him for years, leaving him with a sense of grievance that still fuels him even now that he's a champ. But fighters tend to get old young and he's 30, or, as Hearns's manager, Emanuel Steward, puts it, "30 or so."

The two fighters share one common opponent, Roberto Duran. Hagler decisioned the intrepid Panamanian in 15 rounds in November 1983, while Hearns conked him in two last June. Advantage Hearns, right? Not according to Hagler. "After I was done with Duran, only the shell was left for Hearns," says he.

No one here is predicting the outcome with great certainty. In Las Vegas, where gambling is regal as well as legal, the odds opened at 7-to-5, Hagler, in deference to the fact that he is fighting at his natural weight. The odds now stand at even money, and may tilt to Hearns by fight time because he has been working out under the gaze of the gambling multitudes in a Caesars Palace ballroom while the solitude-loving Hagler has hidden out in funkier quarters at Johnny Tocco's Gym downtown.

No less an authority than *Sports Illustrated* magazine has forecast a draw for the bout. That would be financially pleasing to some because, once eyebrows were lowered, they could stage the thing all over again.

A more limited though equally cautious view is this: Sometime in rounds one or two, Hearns will bounce his famous right hand off Hagler's shiny pate. If the Marvelous One merely blinks and keeps coming, Hearns will be in for a tough evening. If Hagler feels he must pause at that moment to consider new information, the joke will be on him.

● *Apr. 12, 1985*

Triumph of the Pit Bull

LAS VEGAS

L
•

ooks can deceive. For example, hotels here in Betsville have grates or other impediments outside their windows not to keep intruders out, but to keep jumpers in.

But looks don't always deceive. Take the Marvelous Marvin Hagler-Thomas Hearns fight here Monday night. If ever a ring warrior looked the part, it was muscular Marvelous Marvin, the Knight of the Shaved Dome and Baleful Countenance. Next to him the tall, slim, curly-haired Hearns looked downright wispy.

"It's the pit bull versus the poodle," growled one Hagler backer, brushing aside the pre-fight rhetoric that had Hearns dispatching the middleweight champion.

And for a change, what the people saw was what they got. Hagler kept his title by knocking out Hearns in three rounds before a "live" audience of about 15,000 people and 45,000 gold chains, and some two million folks in closed-circuit televisionland.

It was a short fight, but nobody here was heard to complain, not even those who coughed up $600 for a ringside seat. The combatants traded more leather than Gucci. It was as good a three-rounder as any in memory, and the best brawl of any length since Apollo Creed took on Rocky Balboa.

Hagler's most effective weapon was a looping, righthand lead over Hearns's low-held left. That was the first punch Hagler fired, and another one was the last. In between, he hit the challenger with the blow a good half-dozen times from his left-handed stance. Each shot seemed to take Hearns by surprise.

Hearns did some pitching, too, catching Hagler with snapping blows that opened ancient scar tissue over the champ's right eye and raised a nasty welt below it. Referee Richard Steele stopped the fight briefly in round three so the ring doctor could inspect the damage. The doc decided that Hagler could see through the blood, and allowed him to finish his job.

The deciding right knocked Hearns about halfway across the ring and to the canvas. Hearns arose at the count of nine, but referee Steele stepped in to call the whole thing off. "Hearns's eyes were glazed and his legs were wobbly," said Steele. "He didn't ask me to let him continue."

Hearns wound up where he did because he fought the way he shouldn't have. Before the bout, he had noised about the intention to attack and dispose of Hagler in three rounds (oh, irony), but it was clear that the boast camouflaged a quite different plan utilizing his superior speed and long-range firepower. "We'll move," editorialized Hearns's manager, Emanuel Steward, after one of his fighter's midweek workouts.

Could Steward foresee any way his tiger could lose? "Only if we fight too much at close range, and stand still," he replied. On Monday night, Hearns committed both fatal sins. Did the devil make him do it? No, Hagler and machismo did. "Marvin ran right at me at the opening bell, and I had to protect myself," Hearns told a post-fight news conference. "He wanted me to back up. I had to show him I deserved some respect."

In retrospect, Hearns's curious performance Monday night pointed up some oddities about the way he prepared for the bout. Last Friday, manager Steward announced with satisfaction that Hearns weighed 165 pounds, five pounds above the middleweight limit. Steward explained that in training for his 1981 welterweight title match with Sugar Ray Leonard, which resulted in the only previous defeat in a 41-bout pro career, Hearns was too weight-conscious. He came in two pounds below the 147-pound limit and ran out of gas in the late going. Steward said that Hearns was determined not to do that again, but he didn't explain how losing five pounds in three days would strengthen his fighter.

Las Vegas lives on rumors, and reports of two training injuries to Hearns enlivened fight week here. Hearns was said to have cut his lip badly while sparring last Tuesday. They had him with a charley horse in a calf the week before.

The Hearns camp confirmed the cut lip (it had to; reporters saw it) but said it was trifling. It denied any equine mishap. For whatever reason, betting odds on the fight shifted sharply toward Hagler just before fight time, but the bout was so brief that neither injury could have figured in the outcome.

Hagler also failed to follow the script that some experts had written. In most previous fights he had started slowly, worn down his foes by pummeling their midsections, and finished them not with one punch but with the weight of many. In this one he came out smoking and stayed that way, brandishing a right hand that would have pleased Rocky Marciano, another famous resident of Brockton, Mass.

The 30-year-old Hagler had said he would knock out Hearns, if only to gain the acclaim he felt had eluded him in a pro ring career that dates from 1973. "I hear a lot about his punch—what about mine?" he said testily to newsmen.

After the fight, Hagler admitted that any notions he had had of waging prolonged battle ended with his eye cuts. He said he was "a bit afraid" when the referee stopped the bout so the cuts could be examined, and decided to "get serious and get it done." Anyway, he noted, in a dig at Hearns's prediction of a third-round KO, "he can't count past three so I didn't want to complicate things for him."

Hearns showed up before reporters 15 minutes later, apparently unhurt. He proclaimed the fight a good one and bravely mentioned his hope for a rematch, "but not tomorrow." He took some solace in his multimillion-dollar purse and said that the loss, while bitter, averted one potential problem. A win would have added the middleweight title belt to the welterweight and superwelterweight belts he's already won, and set the stage for him to tackle the light-heavyweight division and try for an unprecedented four championships. "I saw myself with four belts, around my waist, chest, neck and legs," he said, smiling. "I asked myself how I was gonna walk."

● *Apr. 17, 1985*

Meet Mike Tyson

TROY, N.Y.

T
•

here's nothing in sports quite like the lure of a Promising Young Heavyweight, which is why a full house of 7,600 people were in their seats and ABC-TV's cameras were grinding for a preliminary bout here Sunday.

The fight matched Jesse Ferguson, an ex-marine from Harrisburg, Pa., with the PYH, Mike Tyson of nearby Catskill, N.Y. This would be the 19-year-old Tyson's 18th professional fight. The previous 17 had ended with Tyson erect and his foes either prone or supine. Twelve of the knockouts had come before the end of the first round.

Sunday's go-around ended in a knockout of the technical variety. Referee Luis Rivera stopped the proceedings at 1:19 of the sixth round because Ferguson was devoting his entire energy to clutching Tyson's arms. The fight had been decided for all intents and purposes late in the previous round by a Tyson uppercut that put Ferguson down for an eight-count and left him bleeding from the nose and reeling.

Ferguson later took issue with the referee's action, saying he wasn't out on his feet when the bout was halted. Mr. Rivera defended himself bluntly. "He didn't want to fight no more," the official said of Ferguson.

The TKO satisfied the fans who filled the college hockey arena here to cheer neighbor Tyson before, during and after the bout, and ABC, which has the young man under a $1 million contract for five televised fights this year. Sunday's was the first of that series, and a poor showing by Tyson wouldn't have done much for the ratings of the remaining four.

If all this attention seems excessive for a 19-year-old, Tyson so far deserves it. He has what everyone wants in a heavyweight fighter but rarely gets—devastating punching power with either hand. He has dispatched opponents with lefts and rights, hooks and uppercuts. His 5-foot-10, 217-pound frame radiates muscle and menace. "When Mike answers the bell, people just know something *bad* is going to happen to the other guy," says Jim Jacobs, Tyson's co-manager.

It has helped, of course, that Tyson has come along at a time when the heavyweight division is at a low ebb. The generally recognized champ at the moment is Michael Spinks, who took the crown from a passive, 38-year-old Larry Holmes last summer in a Las Vegas fight of which the American Medical Association would have approved. Spinks had campaigned previously as a light-heavy. He's a tough campaigner, with a surprisingly whimsical twist of mind, but his credentials as a big man are suspect.

The other top heavies—Pinklon Thomas, Tim Witherspoon, Tony Tubbs and Greg Page—all sort of run together in the public mind. They fight one another from time to time, more or less in private. None but the most devoted fight fan could pick them out of a lineup.

To Tyson's appeal as a puncher should be added a personal background of the stuff of which boxing legends are made. At age 13, the Brooklyn-born youth was serving time for robbery in a juvenile reformatory, so angry and recalcitrant that he was judged to be mentally retarded. A worker at the facility devined his boxing potential and sought out Cus D'Amato, the veteran trainer, to help develop it. D'Amato took Tyson into the camp he ran for young fighters in rural Catskill, and eventually became his legal guardian. D'Amato died last November at age 77.

D'Amato had guided Floyd Patterson to the heavyweight crown, but he wasn't every boxer's cup of tea. His wars with the gangster-infested International Boxing Club in the 1950s left him permanently suspicious of—and hesitant to do business with—others in the fight game, and he demanded a kind of monk-like devotion to duty that few were willing to give.

In young Tyson, however, D'Amato found a willing pupil. Tyson holds his gloves close to his head, "peek-a-boo" style, and avoids punches more with a waist-up bob and weave than with footwork.

Both are signatures of D'Amato-trained fighters. Also, Tyson spars without headgear, the wearing of which gave fighters a false sense of security in D'Amato's book.

Tyson is fond of repeating such D'Amato dicta as "the objective of boxing is *not* to get hit." For all his punching power, Tyson lists "elusiveness" as his main pugilistic asset.

That's no verbal ploy, according to Jacobs. "When Mike is compared with Joe Frazier, I have to laugh," says the manager, who, with co-manager Bill Cayton, also owns Greatest Fights Inc., which has the world's largest library of fight films and tapes. "Frazier and Mike are built similarly, but Frazier took three punches for every one he threw, while Mike is developing into a fine defensive fighter. If he gets anywhere in boxing, it'll be because of his ability to dish it out without also taking it."

Jacobs and Cayton plan to match Tyson as much as twice a month for the rest of this year in their campaign to win the crown for him before he turns 21. He's already booked for bouts on March 10 and 29. With the late Mr. D'Amato, they believe that a fighter learns best by fighting.

Against Ferguson, a 29-year-old recently ranked 20th in the division by The Ring magazine (Tyson was unranked), Tyson concentrated on body punching early with good success. He also took a couple of good left hooks and was tied up frequently by the older man. Although all three judges thought otherwise, he appeared to have lost the slow fourth round of the scheduled 10-rounder.

Later, though, Tyson said he saw something in that round that led to his winning blow. "He dropped his left shoulder before he threw his uppercut. I watched until he did it again, and beat him to it. It happened just like I knew it would."

Tyson cheerfully told a post-fight press conference that he was aiming for the tip of Ferguson's nose "to drive the bone into his brain." Later, in his dressing room, he disavowed any intention to maim. "I didn't want to hurt him bad. I just wanted him to stay down." he said.

And if Ferguson lacked the kind of speed that observers say might give him trouble, well, Tyson thought he'd handle that kind of foe, too, in time. "I'll fight 'em all eventually, including the fast ones," he said. "I'd fight a lion if my managers booked one."

● *Feb. 18, 1986*

King of the Ring: Ray Upsets Marv

LAS VEGAS

T**he** name of the sport is boxing, and on Monday night here Ray Charles Leonard showed why. He gave Marvelous M. Hagler a little this and a little that and a lot of air. When it was over, he had Hagler's cherished middleweight championship belt. If Marv had worn a wristwatch into the ring Leonard would have lifted it, too.

It wasn't exactly magic that Sugar Ray practiced, nor was it the burglar's art. But it had elements of both. Before the fray, Leonard said his plan was "to be there but not be there." Before the puzzled looks in his audience had passed, he elucidated. "I mean I want to be elusive, but score some points," he said. A neat trick, but he pulled it off superbly.

The question of larceny was raised by Hagler after the judges' split decision in the 12-round bout had gone against him. Neither he nor his handlers uttered the classic "we wuz robbed," but they muttered aplenty about "politics" and "Las Vegas" decisions.

"I put on the pressure. I took his best shots," grumbled an unmarked Hagler. "I would have won anywhere else but here."

"Twelve rounds sucks," contributed his co-manager, Pat Petronelli. "Fifteen rounds is the true championship distance."

But in fact, the comments merely underscored the extent to which the champ and his retinue had been outmaneuvered in the much ballyhooed Superfight, which took place before a world-wide closed circuit and pay-per-view television audience estimated at 300 million, plus 15,000 or so eyewitnesses wearing enough gold chain to stretch from Caesars Palace to Katmandu.

The object of boxing is to hit and not get hit, and it was Leonard who accomplished this better. Further, the Leonard camp had made the 12-round limit its one inflexible demand in arranging the go-around.

"We wanted a technical fight—in and out—not a war of attrition," said Angelo Dundee, Leonard's veteran trainer. "No way we'd agree to 15."

Twelve rounds was almost too long for the underdog Leonard to win a victory made remarkable by a five-year stretch in which he had fought only one, lackluster bout after "retiring" from the ring with an eye injury. Two of the three judges—Dave Moretti and Lou Filippo—awarded Hagler four of the last six rounds. Moretti had Leonard on top, 115 points to 113 (seven rounds to five) overall, while Filippo reversed those numbers in favor of Hagler under a system that usually gives 10 points to the winner of a round and nine to the loser.

As is unhappily common in these matters, the deciding vote was cast by a judge whose score card indicated he wasn't watching the same fight as his two colleagues, or almost anyone else. Jo Jo Guerra had it 118-110, or 10 rounds to two, in favor of Leonard. Most ringside observers I spoke to had Leonard ahead, but by a two-to-four-point margin.

The Wall Street Journal card (mine) had Leonard winning, 117-115. My total point count was higher than the judges' because I scored four rounds even while they managed to discern a winner in each. Perhaps this shows indecisiveness on my part. Then again, perhaps it shows acuity.

The fight, like a good essay, had a definite beginning, middle and end. Leonard clearly got the best of the first four rounds, flitting out of reach of Hagler's lunges while peppering the champion with light but neat flurries. Hagler expressed his impatience with the proceedings by motioning with his glove for Leonard to close and repeatedly mouthing the word "c'mon." Leonard's smile at the end of round four bespoke his view of things: The rounds were passing in a way he approved of.

In the fifth, Hagler landed his two best punches of the fight, an overhand right lead in the first minute of action and a sharp right uppercut near the bell. It was to be the only round he would capture on all three judges' cards.

The punches seemed to take some spring out of Leonard. He was a more reachable target in rounds five through nine. Most observers had predicted a Hagler knockout in these rounds, and while Hagler generally got the better of the action in this span, his punches lacked snap, perhaps showing the effects of a 14-year ring career. Leonard not only managed to tie up Hagler inside, but also got off some stinging flurries of his own.

To cries of "Box!" from his corner, Leonard was on his toes again in rounds 10 and 11, mixing a double-windup bolo punch and "Ali shuffle" with his again-brisk combinations. The showboat stuff served mainly to emphasize his own, growing sense of elation. Before the bell for round 12 he raised his arms aloft, knowing he needed only to survive the final three minutes to win. Which he did.

The Leonard-Hagler bout was the last on the card, but not the last in fact. Don King, the bulky, porcupine-haired promoter of many fights (but not this one), attempted to enter the ring after the bout. He was rebuffed by Bob Arum, who did promote the thing, and two security guards. A scuffle ensued, leaving King with a torn sports jacket and curses on his lips.

The subject of further fights of a more-polished sort was renewed at post-bout doings. Leonard left the ring with a pledge that he'd see us "six months and 15 pounds later," possibly indicating he covets Tommy Hearns's light heavyweight title, but he refused to elaborate. Donald Curry, the former welterweight champion now campaigning as a junior middleweight, said he'd like Leonard to come *down* in weight to meet him.

Hagler was equivocal about a rematch, but left a strong impression he'd like one. He stands to gross more than $20 million from Monday's action, so who could blame him? Leonard's $11 million purse wasn't rosin, either. It'll take more negotiations than an arms control treaty to put together Superfight II, but it makes cents, so don't bet against it.

● *Apr. 8, 1987*

TRUE–LIFE ADVENTURES

Part 10

Kathy vs. Me

A friend once told me he knew he had become middle aged when, in his recurring fantasy about being a New York Knick, he stopped thinking of himself as Bill Bradley and began imagining he was Red Holzman.

By that standard, I guess I'm not quite middle aged yet. I still have it in me to contemplate what it might be like to try my hand on some of the more exalted fields of play.

Mind you, this doesn't mean I'm a lunatic. I know darned well what would happen if I climbed into the ring with the reigning heavyweight boxing champ, batted against a big-league pitcher, played quarterback for the Detroit Lions or goalie for the Boston Bruins. Besides, Paul Gallico or George Plimpton already did those things, and described them quite nicely.

Of an occasional lazy Sunday afternoon in front of the TV set, though, I have wondered if I could trade shots with a big-time woman tennis pro. Granted that Martina, Chris, Tracy, Evonne and that gang are talented and skillful athletes, but on TV, at least, the baseline game they play didn't seem too different from the one I play with my tennis-court buddies. Thus, when a representative of the Avon women's pro tennis circuit asked me if I'd like to go a set with one of the pros when the tour stopped in Chicago in late January, I said sure.

Before any feminists in the audience start having

217

conniptions, I'd like to make a few things clear. I did not, repeat not, challenge a top woman tennis pro to a match, a la Bobby Riggs. He, after all, was a former national champion and might have had grounds to believe he could win. I had no such credentials or thoughts, and the whole thing was Avon's idea.

Not only did I give myself no chance of winning, I also thought there was little likelihood I could win as much as a game. I'm an avid tennis player but I fancy myself only a bit better than average in skill: I maybe deserve a 4.5 on that 7-point rating scale that's been making the rounds. I simply wanted to find out if I could keep the ball in play and score an occasional point. That's all there was to it, okay?

So the date was set, and I presented myself, racquet in hand, at the Mid-Town Tennis Club in Chicago. The pro they sent to play me was Kathy Jordan. She's not as famous as Martina or Chris, but she's plenty good. Last year she was national women's collegiate champ, made the round of 16 at both Wimbledon and the U.S. Open and was voted the "most impressive newcomer" on the women's tour. At the time of our match she was rated the 11th best woman player in the world (yes, the world).

She is 20 years old (I'm 42), stands 5 feet, 7 inches tall (I'm 6 feet tall when I haven't had a haircut in a while) and is good looking (I'm just average there, too).

The deal was that she would play as though it were a real match. Any doubts I might have had on that score vanished when, after we'd hit for about 10 minutes, I declared myself ready to play but she said she hadn't warmed up sufficiently.

I served first and, lo and behold, after the first four points the score was 30-all! I scored my points on two backhand lobs—one that she hit into the net and one that she only ticked with her racquet.

Alas, that was about it for me. She won the last two points of that game, and I could gather only four more while going down to a 6-0 defeat. The first-game lob was my only winner; my other points resulted from her mistakes.

Her serve was as good as I've ever faced, and I have rallied with several male club pros and college-varsity players. I can handle hard serves pretty well, but hers had a kick to it to boot. I got most of them back, all right, but usually she was right at the net to put away my return.

I got the best idea how good she was during one of the middle games. I hit a crisp (for me) serve wide to her backhand and followed it with a hard cross-court forehand. That's a sure point against anyone I play regularly, but while I was congratulating myself she retrieved my shot and rifled it past me down the line for a winner.

Our longest rally, I think (I couldn't take notes while I was playing), lasted six hits. Every time I hit a weak shot, she put it away. The match was, literally, no sweat for her. She looked as fresh after it as she did before.

We chatted a bit, and she admitted to having been put off by the idea of playing an everyday player like me. She said that anyone who knew anything about tennis would know I would get creamed. She said she frequently beats male players far better than me.

After awhile, though, she got the idea how I might have been curious to see how I would fare. "When I was a little girl, I used to watch the top women pros play on TV," she related. "When they muffed a shot I'd think, 'I could have got that one.' What I didn't see was the amazingly high level of the game they were playing. I guess you can't really tell that unless you get onto a court and see for yourself."

- *Feb. 15, 1980*

Burning Rubber on Ice

I
•

get more come-on mail about auto racing than any other sport, so it's fortunate that I have a large receptacle in which to store it. It's 30 inches high and stands next to my desk. I empty it into the garbage every Friday.

I've always had serious doubts about whether auto racing is a sport. It take guts and a steady hand, but so does forgery. TV highlights of races usually show cars rolling around and crashing into one another. Drivers get hurt and sometimes take spectators with them. It looks like Death Wish City to me. The American Medical Association should look into it.

On a social occasion I expressed this view to Bill Siegfriedt, an engineer and neighbor of mine, and he took exception to it. I expected that he might, because I had seen him up to his elbows in grease of a weekend, messing around with a little white sports car he owns. Turns out, he races the car sometimes, although not in ways you see on television.

"My wife and I do vintage-car events [the little white job is a 1958 Alfa Romeo], rallies and an occasional solo. A solo is where you take your car around a course against the clock," he said mildly. "It's fun and nobody gets hurt. You ought to try it."

Yeah, sure, I thought. Driving the Chicago expressways more than keeps me supplied with motor thrills. Let Dan Gurney try the Dan Ryan sometime.

Bill meant what he said, though, and a few weeks later he phoned me with a concrete proposal: "I've got an event you'll love—ice racing."

My gasp must have been audible, because he chuckled. "It's not like what it sounds," he explained. "We go out on a frozen lake in Wisconsin, mark out a course and drive it against the clock. The ice doesn't let you go too fast, and because you're out alone the worst you can do is skid around some."

I told him my Ferrari was in the shop, but he chuckled again. "You don't need a Ferrari. It's a Sports Car Club of America event, but most of us take our family cars because they're better on ice. A couple of years ago, one guy towed his sports car out for an ice race with his old Chevy station wagon. He ran the course with both cars, and won with the wagon."

Now that's the kind of story that appeals to me, so I said OK, I'd go. I've got a station wagon, a rusty 1977 Plymouth Volare with 60,000 miles on it, and the idea of racing it tickled me. Upon reflection, though, I began to worry that the wagon might not make the 120-mile trip to and from the site of the race, so I opted instead for the second component of my household's fleet, an '81 Chevy Citation. Good choice, said Bill; the car's front-wheel drive goes well on ice. (Even I knew that.)

The appointed Sunday dawned cold and clear, and we set out for Lake Maria, near Twin Lakes, in my Citation and the Siegfriedts' immaculate Volkswagen Jetta, which was piloted by Bill's wife, Corky, herself an enthusiastic racer. I wasn't thrilled by the single-digit temperature. Racquetball is my idea of a winter sport. But I took solace from the fact that the frigid reading was good for the ice.

We arrived at the lake to find a veritable winter carnival in progress. Skaters, cross-country skiers, ice fishermen and snowmobilers were everywhere. We ice racers agglomerated in a small corner of the big lake, our 50 or so vehicles looking like those you'd see at lunch time in any McDonald's parking lot. True to Bill's word, spiffy was out, and sturdy was in.

And instead of the frenetic preliminary activity one associates with racing, the assembled car nuts chatted and exhaled steam in outdoor groups, or sipped coffee in a nearby restaurant. "Not much you can do to prepare for a race like this," said burly Don Smith, a Chicago suburbanite. His BMW was equipped with Goodyear F32 cold-weather tires (F32, get it?), which he deflated a bit to improve traction, but he didn't think it would help much. "This whole thing is more social than competitive," he observed.

The sole exception to the affair's laid-back spirit was Bob Kamholtz, a red-bearded chemical worker from Genoa City, Wis. A couple of hundred ¾-inch bolts protruded from the rear tires of his beat-up '75 Chevy Monza, making it look like something out of "Road Warrior." He said his aim was to hit 75 miles per hour on ice, but he admitted he wasn't sure how he'd take the curves at that speed.

Mike Fernandez, an accountant and the meet's director, showed me the course, a large oval with a small one inside, marked by pylons and measuring about a half-mile. Not to worry about accidents, he declared, echoing Bill and everyone else there. "Nobody gets hurt on ice."

Then he thought a second and recanted. "A couple of years ago a kid drove a snowmobile across our course, got hit by one of our cars and broke a leg," he said. "You gotta watch those snowmobilers. They're crazy."

Entrants were divided into 10 classes based on car type and engine size and placement. Lots of time was spent signing in, lining up cars by class and fiddling with balky timing gear. Three runs for everybody, about 4½ minutes of track time each, consumed more than five hours. Eating and chatting filled the hours, so nobody much minded. Like the man said, it was mostly a social event.

It was a pretty one, too: the snow that covered the lake sent up picturesque plumes behind the hurrying cars. Bob Kamholtz's bolt-tire Monza made the biggest and prettiest plumes, but some of the slowest times. It couldn't handle the tight, inner-circle turn that separated the sheep from the goats all day. And yes, nobody got hurt, although a few snowmobilers tried.

My Citation bounced home seventh in our eight-car class, and 33rd of 67 drivers overall. I don't know how fast I went. Who had time to look at speedometers? But it was fast enough so that I botched some turns and made me a little uncomfortable, which meant, according to a fellow contestant, that I had attained a good first goal for a novice racer.

Neighbor Bill copped a second in his class, adding to his Ivan Lendl-sized trophy collection. "Some fun, huh?" he said. "Not bad," said I. If they lined up parked cars along both sides of the course, it would have been as tough as driving down the street we live on.

● *Feb. 15, 1985*

Notes from Under Water

I.

have spent my life avoiding events with "marathon" in their titles. The idea of going beyond normal levels of human endurance in the name of sport has always struck me as neurotic, not admirable. My picture of a marathon runner, the most prominent member of the species, is of a skinny guy with sore knees and a permanently contorted facial expression. Not only don't I want to be such a person, I don't want to watch him (or even her).

Thus, I was surprised at my reaction when a friend, Nick Farina, suggested last winter that I take part with him in something called the Des Plaines River Canoe Marathon, a 19-mile race down a river that winds lazily through the suburbs west of Chicago. Instead of images of pain and suffering, the vision that leaped to mind was of Burt Reynolds digging down the Chattooga River in the movie "Deliverance." Whatta movie! Whatta scene! One of the great moments in cinema!

While I was musing about Big Burt, Nick fleshed out his description of the affair. It wouldn't be like a marathon run, he said, because we'd be in a boat going with the current, so the water would do much of the work. He noted that the race was set for May 19, when the weather was almost sure to be nice. He said I should think of it as an outing as much as an athletic event.

I pointed out that I'd been in a canoe maybe twice, but Nick was reassuring. Despite following the sedentary occupation of public relations, he's a husky guy who drives a Jeep and looks comfortable in a lumberjack's shirt. His more specific qualifications included the possession of a canoe with all the trimmings. He said he'd done a lot of canoeing and would pilot our vessel from the rear seat. All I'd have to do is sit up front and paddle. I could handle that, couldn't I? "Sure, sure," said Fred-Burt. "Piece of cake."

As race day approached and Nick's resolve remained firm, I felt a need to learn more about what I was getting into. I visited Ralph Frese, who was running the event.

Frese is the sort of man you'd expect to meet in the Wisconsin North Woods, not Chicago. Bearded and Lincolnesque, he owns the Chicagoland Canoe Base on the city's landlocked northwest side. He builds, sells, rents and collects canoes and is an expert on their use and history. He has canoed all over the U.S. and Canada. A few years back he organized reenactments of the river voyages of the explorers LaSalle and Marquette and Joliet, which opened the Midwest to settlement. "The canoe was as important in the history of this country as the covered wagon," he declares.

Frese started the marathon in 1957 as a Boy Scout event. Twenty-five canoes participated in the inaugural. This year, only the first 1,000 boats that entered were accepted.

"It's a race for people who want to race, and a chance to enjoy the river for the rest," Frese said. "I think it's done quite a bit to draw attention to the Des Plaines as a natural resource. Every year we run we see less junk along the river, and more wildlife. It's very encouraging."

Frese said I shouldn't worry about being a novice in the race, because many others would share my status. He said that a "respectable" time for the course was about 3½ hours, but that times probably would be slower this year because lack of spring rain meant a low water level and a slow current.

"Any advice?" I asked.

"If you fall in, don't swallow the water," he replied. "It's cleaner than it was, but not that clean."

Sunday came up sunny and cool—perfect for canoeing. I arrived at the Libertyville, Ill., takeoff point to find scores of people lugging canoes toward the river.

I'd passed over the Des Plaines by car hundreds of times, but Sunday I got my first close look at it. It's the color of chopped liver, but less appetizing. It occurred to me that Frese's warning about the water might have been too mild. I wondered when I'd had my last tetanus shot.

Entrants were grouped officially by age, sex, expertise and canoe type. Contestants' self-classification was simpler: "serious" canoers and "big-cooler" types.

The serious teams—female as well as male—tended to be trim, wore matching T-shirts or tank tops, and had water bottles strapped to their backs and connected to their mouths by tubes. The cooler-carriers brought more substantial refreshments, and stopped frequently along the route to enjoy them.

Nick and I decided to try to give a good account of ourselves, stopping only when necessity dictated it. Our combined age was 89, and we felt obliged to show that middle-aged guys had guts (er, I mean fortitude).

Our determination was tested at the outset when, saddled with an outside post position in shallow water, we flailed the water ineffectually before an amused starting-line throng. By the time we were headed in the right direction (south), the rest of our 10-canoe heat was around the bend.

Nineteen miles is a good leveler, however, and I'm proud to report that we caught and passed some earlier starters. Among them were a lot of big-cooler types, some teen-age girls, two fellows who said they'd eaten Mexican food the night before, and two guys wearing caps that looked like bear heads.

And we, in turn, were passed aplenty. We knew we were in trouble when the occupants of canoes coming up on us chanted "hut" as their signal to change strokes, drill-team style. Some of 'em made wakes as they went by.

Both Nick and I got wet before the race was over. I stepped out to haul us ashore to portage around a dam and wound up in water up to my waist. My video-club membership card is still soggy. Nick got out to push when we were stuck on another dam (now I know why they call them that), and followed the canoe a ways downstream.

We were fine for our first two hours on the river and bravely cheerful through the next. The rest of the way was sheer survival. We crossed the finish line here after four hours, 27 minutes, more than an hour slower than the winner in our aluminum-canoe class. Race officials said our performance was "almost average." I considered that a compliment.

On the negative side of our experience was soreness in every muscle from the waist up. On the positive side were a couple of nice suntans and the ducks, geese and scenery we glimpsed along the way through our sweat.

Every finisher got a handsome patch to commemorate the occasion. I notice now that the buckskin-wearing *voyageur* pictured on it is sitting with his back against his canoe, not paddling it. That guy was no dummy.

• *May 24, 1985*

High Anxiety

MOUNT MASSIVE, COLO.

I have never found compelling the notion that one should attempt to surmount natural obstacles because they are *there*. On the occasions I have tried, I wound up eating or drinking too much, or both, and regretting it. My general rule is that it's better to ignore the implied dare than to court heartburn or its equivalent.

Nonetheless, I find new experiences stimulating, and when Ray Sokolov, who edits the "Leisure & Arts" page, suggested a sports-related one, I took notice. I did so because (1) he's my boss and (2) as this newspaper's sports columnist, I have a certain position to maintain. How would it look if I let a desk-bound editor one-up me on my own turf, even if he did manage his high-school wrestling team?

Ray proposed that we climb a mountain together. He said that he'd climbed a lot of them, and that it was great fun. He once even baked a cake atop Mount Whitney in California. The scenery would be breathtaking, he said, and the mountain air invigorating after a soggy summer at sea level.

I replied that I had spent most of my life around Chicago, which is so flat that you can roll a bowling ball from one end to the other. The tallest peak in Evanston, Ill., where I now reside, is Mount Trashmore, a 60-foot toboggan hill that used to be a garbage dump. I get dizzy looking out of second-story windows.

There are mountains and there are mountains, Ray countered, and the one he had in mind took no technical skill to climb, just good legs. He said I should think of it as a day's hike. Saving the best for last, he revealed the place's name: Mount Massive.

That grabbed me, all right. Whatta dateline for a column! Whatta brag! There being nothing wrong with my legs at the time, I said OK.

When more sober thoughts took over, I figured that a bit of research might be wise, and I phoned the appropriate Colorado officials. Yes, one said, there surely was a Mount Massive in the Sawatch Range near Leadville in the central part of the state. It stands at 14,421 feet, third tallest in the contiguous U.S. behind only Mount Whitney at 14,494, and Mount Elbert in Colorado at 14,433.

Mount Massive wasn't a difficult climb, the fellow confirmed, pointing out that it's a stone's throw from Mount Elbert if you have a good arm, and that several hardy mountaineers had climbed both peaks in the same day.

For further information I called the U.S. Forest Service in Leadville and spoke to forester Jamie Lind. He said there was little danger in a novice like me attempting Mount Massive if I followed a few simple rules. The first was that I not go alone because even an experienced climber can get into trouble if he sprains an ankle. The second was to try to reach the peak and start down by noon because afternoon thunderstorms sometimes well up quickly, and being inside one isn't one of life's great treats.

A third rule was to drink plenty of liquids and bring warm clothes to guard against hypothermia, a drop in body temperature caused by a sudden chill on high. Mr. Lind said I'd know if my partner was becoming hypothermic because his conversation would stop making sense. "Fine," I thought, "but with Ray, how could I tell?"

Mr. Lind said it was a good idea to spend as much time as possible in the mountains before climbing in order to get used to the thin air. Unfortunately, our schedules didn't permit a long acclimation (busy, busy), but we weren't about to let a small thing like that stand in our way.

I arrived in Denver Tuesday evening last week and spent the night breathing the mile-high air. I met Ray at the airport Wednesday and we drove to Aspen, Colo., where we inhaled and exhaled at about 8,000 feet while quaffing some of the complex carbohydrates that climbing experts recommend.

On Thursday, Ray thought that a hike up to Buckskin Pass, at 12,462 feet, would be a good warm-up for our assault on Mount Massive the next day. Getting started as early as a windy, eco-nut bus driver would permit (he stopped our trip to the 9,500-foot trail head every few minutes to deliver paeans to the panorama), we reached the pass over a narrow, rocky trail in just over three hours.

The view from the top was, indeed, breathtaking, but even more so was the effect of the altitude. Toward the end, we two lowlanders were stopping every 50 feet or so to catch our breath, which, like us, came in short pants. Among the other revelations of my first taste of mountain hiking were that walking on rocks was tough on the feet and that going down a steep grade was more painful than going up.

Ray, experienced as he was, learned that his newish boots didn't fit quite right in back. He had two nasty blisters to show for his day.

A combination of adhesive tape and moleskin calmed Ray's dogs, and a night's rest soothed my mooing calves. The next day we were up and at 'em early to tackle the Big One.

It turned out that Mount Massive was a much different climb than Buckskin Pass. The latter was a steep but mostly steady ascent. The Mount Massive trail meandered for a couple of miles while gaining less than 1,000 feet. Then it shot upward from about 11,000 feet to the 14,421-foot peak in roughly the same distance.

Where the Buckskin Pass trail was visible and much traveled, the one up Mount Massive was neither. Using a 1978 guidebook map and following man-placed piles of stones called cairns, we got to within 1,000 feet of the top. Then the cairns and trail disappeared.

We followed what looked like the most direct route to the summit from there, but wound up about 150 feet short, with craggy boulders above, left and right. Ray said that was what the Matterhorn looked like all the way. I wasn't schooled for such climbing and, huffing and puffing in 14,000-foot air, neither of us was up for further progress. Newspapermen aren't completely crazy. Having climbed hard but not smart, we declared a moral victory and called it quits.

In our defense, we weren't the only ones to go astray on Mount Massive that day. We encountered two other pairs of climbers, both of which had lost their way. A young man and woman said they took a wrong turn and wound up at a lake well east of the peak. A couple of men with fishing gear were wandering in search of the lake the other two had blundered near.

Forester Lind said the lack of onsite path marking reflects Forest Service philosophy. "We want to keep the big, wilderness mountains primitive," he said. I suggest, then, that routes be marked in caveman language.

Coming soon: The Descent! Or, Where's the Railing?! Or, Me and Scree.

● *Aug. 30, 1985*

Something's Fishy in Eagle River

EAGLE RIVER, WIS.

I have vacationed in this northern Wisconsin resort area for a dozen summers, man and boy. It's a lovely place, covered with pungent pine trees and sparkling lakes. Also, some of the restaurants are first rate.

I had, however, always looked askance at the region's claim to be the nation's muskie-fishing capital. In all my summers here, I had never seen a real, live muskellunge, the square name of the predator that draws sportsmen from far and wide.

Sure, I'd seen those huge, waxy, mounted fish labeled as muskies, their backs arched orgasmically in trophy pose. Every hardware and bait store hereabouts has one. But my lack of firsthand confirmation of the beast's existence led me to suspect that there's a factory somewhere turning them out to entice the tourists.

My contacts with the natives served only to heighten my suspicions. Whenever I chose to fish was the wrong time to catch a muskie; wherever I chose to fish was the wrong place. The times and places they recommended were, invariably, inconvenient and unpleasant. I mean, when you're on vacation, who wants to get up at 4 a.m. and sit in a boat on a weedy lake, surrounded by biting insects?

My curiosity about the fish finally led me down the classic American path: I sought out an expert. I asked around, and when more than one person mentioned Tony Rizzo, I phoned him.

Rizzo told me that he certainly was an expert on muskies. He said he'd caught about 1,300 of them in his 26 years as a fishing guide here. He'd even written a book titled "Secrets of a Muskie Guide." He sent me a copy. The photo on the cover showed a dark-haired, smiling Rizzo, T-shirt peeking from his open collar, hoisting a thick-bodied, long-nosed fish that looked about 5 feet long. That was a muskie, I presumed.

Impressed, I phoned him again to talk business. He said his daily fee was $140. I blanched but pressed on. Would he guarantee that we'd catch a muskie? He replied in the negative. "I'll guarantee walleye, but not muskie. If they were easy to catch, you wouldn't pay a guide $140 to help you find one, would you?" he said with unassailable logic.

We discussed time of year. He said any time would be good but midsummer, when most people vacation; fish generally don't bite well then. (It figures.) We settled on a day in the first week of May, partly because he had some free time then and partly because I wouldn't have to get up at dawn to catch fish. "It's usually so cold up here in May that the fish sleep late, too," he quipped.

And so on May 7 we met at Rizzo's Silver Muskie Resort on Star Lake. It's a Spartan, eight-cabin affair that his wife and son run while he takes people fishing.

One glance at Rizzo and I revised my estimate of the size of the fish on his book's cover. He stands closer to 5 feet tall than 6 feet, so the fish must have been about 4 feet long. That's still a heckuva fish, though.

One sentence from Rizzo revealed his Chicago nativity. He spent his early summers here fishing and the rest of his time in Chicago wishing he were fishing. He worked as a printer in a bottle-cap factory until he saved enough money to buy his resort in 1960. He says that life in the woods isn't all fish fries and Old Milwaukee. Winters are long, cold and dreary. Nonetheless, it beats being a printer in a bottle-cap factory.

Rizzo latched his handsome Lakeland fishing boat to his station wagon and we set out for nearby Lake Irving. It's a shallow lake that warms quickly and thus yields fish readily in early spring. On the way, he expounded on the muskie's allure.

"It's a good-eating fish, but walleyes taste better," he said. "It's a fighter, but pound for pound the smallmouth bass fights harder. The thing about the muskie is that it's so hard to catch.

"First off, there aren't that many of them. Second, they've got mouths like leather, so they're hard to hook. But mostly, it's that they're so smart it's uncanny. A muskie'll swim all around your boat and never strike. Or he'll hit your lure and let go. Or he'll take the bait, let you reel him in, and snap your line at the last second.

"With most fish, you measure your day by how many you catch. With the muskie, it's by how many you see. You'll see a dozen for every one you'll land. But believe me: Seeing a 50-inch muskie in the water is a thrill."

Rizzo said that this day we would cast with live minnows and seek muskie and walleye together. Muskies aren't ready for bigger bait this early in the year, he noted. He said he doesn't use artificial lures until the water temperature tops 56 degrees, and the large muskie plugs until summer. "A lot of fishermen lose out by using big plugs too soon," he opined.

We had cast for about an hour on the cool, breezy morning, with two walleyes to show for our efforts, when Rizzo hooked something that bent his rod double. He handed it to me, saying "Here's your muskie."

I took the rod and pulled. The fish pulled back. "Back reel!" Rizzo commanded. I responded with such alacrity that I snarled the line. Fortunately, the fish was patient until we got it unsnarled.

I performed better thereafter. When the fish pulled, I back reeled slowly. When he stopped, I reeled in. We reached a standoff for a minute or so just out of netting range. Then he relented a bit, and we had him.

The fish measured 32 inches, the Wisconsin legal limit. It weighed about six pounds. It looked like the one on Rizzo's book cover, only smaller. It was a muskie, all right. We both smiled.

Tony said that he preferred to keep the muskie population up by throwing back the ones he catches. I agreed, and back it went.

That was it for muskies for the day. We caught 16 or 17 walleyes, keeping the biggest 10. They averaged about 16 inches long.

The sun came out at noon, warm enough to redden my forehead and hands. We saw an eagle circle the lake and, later, deers feeding along the roads. The filleted walleyes cooked up great. It would have been a wonderful day even without the muskie.

● *May 23, 1986*

ODD BALLS

Part 11

Long Day at the Indy 500

INDIANAPOLIS

et me begin this account of my visit to the Indianapolis 500-mile auto race last weekend by saying that I have never understood what people see in auto racing.

Watching a bunch of guys drive cars around a track at dangerously high speeds might have a certain morbid fascination, but as far as I'm concerned it ain't sport.

Where is the physical grace one associates with athletics? Where is the drama of men (or women) testing their inner resources?

Where, indeed, are the "athletes" themselves? All the spectators at Indy see of the drivers while the race is on are the tops of their helmets, and when they do emerge from their machines they are so plastered with advertisements for auto products that only the seats of their pants are unobscured.

I've always doubted whether auto racers could be called athletes in any real sense, and two years ago a study came out that supported me in this. Glenn Dawson, then director of physiological studies at the University of North Carolina at Charlotte, tested 10 professional race-car drivers for various physical aptitudes and compared the results with those taken from a cross-section of the male population of the same general age (about 35). He found that the drivers were above average in grip strength and abdominal endurance (?), below average in cardiovascular fitness and average in other respects.

Prof. Dawson's tests disproved the widely held notion that race-car drivers have quicker reactions than other people; in a test that required them to press a button when a light came on, they were a trifle slower than the average-man group.

Auto racing certainly takes courage and a steady hand, but so does high-rise window washing, and they don't give prizes for that. About the best thing I can say for it is that it keeps a few speed de-mons off the roads once in awhile, making them a wee bit safer for you and me. As for the spectators, I guess they've had no place else to go since cock-fighting became illegal.

In light of these views it might reasonably be asked what I was doing at the Speedway last Sunday. The answer is that, for better or worse, the Indy 500 is acclaimed as one of the four premier annual sporting events in the U.S., the other three being the Kentucky Derby, the pro football Super Bowl and the baseball World Series. It's an Event with a capital E, and one must attend it at least once in his life to be considered a true sports fan. Heaven forbid that anyone should have cause to doubt my credentials in that department.

As an Event, the race measured up very nicely, I thought. An es-timated 350,000 people showed up, same as every year, and they put on quite a show.

Standard dress for males was shorts and sneakers; standard dress for females was shorts and some kind of skimpy top. There was lots and lots of beer, quite a bit of Southern Comfort and plenty of pot. I'd venture to say that between a quarter and a third of the crowd only peeked at the race, spending their time sunbathing, drinking or wandering around the huge infield. If you'd have asked them who Johnny Rutherford was, they would have guessed that he played bass guitar for The Who.

Most of the people who actually came to see the cars go round and round saw only a fraction of it: the track is so big (2½ miles around) that very few seats provide a complete view. I sat on the first turn and saw maybe 20% of the proceedings. The rest of the time, I had to rely on the gabby public-address announcer to tell me what was happening, a not-too-satisfying arrangement.

From a sporting standpoint, the Indy 500 provides little direct competition between drivers. Cars pass one another infrequently; most position-changing takes place while cars are off the track for pit stops.

There were quite a few slow-downs for wounded cars—13 by official count. The pace car comes out and leads the field around, and no one is supposed to pass. That puts a definite damper on the action. It seemed to me that the pace car spent more time on the track Sunday than some of the entrants.

Otherwise, the Indy 500 is noisy from the sound of the cars' engines, and smelly from exhaust fumes. Add the heat and the event's length (3½ hours on Sunday), and you have a long, long day, punctuated only by occasional crashes. I dozed a couple times.

Afterwards the traffic outside was monumentally jammed, thanks in part to local police whose methods of traffic control were eccentric, to say the least. Service in the restaurants of Indianapolis was the slowest I've ever seen. A motel room cost $228 for a three-day package, the only kind of accommodations that were widely available. That's about twice regular rates.

What did I think of the Indy 500?

The judge should have given them a tougher sentence.

● *May 30, 1980*

Cheers and Boos

I
•

t happens almost every weekend during football season: I'll be sitting in front of the television set watching a game and one of my children will join me and ask who I'm rooting for.

I reply that unless a Chicago team is playing (I was born and raised in Chicago, and live near there now) I merely root for a good game. Sometimes I can't resist adding a testy lecture on the virtues of enjoying sports for their own sake. I especially like paraphrasing Grantland Rice to the effect that it isn't who wins or loses that counts, but how the game is played.

I'm testy on the subject partly because it's a sensitive one around my house. I realize that television has made young fans far more cosmopolitan than those of my own, pre-TV, formative years, but I still dislike the easy attachments to teams that my kids form, and even more their propensity for adopting winning teams as their favorites for the day, week or season. I interpret this as a flaw in their characters, and I am trying to correct it.

For home consumption, my position on sports loyalties is simple: You root for the teams that represent the city where you grew up; otherwise, neutrality is best. In other words, you play the cards you are dealt. I think that has the clear, solid ring of a precept with value beyond sports.

I must confess, though, that my irritation stems

partly from guilt, and that my righteous prose oversimplifes my true feelings. When two non-Chicago teams play, I usually do pick a team to root for, however faintly.

I don't choose the team I think is most likely to win; that would be reprehensible by my lights. In the interest of honest and responsible parenthood, I have subjected my beliefs on the matter to intense scrutiny, and I have compiled a list of criteria for transient rooting I consider valid.

—I root against teams that represent so-called Sunbelt cities and for teams from cities that are run down and depressed. The folks out there in the West and South have sunshine, prosperity and lots of beautiful women; that should be enough for anyone. People from towns like Buffalo, Cleveland, Baltimore and Detroit need something to perk them up.

I have one exception to that rule: I root for teams from Oakland, Calif. I've never been there, but I understand it's a workingman's town, a kind of Detroit of the West Coast. Also, it's next to and a rival of San Francisco, my least-favorite sports town. San Franciscans are so busy patting themselves on the back for living where they do that they have little energy left for applauding teams that bear their city's name.

—I root against teams that are led by maniacs, and for teams whose coaches seem homely and reasonable. For some reason, manic coaches seem to show up most in colleges; Bobby Knight of Indiana and Bo Schembechler of Michigan top my current list. I was sorry when Woody Hayes and George Allen were fired, because I enjoyed rooting against them.

I like the New Orleans Saints because I like Bum Phillips's crew cut, cowboy hats and post-game witticisms. I like the Cleveland Browns because of Sam Rutigliano. I read the other day where he told his players that he hated practice as much as they did, but that they all might as well stick it out because they're getting paid for it.

—I root for teams that feature speed, deception and finesse, and against teams I perceive as plodding and brutish. Hurray for the Dallas Cowboys and San Diego Chargers, boo for the Denver Broncos and Los Angeles Rams.

I had one exception to that rule: I liked the Detroit Lions teams of the early 1960s that were in trouble only when they had the ball. Alex Karras, Joe Schmidt, Yale Lary and that gang gave defense a pizazz it hasn't had since. Also, their main rivals were the Green Bay

Packers, whom I didn't like because of Vince Lombardi. (I like them now; see reason number one.)

—I root against teams that win too many championships; say, more than one every half-dozen years. We in Chicago are satisfied (indeed pleased) with one championship a decade in *any* sport; why should others have it better? If the New York Yankees never win another pennant it'll be too soon for me.

—Finally, I root against teams whose fans bother me. There used to be a fellow from Boston in my office, and he never stopped talking about that city's teams. "How about those Celtics?" he'd say, or "The Bruins are looking great again this year." When he talked about the "Sox" he meant the Red Sox, not the White Sox, for heaven's sake! I rooted against Boston because I hoped it would shut him up. Now that we don't work together anymore we get along fine and I'm neutral again about Boston teams.

So there it is, kids, your pop's philosophy of rooting in all its complexity. You're free to frame your own, of course, and it needn't agree with mine. But if it doesn't, keep out of my way on game days.

● Oct. 6, 1981

Sports Talk with a Non-Fan

I never have trouble making conversation with people I meet on airplanes. All I have to do is tell them that I write about sports and they open right up. Sports are a great bond among men (and some women, too), and even the dumbest guys have something to say on the subject.

Thus, I was taken aback some weeks ago when, on a Miami-to-Chicago flight, I found myself sitting next to someone who merely grimaced when I revealed my occupation. "It has always been my bad luck to be thrown in with sports fans," he said. "I can say without hesitation that I am not one."

The gentleman introduced himself as Robert Anderson, an agronomist on the faculty of the University of Minnesota. A few minutes of general chitchat revealed him to be an intelligent fellow, and a good-humored one to boot. After we got to know one another a bit, I expressed surprise that he, a middle-aged American, could expect to avoid sports. He conceded he had had some contact with them over the years.

"I've gone to two baseball games in my life—my first and my last," he quipped. "It was at Wrigley Field in Chicago, and I remember that the weather was chilly. Someone sang the national anthem nicely, but it was downhill from there. If it had been up to me, I'd have left after the third inning.

"I went to one football game in Minneapolis. Minnesota played the University of Nebraska, where I went to school. The only thing that kept it from being a total loss for me was that a dog got loose and ran around on the field.

"I took a group of Cub Scouts to see a hockey game once, but I didn't see much of it, because the kids kept racing off for hot dogs or to go to the washroom. I spent the whole evening worrying that the game would end and I'd have fewer kids than I brought."

Mr. Anderson said that he had made several stabs at informing himself about sports by reading newspaper sports pages, but the experiences left him feeling like a man from Mars. "Sports pages are written for the cognoscenti," he said. "You can read whole, long stories that never mention what sport they're about." (I've checked this out, and he's right!)

He said that he's not totally oblivious, and as a resident of Minneapolis knows who the Twins and Vikings are, but other sports-page terms still throw him. "What is the Stanley Cup?" he asked. "What is the USFL?" (What, indeed?)

"It's not because of lack of exposure that I'm not a fan; goodness knows, I've had my chances," he said. "As a scientist, I can only conclude that my aversion to sports is congenital. There must be something in me that doesn't allow them to 'take.'"

(I have long suspected the same thing. My 12-year old daughter, Jessie, has grown up in a household of avid fans, and has been dragged to numerous athletic contests. Yet every time the rest of us settle in for an evening of ballgame-watching on television, she wails "Sports again?!" and stomps away. I guess I'm going to have to get her a set of her own one of these days.)

Nonetheless, my flying companion noted that being a non-fan hasn't spared him the company of sports nuts. To the contrary, "at meetings and such, they seem to sense my presence and seek me out," he said. "For a long time I was faced with the choice of being rude and telling them to buzz off, or standing there and being bored."

Then, he went on, he discovered how to avoid both of those unpleasant alternatives. "I found out that if I could throw out one little line about sports—anything at all—they'd grab it and jabber on, ad infinitum. I could think my own thoughts while they were talking, and slip away gracefully after they were done."

Mr. Anderson's line was "the Twins haven't been the same since they traded Vic Power." He said it worked great for quite a while, but recently it has been getting him some funny looks. I said that was no wonder, because the Twins traded Power in 1964, and the memory of him might have dimmed for some.

He said he didn't realize that, and asked me if I could suggest another one. I told him I thought "Cal Griffith should sell the team" might do. He thought that seemed too obvious ("you have to show *some* sophistication"), but he said he'd think it over.

I've thought it over, too, and I've decided that a sports column ought to be of use to everyone once in a while. So here are a few get-away lines for you non-fans out there:

"The Phillies blew the pennant when they traded away Reed and Hernandez."

"Bob Horner would be a heckuva lot better hitter if he'd lose 20 pounds."

"If the refs called all the fouls they should on Moses Malone, he'd never finish a game."

"Joe Namath was a better quarterback than any of those guys who are around now."

"The Vikings will never be the same without Bud Grant."

Oh yes. The sports involved in the above statements are baseball, baseball, basketball, football and football. And the Twins are a baseball team.

● *May 11, 1984*

Real Tennis

H•enry VIII, the Italian painter Caravaggio and I have something in common. We all played court tennis.

Actually, that's a bit of an overstatement. I didn't really play court tennis, I just batted the ball around some. Still, I got a taste of the game, which is more than most people can say.

I almost didn't get my nibble. When I phoned a club that has a court and expressed an interest in trying the ancient and intricate game in order to write about it, I was put in touch with Clarence C. Pell. He's a steady-eyed, straight-backed gentleman of 73 years who is a many-time national champion and authority on court tennis and other racket sports. He wasn't keen on my idea.

"We're not looking for new players. Our courts are full now, and we wouldn't like to see happen to our game what happened to lawn tennis," he said.

"What's that?" I asked.

"People like that McEnroe playing it. All the young players mimic him. I think it's terrible.

"They also stole our name, you know," Mr. Pell continued.

"Who?"

"The so-called tennis people. Tennis means court tennis. The other game is lawn tennis. It was invented to give the ladies something to do because it was thought

246

that tennis was too difficult for them. We're quiet little people, and we didn't fuss over the theft, but it was very fresh of them."

He promised to give my request some thought, though, and finally agreed on the condition that I wouldn't name the club where we would play or the city in which it is situated. "Every time the club gets in the newspapers it comes to grief," he said.

I told him it was customary for papers to begin stories with "datelines" indicating where they were written. "Just put down 'Somewhere in the East,'" he suggested. "All the courts in this country are there."

There being only nine such courts, my options were limited, so I said OK. I've played tennis, squash, handball, racquetball, badminton and even cestaball, and I wanted to try the sport that spawned them.

And court tennis, called "real tennis" in England, "royal tennis" in plebian Australia and *jeu de paume*, or handball, in France, where it was born, has one heckuva history.

Its roots go back to the 11th century, where it was a recreation in monastery cloisters. The monks went so wild over the game that their bishops soon were firing off edicts against it, but to little effect.

It was played first with the hand, then with a glove and, finally, with a racket. By the 16th century it had spread over Europe, and its popularity exceeded that of any game until recent times, with between 1,100 and 1,800 courts in Paris alone.

Court tennis had the first corps of sports professionals and, yes, the first pros' unions, recognized by King Charles IX of France in 1571.

French and English kings were among the earliest tennis nuts. Francis I of France was supposed to have had a court on his battleship, if you can believe it. Henry VIII of England built one in his Hampton Court palace that's still in use, but his records show gambling losses that indicate he was a poor player (too chubby, probably).

As Manuela Hoelterhoff informed us on these pages recently, Mr. Caravaggio of Renaissance fame took the game so seriously he killed a fellow player during an argument.

Court tennis began to fade around the early 17th century, and has continued to do so since. Today there are only 30 courts in the world: 15 in England, nine in the U.S. (all private) and three each in France and Australia. There are about 7,000 players world-wide,

1,500 of them Americans. The reigning world's champ is Chris Ronaldson of England, who plays out of old Henry's club at Hampton Court.

One reason the game isn't more popular is money. The court at Newport, R.I., on the grounds of the National Tennis Club, cost some $400,000 just to restore a few years ago. Another is that it's tough to play, although Mr. Pell declares that it's a "scurrilous rumor" that court tennis takes two years to learn and a CPA to referee.

At any rate, the court on which court tennis is played is the busiest in sports. It's a finished-concrete room about 96 feet long and 30 feet wide divided in half by a net that droops from five feet at the end posts to three feet in the center.

You can play shots off the side and back walls as in squash, but those walls aren't flat or featureless. A sloping roof, called the penthouse, runs around three sides, there are netted openings in the rear walls and one side wall, and a buttress, called the tambour, protrudes into the service-receiving, or "hazard," side. When a player hits a ball into one of the wall-openings on the other side of the net, or off the tambour, he has a winner.

Rackets are made of wood with gut strings. Their smallish heads are cocked so they can reach into corners better. Balls are heavier and a bit smaller than tennis balls. They're made by hand with wound-tape centers and stitched-felt covers, and they tend to be lumpy. Proposals to make them uniformly round have been squelched as untennislike.

Service is always from the service side of the court, and the serve must be hit off the penthouse roof into an area on the floor of the hazard side. Play and scoring are similar to lawn tennis with one big exception: the "chase."

A chase is a point held in suspension. It occurs when one player hits what in tennis would be a passing shot. The spot where the ball touches the floor the *second* time is noted. The point is later replayed, and the player who lost the original point can recapture it by hitting a winner closer to his opponent's rear wall than the first winning shot. The chase, one commentator noted, "makes what otherwise would be a stupid display of hard hitting a game of skill and fine judgment." It's harder to grasp in theory than in practice.

Mr. Pell and I took the court for the promised demonstration. Trying to give a good account of myself, I removed jacket and tie and laced on my sneakers. He merely stripped off his suit coat, leaving tie and street shoes in place.

I learned a basic, underhand serve quickly, but rallies were something else. The ball, skidding low off the slick concrete floor, was hard to pick up, and I hit a lot of shots off the racket frame. When Mr. Pell wanted to, he dropped his service so neatly into a corner that I couldn't swing at it, much less strike it. The erratically bouncing balls complicated everything.

Mr. Pell told me not to feel too bad. He said Martina Navratilova tried the game at Newport last summer, and didn't do much better.

"She'd be good if she practiced, of course, but I think we opened her eyes to our game's complexity," he noted drily. "It's to lawn tennis what chess is to tick-tack-toe."

● *Apr. 5, 1985*

Steroids and
Mr. Universe

ORANGE, CONN.

Y
.

ou know the story about the 96-pound weakling who muscled up and punched out the local beach bully, don't you? Well, here's a twist on that tale.

Ten years ago, Ken Passariello, the holder of college degrees in English and philosophy, was a high school English teacher. He stood 5 feet 5 inches tall and weighed 260 pounds. "You could have rolled me from one end of town to the other," he recalls.

Fed up, he read up on nutrition, dieted, and lost 80 pounds in six months. He then took to body building to complete the transformation. Four years later, in 1980, he won the Mr. America title in the lightweight (154-pound) division. He repeated that triumph in 1981, and captured the Mr. Universe crown besides.

Passariello now competes as a professional body builder, and he and his wife, Georgianna, own and run a spiffy gym with the poetic name of Passariello's Quest in this suburb of New Haven. He also has launched a promising pro wrestling career under the billing of "The Prince of Pain." Dressed in studded collar, belt and wristbands and S&M harness, he plays the bouncing bad guy in arenas around the East.

The wrestling, he says somewhat apologetically, is for fun and money. The body building is serious. "It's a sport like any other, and a lot harder than most," he avers. I was not about to argue the point with a man who has a 54-inch chest and thighs that measure 29 inches each, the same as his waist.

However you look at him, the blond Passariello is a remarkable specimen, and he makes no bones about what made him one. "I owe it all to clean living, hard work and steroids," says he.

Not only does Passariello 'fess up to using anabolic steroids, the substances that simulate the actions of male hormones and are big-time sports' worst-kept secret, but he consults with other athletes on their use, as well as on diet and exercise. He says his client list has numbered several hundred over the past few years.

"It's no big, formal business, and I never went out looking for customers," he says quietly. "I don't advertise, and I don't even have business cards. I guess it got started because I'm one of the few athletes who really has looked into steroids and is willing to talk about them. I'm just that kind of person. When somebody asks me how I train, I'm not about to give them a lot of B.S. about eating tuna fish."

Passariello believes that he is filling a "crying need" for someone to give athletes factual information about the drugs that so many of them use surreptitiously. He felt that need himself when he first investigated using them a half-dozen years ago.

"I was just starting to compete in body building on the national level, and I knew I had to use steroids to have a chance. I knew that every top body builder used them, no matter that they said in public," he says. "I went to my physician. He said 'Don't use them, and don't ask any questions.' That's the standard medical answer, and it's what the guys in suits who run sports tell you. They're the daddies and the athletes are the kids. We're supposed to do what we're told.

"The trouble is that steroids work, and every athlete knows it. They give you bigger, stronger muscles, increase your endurance, and help you recover from injuries faster. Also, you can get them about anywhere. Almost every gym has a pusher. A lot of them will take you into a back room and shoot you up with about five times what you need. At a nice profit to them, of course."

Passariello says he went that route for a while, but started experiencing the "weird" side effects that go with drug overuse. He did some reading on the subject, and then some research, and found a physician who would monitor his intake. Eventually, he and Stanley Morey, a fellow body builder with a Ph.D. in chemistry, wrote a 68-

page booklet on the drugs. They offer it for sale through ads in body-building magazines.

The booklet is no pro-steroids tome. It describes how the drugs work and what their negative effects are, among them possible liver damage, prostate problems, reduced sexual drive, sterility, acne and depression during withdrawal. It makes the point that everybody reacts differently to the substances, so side effects can't be predicted with certainty. It states that steroids "aren't the answer to success" in sports and are no substitute for traditional athletic values.

Passariello says he tells his fellow athletes much the same things when they ask him for advice. "I don't tell people to use steroids," he declares. "I'm not a doctor so I can't write prescriptions, and I don't sell the stuff. I just tell guys what I know, including the bad things, and let them draw their own conclusions. Athletes being what they are, most of them will run a risk if they think it will help them win. That includes me. Like it or not, that's sports in America today.

"Who uses steroids?" he echoes. "Every top male body builder, and a lot of the women ones. Every top weight lifter. Most Olympic-level weight throwers. About 80% of the linemen in the National Football League. I think the last is a good guess, because I've consulted with about 100 of them."

Both the National Football League and the National Collegiate Athletic Association have rules against the use of steroids to improve performance. Neither organization has a drug-testing program, and neither professes to know how many football players use the drugs.

"That's a laugh," says Passariello. "I can look at a guy and tell whether he's a user. There's puffiness in his face, extra fluid in his joints and sometimes swelling around his breasts. Every coach knows that, too. They make locker-room speeches against steroids, and look the other way while their strength coaches pass them around.

"I'd say use is way up among college football players. You see kids going from 210 pounds in high school to a strong 260 in college. They can't do that just by drinking milkshakes.

"Most of the young pros who come to me tell me they took steroids in college without any decent guidance. Letting them do that is a crime in my book. Some of the older guys in the NFL didn't come up that way, but now they're worried about losing their positions to the younger players. They ask me what to do. I tell 'em, 'it's up to you, brother.' That's what I tell 'em all. They're adults. What more can I say?"

● *May 10, 1985*

No Action, Please . . . We're British

LONDON

I
•

first visited England a dozen years ago, and one of my main memories of the trip was picking up a British newspaper, reading a long story on the sports page, and not understanding a word of it. Even the identity of the sport was obscure.

I later learned that the game was cricket, which has a vocabulary all its own. This is mostly because British sportswriters have had much longer to hone their cliches than we Yanks. Reading about cricket now is what reading about baseball will be like in 100 or so years.

Here's a brief sample of what I mean, from last Monday's Times: "Gilbert had Gladwin held at long leg from a hook; Pritchard was caught behind against a lifting ball; and Lilly was leg before to one that kept low. In the first over bowled by Matthews, Gooch played a forcing stroke off his legs and was well caught, low down at short midwicket by Hilditch."

The experience left me with two resolves: First, never to write a sports story without mentioning the sport, and, second, to see a cricket match. Anything that obscure must be interesting.

Summer is cricket season in England, so witnessing a match during my present trip was high on my agenda. Just where cricket ranks in the hearts of Englishmen was brought home to me on my first evening here, when I attended a function linked to the Wimbledon tennis tournament. I was introduced to a British tennis promoter, and was having a hard time making chitchat with him about the sport that provided his livelihood, until I told him I hoped to catch some cricket.

"Ah—there's the sport! The ultimate civilized game!" he exclaimed. "In football [soccer to us] the players generally behave well but the fans carry on. In tennis, the fans behave but the players fuss. In cricket, *everyone* is gentlemanly."

But cricket's typical Britishness goes beyond an upper-class emphasis on manners. Like many sports, it was invented here, and the British don't play it all that well any more. The recognized champs are the West Indians, who gave the English an unprecedented five-matches-to-none trouncing in a Test series last year. The Australians now are here for another such international all-star game, and while the Test is deadlocked at one win each, English confidence isn't overwhelming.

Like most things British, cricket matches take awhile. Countries play for five days, and county matches—the staple of English cricket—last for three. In recent years, one-day cricket has taken hold, but rarely for important events. "Can't develop any decent strategy in just a day." I was told.

Furthermore, as often as not, matches end in draws. We Americans find standoffs intolerable and invent tie-breakers and shoot-outs to eliminate them. The British merely shrug and point out that life often is inconclusive.

Cricket is played on a large lawn that's more or less round. Most of the action takes place on the "pitch," a rectangle 66 feet long in the center of the field. At each end of the pitch is a wicket, three 28-inch high sticks with a bridge, or "bail," across the top. There are 11 players to a side. A team bats until 10 outs, or wickets, have been recorded against it. Then the other team bats. One turn at bat for both teams equals an inning, as in baseball. Two innings (not nine, thank goodness) make a game. If the trailing team can't complete its innings, the match is a draw.

The main actors are the pitchers, called "bowlers," and the batsmen. Batsmen take the field two at a time, one guarding each wicket. Most wear protective leg and face guards.

Batsmen wielding paddle-shaped bats attempt to score runs by hitting the ball between or over the fielders in any direction (there are no foul balls) and crossing to the opposite wicket without being caught. Each cross is worth a run. If their hit clears the boundary of the field on the ground, their team gets four runs. If they clear it on the fly, it's worth six. That's exciting, but it rarely happens.

The bowler takes a running start and tries to retire the batter by hurling the ball past him on a bounce, knocking the bail off the wicket behind him. A batter also is out if his hit is caught on the fly, if a fielder knocks off a bail while he's running, or if the umpire rules that he blocked a pitch with his body that would otherwise have hit a wicket. The game is a lot more complicated, but that's the general idea.

A batter's turn lasts as long as he protects his wicket. He won't run unless he's reasonably sure he can score. That's what makes games so long. Most matches start at 11 a.m. and run until 6:30 p.m. or later, with breaks for lunch and tea, of course.

The match I saw on Wednesday took place at Lord's, home ground of the Marylebone Cricket Club, which codified cricket's rules about 200 years ago. The club's ancient brick building sits at one end of the grounds and commands the best seats. It's for men only, and nobody gets in without tie and jacket.

The contestants in the county match were Middlesex and Nottinghamshire. The good news was that Middlesex was in first place in the league. The bad news was that four of its best players were off playing for England against the Aussies. Oh well, can't have everything.

The day got off to a rousing start. Barlow, Middlesex's leadoff man, slapped the ball to and fro and was approaching an individual 100 runs before lunch, a signal achievement. Alas, at 97 his tipped shot was caught by the wicketkeeper, cricket's version of a baseball catcher, and he was out. Run production slackened after that, although my press-box colleagues were divided on whether good bowling or poor batsmanship was the primary cause. One fellow stayed put for 20 or so hits before risking a dash for the opposite wicket and a run. The crowd cheered derisively. His effort was too slow even for cricket.

About the best thing that happened in the afternoon is that I learned a cricket joke. To get it, you need to know that a "maiden" in cricket is when a bowler completes his turn of six pitches, or "over," without surrendering a run.

Joke: "Cricket is the only place where a fellow can bowl a maiden over and remain a gentleman." Ho ho ho.

Middlesex tallied 246 runs before going out at 5:35 p.m. Notts posted 66 in only one wicket by quitting time, and its prospects for the match looked good. It would have to proceed without me, however. If nothing else, cricket made me appreciate the hours for baseball writing.

- *July 12, 1985*

Push-Up King

I
•

t is pleasant to report that, at a time when the words "exercise" and "machine" go together like "golf" and "cart," the humble push-up is making a comeback.

There always has been a lot to say for the push-up. It's free. Anyone can do it anywhere, any time, and in whatever garb one happens to be wearing. It isn't boring, and it's easy on the knees.

Moreover, the push-up has been acclaimed as the Best Single Exercise. While its basic, up-and-down arm pump directly benefits your arms, chest and shoulders, other muscle groups, including the abominables (oops, abdominals), thighs, hip flexors, gluteals and extensors (they're in your back, or should be) are working to keep the rest of you rigid. Physiologists call the latter phenomenon "muscle co-contraction." Aren't you glad you know that?

The fellow who has given the push-up its biggest boost of late is Herschel Walker. He was quite a running back at the University of Georgia before he ran away to join a carnival. In 1982 he won the Heisman Trophy as the nation's best college football player.

Walker stands 6-foot-1 and weighs 222 pounds. His physique suggests a pile of smooth rocks, artfully arranged. In his just-published book, *Herschel Walker's Basic Training*, he reveals that he never pumped iron or used workout machines until very recently, and then only a bit. His main fitness formula remains the same as when he was a farm boy in Johnson County, Ga.: Push-ups, sit-ups and sprints. When somebody gets in Ol' Herschel's way on a football field, he whups 'im country-style.

Nowhere, however, is the cult of the push-up stronger than here in Buffalo. This city on the shore of Lake Erie had been best known heretofore for its winter weather, which comes in several shades of gray, and for being the one-time home of O.J. Simpson. Now it bids fair to become the world's push-up capital.

That reputation stems largely from the labors of Jeff Warrick, a 23-year-old high-school dropout. Last June, taking only brief rests, he reeled off a mind-boggling 24,300 push-ups in just under 15 hours at a local YMCA. The people in England who put out the Guinness Book of World Records accepted the mark for inclusion in their 1986 edition.

Things start getting a bit complicated here. Some who witnessed Warrick's feat raised questions about his style; many of his push-ups weren't "regulation," they contended. A particular objector was Brian Perry, a 38-year-old Buffalo veterinarian, fitness buff and aspirant to the push-ups crown. "Warrick wasn't doing push-ups—he was doing little flutters," Perry maintains. "It just wasn't right."

A videotape of Warrick in action was dispatched to England to resolve the dispute. The Guinness folks hemmed and hawed some, and, finally, disallowed Warrick's record, although it was too late to recall it from print.

"Unfair!" cried Warrick. "Maybe all my push-ups weren't perfect, but nobody who runs a marathon looks pretty at the end," he says. David Boehm, Guinness's American editor, thinks Warrick has a point. "Frankly, we can't say with certainty that any applicant for the push-ups record did them all properly," Mr. Boehm says. "Our verification procedures are a bit of a mess."

But while Guinness is getting its act together, Warrick and Perry are huffing and puffing, both physically and verbally, in preparation for a Great Push-Ups Showdown. When and where— or, indeed, if—it will take place, remains to be determined. The two men live in the same city, but communicate mostly by rumor.

Still, a match between the muscular middleweights (both stand 5-foot-6 and weigh about 155 pounds) shapes up as a humdinger. It would be youth vs. middle age, Uptown vs. Downtown. "I'd be like Rocky," Warrick smiles in anticipation. "I'd be the champ who's the underdog."

Warrick makes it clear he takes his push-ups seriously. He admits to having had a hard time "getting things going" after he dropped out of school after the 10th grade seven years ago. He has since worked as a karate instructor, security guard and nightclub acrobat, among other things. He'd like to get into show business—maybe as a kung-fu movie star—but says he figures he has to "get known" first.

That's where the push-ups record comes in. "I never liked sports, but I always liked working out," he says. "I'd do a couple thousand push-ups in an afternoon, just for fun. Then one day I got a Guinness book and read about the record. I thought I'd try to break it. When I did, I got a lot of recognition in the community. It doesn't matter what Guinness says now; I'm the real push-ups king. The people here know it. And when I break the record again, as I surely will, everybody else will."

The mustached Perry affects a more laid-back mode. "In the great scheme of things, the question of who can do the most push-ups ranks with whether Stove Top stuffing tastes better than potatoes," he observes.

But around the Village Glen club in suburban Williamsville, Perry is anything but relaxed. His thrice-weekly workout consists of several hundred push-ups, chin-ups, sit-ups and parallel-bar dips, a couple of brisk turns through a line of Nautilus machines, and a good deal of running. The routine lasts a couple of hours, with only brief breathers. "Fitness got habit-forming with me," he shrugs in explanation.

Perry hasn't yet launched a direct assault on the Guinness push-ups mark, but his recent warm-ups include 1,998 repetitions of the exercise in a half-hour period, and 10,000 in four hours. All the push-ups were "strictly regulation," he avers.

"I want the record, but I want to do it right," he says. "The way it is now, one guy runs the mile and another takes a cab, and the two times are compared. If we both do 'em the same way, there'll be no problem. I'll win."

Whaddaya say to that, Jeff? "Hmmph. He talks, I do. Whatever it takes."

And so the battle lines are drawn, and all Buffalo waits. O.J.? Who's he?

• *Dec. 20, 1985*

Sultan of the Airwaves

I.
'm Arthur George Rust Jr., and this is Sportstalk. You're on the air.

    Caller: Mr. Rush?

    AGRJ: It's Rust, with a T.

    Caller: I'm a big fan of yours.

    AGRJ: Not that big. You don't know my name.

    Caller: I was nervous.

Who wouldn't be nervous? We're talking radio station WABC here, 50,000 watts from the Big Apple, with a national audience of millions after the sun goes down, not to mention Canada.

And the guy on the other end of the phone is Art Rust Jr., 58, the World's Greatest Authority on sports. Don't believe it? Just ask him.

"You've heard about walking encyclopedias? Well, I'm a walking computer," says Mr. Rust with nary a blush in his Manhattan broadcasting studio. "I know so much it scares me sometimes.

"One time we're in Flushing, doing the show outdoors. There's a couple hundred people watching. A fellow stands up with a piece of paper in his hand. He reads off the names of a dozen old-time Puerto Rican ballplayers for me to identify, guys like Hi Bithorn and Looie Olmo.

"I reel 'em off: 'Hiram *Gabriel* Bithorn, Chicago Cubs, 1942 to '46, White Sox, 1947. Louis *Rodriguez*

Olmo, Dodgers, 1943 to '49,' and so forth. The guy's mouth drops open. It was just me up there, by myself. No script. No books. No flunkies looking things up. I tell you, brother, I'm a bitch!"

Art Rust Jr. amazes and amuses the multitudes between 6 and 9 p.m. weekdays on WABC. A veteran of radio and television who does a weekly sports column for the New York Daily News on the side, he has done the Sportstalk show for six years now. It's different from the others that clog the airwaves nightly, he avers.

"First, I'm the biggest—nobody else has a fraction of my audience," he says. "Second, I'm black. That gives me a whole new dimension—a different way of looking at things. Third, I deal strictly in sports facts, not trivia. That's because I don't think there's such a thing as sports trivia. One man's trivia is another man's history. What's more important to most people: Joseph Paul DiMaggio's lifetime batting average, or the Congress of Vienna?"

> *Caller: Hi, Art. This is John from the Bronx.*
> *AGRJ: How are you, John. Do I hear water running?*
> *Caller: I'm taking a bath.*
> *AGRJ: What's on your mind?*
> *Caller: Those guys running the Yankees! PU! They stink! We acquire Britt Burns! Britt Burns!*
> *AGRJ: I was in Florida and I broke that story on his injury. I knew he could play in pain, but I didn't expect that.*
> *Caller: And they traded Baylor to the Red Sox! That's why the Red Sox aren't folding.*
> *AGRJ: Mike Easler's not chopped liver.*
> *Caller: He's not Baylor. Besides, the Yankees have no catcher, no shortstop and nothing resembling a pitching staff. Where's George? Get him on the show!*
> *AGRJ: I'll do that.*

"Anyway," Mr. Rust continues, "people don't call in with fact questions all that often. We deal mainly with issues here. Racism in sports. Drugs. The pernicious influences affecting college athletics. I'm an educator. I'm a sociologist. I'm a catalyst. I get people thinking.

"I go right at 'em on the racial thing. Anybody who thinks racism went out of baseball when Branch Rickey signed Jack Roosevelt Robinson in October of 1945 has another think coming. Don't believe me? See how many black, fringe ballplayers you can name.

There ain't many. If you're black and not a star, you're out. George Foster had it right.

"Same goes for the media. People ask me why, with all my knowledge, I never did play-by-play for a big-league team. I tell 'em that when I wanted that job, there was no way they were gonna have a black in the booth. Now, of course, they can't afford me. I get some satisfaction from that.

"I aggravate some people because I'm a brilliant black SOB, and I'm on top. I'm arrogant. I don't take a back seat. I live plush. But I can relate, too. You might be surprised who listens to my show. Mario Cuomo does. And Robert Merrill, the opera star. Richard Nixon's an Art Rust Jr. fanatic! He says he's gonna come on my show some day. What do I think of him? Well, he got caught.

"But it's the ordinary people with brains who really dig me. My call-in regulars and I have a love affair going! Four birthdays ago, Billy from Brooklyn phoned up from the lobby with 10 buddies. He had a case of champagne and a huge cake. Whatta party! When my man Mario from Manhattan got married, he invited me. And I went! You'd better believe I broke some color lines that day.

"The bottom line, though, is the show. This is a performance business, like sports, and if you don't perform, you're history. That's why I understand athletes so well. And you know something? I've never done a bad show. Believe it! I can make roaches running across the floor sound like the Kentucky Derby."

Caller: It's Teddy from Brooklyn, Art. Thanks for taking my call.
AGRJ: The pleasure is all yours.
Caller: My question is about Clete Boyer and Brooks Robinson. One year Clete had a better fielding average, but Robinson got the Golden Glove award at third base. Why was that?
AGRJ: More than the averages go into the award.
Caller: Who'd you like at third?
AGRJ: My guy was the pencil-thin Brooklyn Dodger, Mr. Billy Cox. That man could pick 'em. I'll tell you about another gentleman. His initials were Aurelio Rodriguez. Had a shotgun for an arm! Came up with the Angels in '67. They traded him to the Senators in '71. Then he went to . . .

● *Sept. 26, 1986*